This book is dedicated to my long-suffering family who have supported me through the years of my Spitfire obsession.

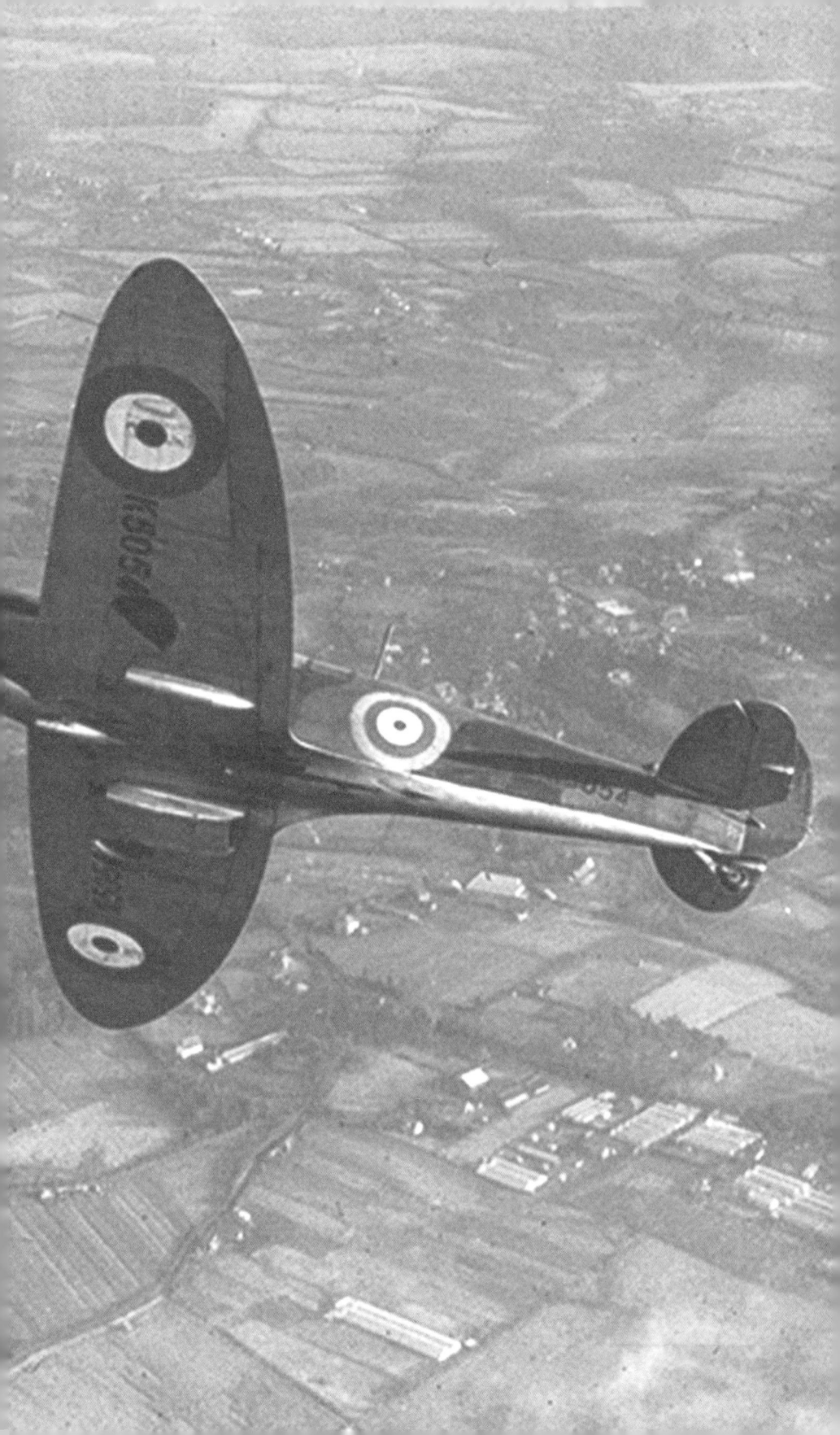

Mitchell

Mitchell

Father of the Spitfire

PAUL BEAVER

 Elliott&Thompson

Jacket images:
Front: Reginald Mitchell, the father of the Spitfire, pictured with his favourite pipe in 1936; the Spitfire Mk I is flown by Squadron Leader Henry Cozens, OC No. 19 Squadron, at RAF Duxford on 31 October 1938.
Back: The Type 300 Spitfire prototype on a test flight in 1936.

First published 2025 by
Elliott and Thompson Limited
2 John Street
London WC1N 2ES
www.eandtbooks.com

Represented by:
Authorised Rep Compliance Ltd.
Ground Floor, 71 Lower Baggot Street
Dublin, D02 P593
Ireland
www.arccompliance.com

ISBN (hardback): 978-1-78396-903-6
ISBN (trade paperback): 978-1-78396-926-5

Map (page ix): JP Map Graphics Ltd

9 8 7 6 5 4 3 2 1

A catalogue record for this book is available from the British Library.

Typesetting by Marie Doherty
Printed by CPI Group (UK) Ltd, Croydon, CR0 4YY

Contents

Map of Southampton   ix

Foreword by Air Chief Marshal Sir Rich Knighton   xi

Introduction   xiii

Prologue   xxiii

1	In the Beginning	1
2	Super Marine	9
3	Gateway to the Empire	23
4	First Designs	41
5	Schneider 1922 and 1923	53
6	Southampton: the Game Changer	65
7	Need for Speed	83
8	Vickers Takeover	97
9	Schneider 1929	113
10	Leave It to Lucy	125
11	Back to Business	137
12	Towards a Fighter	159
13	Towards the Icon	175
14	A Legend Is Born	193
15	Future Imperfect	201

16 Last Days   215
17 Legacy   223

Epilogue   229
Appendix 1: Timeline to the Spitfire   233
Appendix 2: Air Ministry Specifications of the 1930s   237
Appendix 3: The Mitchell Designs   241
Acknowledgements   289
Endnotes   293
Sources and Bibliography   299
Picture Credits   303
Index   307

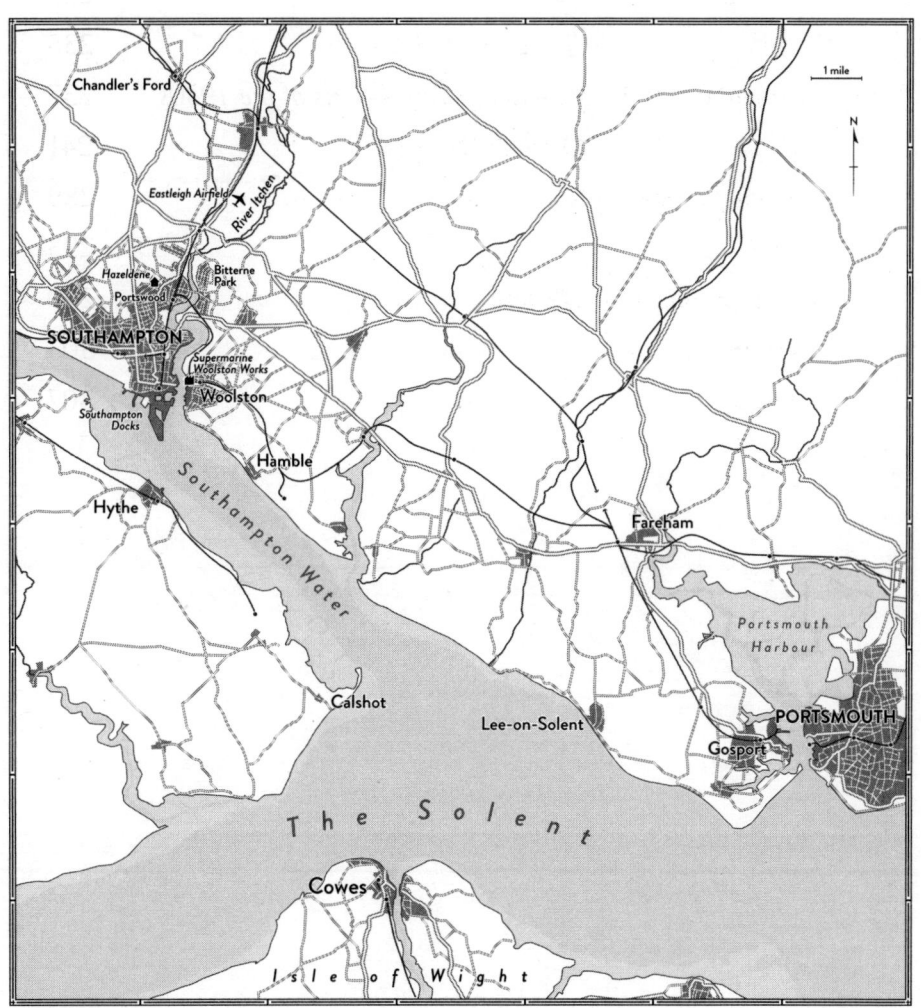

Map of Southampton

Foreword

Ask anyone, not just in Britain, to name an iconic aeroplane and I would wager that the overwhelming answer would be the Spitfire. It is the iconic fighter of the Royal Air Force's contribution to winning the Second World War and it was the chosen mount of so many of our Allied and Commonwealth nations.

For more than eight decades, people have linked the Spitfire and Supermarine's chief engineer and designer, Reginald Mitchell, in the same breath. As well they should as Mitchell was, as Paul Beaver says, the Father of the Spitfire.

But as Paul shows us in this book, Mitchell was much more than Supermarine's point-man to whom so much credit for the racing seaplanes of the Schneider Trophy, the giant flying boats and the first passenger seaplane must go; he was a genuine visionary and innovator before such things were in the popular mindset.

As Chief of the Defence Staff and an aeronautical engineer, I fully understand Mitchell's passion for technology and all it could bring – and still does bring – to the Royal Air Force. I look back at history and marvel.

At Britain's most vulnerable, ejected from the European continent and facing a potential German invasion, it was the modern, sleek and deadly Spitfire that made the critical difference – ably assisted (obviously!) by the Hurricanes and the Dowding integrated air defence system. While 'the Few' get much of the deserved glory, it was 'the Many' that truly made the difference, and they include the Supermarine workers as much as anyone else.

At a time of significant national strain, Team Spitfire made a difference, made history, and created an icon. The Battle of Britain brought the UK and our Allies precious time to organise, build, train and project the multi-national armada into Europe that would, ultimately, secure victory. As the clouds of war cleared from continental Europe some five years later, the Spitfire was still in the skies in 1945, finishing what it had started.

The Nation, the Commonwealth and the Free World owe much to the Father of the Spitfire, R. J. Mitchell. I would have loved to have met him.

Air Chief Marshal Sir Rich Knighton
Chief of the Defence Staff
Chief of the Air Staff 2023–25

Introduction

It is 5 March 1936. For this time of year, the weather is not unpleasant. The gravely ill engineer, still in his forties, has left his convalescence at home and driven himself three miles to Eastleigh airfield, even neglecting his tie for once in his life. Sitting on the running board of his yellow Rolls-Royce, surrounded by his team, he manages to make a good show of watching his creation take to the air for the first time, despite the pain that many know he is bearing. The engine roars as the light-grey fighter aeroplane departs towards the Solent. Sadly, he will not be there to see the Spitfire's finest hour; but at this moment he knows he has fathered a winner.

Reginald Mitchell is one of the greatest names in aviation history. He will always be linked to the Spitfire, that celebrated fighter aeroplane that arguably saved Western democracies from Nazi German tyranny in the Battle of Britain; yet his career is far more interesting and varied.

If asked to sum up Mitchell's talent, I call him 'the Father of the Spitfire', or 'the great conductor', as he led an orchestra of 150 young men and women who helped create racing seaplanes and flying boats that travelled around the globe, as well as one of the world's most famous aeroplanes. He was in the vanguard of the first generation of aeronautical leaders to develop their people and allow subordinates to come forward with ideas. He supported innovation and he liked to nurture the talents of the team at Supermarine, including women, often shunning the limelight even when his designs won the Schneider Trophy races – the aeronautical 'World Cup' of their day.

This book will challenge many of the myths that surround Mitchell's life and work, taking us behind the scenes to explore the creative genius of an engineer devoted to pushing the boundaries of technology. It also brings to life an era in which the race for technological mastery was driving conflict between the great powers. Mitchell came into aeronautics at a time when anything was possible, and achieved what many believed to be impossible.

Mitchell's legacy was felt throughout the Second World War, influencing the P-51 Mustang and other American designs. US designers had watched Mitchell's flair for adaptation and streamlining, seen his ability to harness new engines and to innovate in the fuselage as well as the structure. Mitchell seems to have had a passion for continuous improvement that today's military calls spiral development. He was ahead of his time and deserves that recognition.

Mitchell's story begins near the industrial city of Stoke-on-Trent in Staffordshire, where young Reginald displayed a flair for making and flying model aircraft before completing an engineering apprenticeship and learning his craft against the backdrop of the First World War. By 1916 he was at Supermarine, now an iconic name in world aeronautical history. Its accolades include the first passenger flying-boat service in Britain, the Schneider Trophy winning designs and, of course, the Spitfire. But it had humble beginnings.

Here, with some of the greatest aeroplane designs in history, Mitchell would rise to fame when still only in his early twenties. It was the beginning of what would be a career of less than a quarter of a century and yet his contribution to aeroplane design, manufacture and development would be significant. Mitchell developed his engineering and design talents in four basic areas at Supermarine: single-engined amphibians (an aeroplane that is capable of taking off and landing on both water and land); twin-engined flying boats; racing seaplanes; and single-engined monoplane fighters. In his last months, he would add a four-engined, high-flying bomber to that list. He imagined engineering solutions to over forty different designs, concepts and schemes.

The immediate post-First World War period saw national rivalries between the victors intensify. The forum for this competition was the Schneider Trophy race, a headline-grabbing festival of speed that pitted the finest pilots and engineers of seaplanes in France, Italy, the USA and the UK against one another between 1913 and 1931. At Supermarine, Mitchell took on the challenge of speed with gusto, using his racers to test new ideas – today we would call them technology demonstrators – and fostering a close working relationship between the aeroplane design team at Supermarine and Sir Henry Royce, doyen of the engine manufacturer Rolls-Royce.

But it wasn't just at the cutting edge of speed where Mitchell was making his mark. Mitchell's other two key designs were the Southampton and the Scapa flying boats, and their epic journeys to Australia and Hong Kong demonstrated both his design and engineering prowess as well as the vision of the Air Ministry in London to invest in the expertise to design, build, maintain and operate these magnificent machines. It is a testimony to Mitchell that their arduous journeys were accomplished without loss. For the first time, a European nation was able to police its trade routes, naval harbours and commercial interests from the air. Mitchell had shown his ability to transit from an apprenticeship in the railway industry to the new engineering science of aeronautics and to have the vision to embrace it. His design philosophy was not linear progression but a process of continuous improvement – in other words, taking the best from each design, yet finding time to add new technology.

As Europe's politics darkened in the 1930s, the work of Mitchell and his team became crucial to a nation preparing for war. Europe's first global conflict had ended in an uneasy peace. Watching developments in Italy – the first European fascist dictatorship – and in Germany – secretly building up an air force even before Hitler came to power – Britain was especially concerned. In 1931 the government released a specification for a bomber-destroyer fighter to counter the new generation of fast bombers being built by Dornier, Heinkel and Junkers. These German machines were frequently announced as fast mailplanes or passenger aircraft, however unlikely the cabin space might appear.

Mitchell had a first attempt at a fighter immediately after the 1931 Schneider contest but the monoplane Type 224, which could be dubbed the first Spitfire, simply did not cut the mustard. 'If it doesn't look right, it won't fly right' is a well-used but apt adage.

Back in 1916, the Dutch designer Anton Fokker had pioneered the monoplane Fokker Eindecker fighters, known to the Allies as the Fokker Scourge on account of their outstanding flying characteristics and their use of the latest technologies. The Allies were slow to take up the notion of a fast monoplane fighter, preferring instead the known manoeuvrability and the comfort of the biplane fighter. However, partly due to decisions made by Supermarine's parent company, Vickers, and partly due to the relationship between Mitchell and the Air Ministry, in 1934 Supermarine embarked on the development of a new, radical and game-changing monoplane fighter with the latest engine technology from Rolls-Royce.

Mitchell had built a team of young men who were able to take on the mantle of design and development when he was ill with cancer. The result, under his orchestration, was the Type 300, which became the Spitfire, arguably the best performing fighter of the Second World War.

Mitchell's role in the development of the Spitfire is supposedly encapsulated in a 1942 propaganda film called *The First of the Few*, which depicts Mitchell as a lone hero solely responsible for its design. The film is pure fabrication and has led countless writers to make erroneous claims about Mitchell's motives, desires and illness.

I have wanted to write this book for forty years to tell the real story of the Spitfire. As I researched the Spitfire it became clear that the man credited with single-handedly designing the fighter was a great engineer and pioneer, but the creation of a masterpiece wasn't a single-handed enterprise. It took a team, and it was the result of two decades of hard graft and experience. In addition, Mitchell was seriously ill at the pivotal time of the Spitfire design work. This perspective is enhanced and supported by my exposure to those who were there and are not long passed. For nearly a century after his death, Mitchell was eulogised more for the Spitfire than for the other twenty-three designs on which his fingerprints are all too apparent.

Mitchell was an outstanding brain and brilliant engineer, but his genius was not so much the pencil and the use of the eraser on the Spitfire's design but rather bringing together a team who could take his vision forward. The movie and the books passed over the likes of Joe Smith, Alan Clifton, Alf Faddy and two hundred others who made the projects literally fly. He could not have done it alone, if only because he was painfully ill from 1933 and knew he would die early if his cancer returned. He trusted Faddy, his lieutenant, to develop the initial concept.

At a time when Britain and its allies needed a 400-mph fighter to redress the menace of the German Luftwaffe, the Spitfire rose to the challenge. The Spitfire did not win the Battle of Britain alone – there were fewer than twenty squadrons in service when the great aerial contest began – but it can be said with confidence that the battle would have been lost without it.

Nevertheless, the Spitfire is the most renowned aeroplane in the world. It is not just the pleasing shape, the amazing elliptical wing form, or the music of the Merlin or Griffon engine that makes the Spitfire stand out. It is an engineering masterpiece that was ahead of its time. The complex construction of monocoque elegance – where the chassis is integral with the body – would challenge the initial production team yet provide the basis for development into seventy-two variants, including a floatplane fighter and long-range reconnaissance fighter with no armament, relying only on speed to protect it. Traditionally, aeroplanes were built of wooden or light alloy frames covered with Irish linen and tightened by cellulose dope, but Mitchell's team had experimented with the Schneider Trophy racers to create a new form where the skin of the aeroplane was very much part of the overall structure. These attributes attracted users from Australia to Norway, America to Thailand.

As a schoolboy, I grew up twenty years after the Second World War with tales of derring-do in the skies of Europe – Spitfires and Hurricanes in the Battle of Britain particularly caught my imagination. As I grew older, I understood more about the genius of the Spitfire's design and the engineering behind it. I then began to fly as a teenager with the dream of piloting a Spitfire, never expecting that the opportunity would arise to learn the skills needed to fly this wonderful icon. To quote veteran Auxiliary Air Transport pilot Joy Lofthouse: she's a goddess in the air and a bitch on the ground. Landing the Spitfire required more concentration than anything I had ever done before or since. Yet in the air, she is a bird. To turn, one just thinks the fighter into the turn rather than guide her with the controls.

But it is also the feats achieved in every theatre of the Second World War that define the Spitfire. Ask any Norwegian, Dane,

Dutchman or Belgian and they would all say the Spitfire 'saved' them – even the French agree, begrudgingly. I can testify to those feelings being expressed when I flew a Spitfire from Norway to Goodwood in the UK, stopping for fuel in Denmark, Germany, the Netherlands and Belgium on the way. Most surprising was a German airport worker who confided in me that the Spitfire was the venerated liberator of Germany from the Nazi rule of Hitler and his cronies. In Britain, in Europe, even in New Zealand, no air show is complete without a Spitfire display.

This is Mitchell's legacy. But perhaps his greatest work was just out of reach when he died. Three programmes took all his energy: the fast-long-range bomber programme, a fast amphibian and a twin-engined Spitfire replacement armed with cannon for the war he saw coming. Little has been written about these projects or the progress Mitchell had made in their design and engineering specifications. They account for his lack of direct involvement in the Spitfire.

Had Mitchell lived, his brilliant – and there is no other word for it – long-range bomber design could have changed the balance of the strategic air war in 1942. It was faster, flew higher and carried a greater war load than even the legendary Lancaster. His design was for a bomber that would have been faster at altitude than the early Messerschmitt fighters – Supermarine knew a thing or two about speed, so the figures quoted stand up to scrutiny. Mitchell was, after all, the king of speed, with his design having been crowned the fastest aeroplane in the world in 1931, breaking the 400-mph barrier.

He also knew that the Spitfire needed better armament than the standard-rifle-calibre Browning 0.303-inch machine guns that were specified by the Air Ministry. He believed rightly that the clever elliptical wing that gave the Spitfire such agility in the air was so thin that it could not mount cannon without time-consuming modification. To destroy armoured bombers, cannon were vital. He was working on a new model that would fulfil these requirements. He also thought that no fighter based in Germany could reach British airspace so he wanted his fighter to have the range to cross the North Sea and engage the Germans over their own territory and win the air battle there.

These areas have rarely been touched on by historians but are vital to understanding Mitchell, who had a genius for design born out of his dedicated engineering background. He was an engineer who designed, not a designer who understood engineering. He might well deserve the accolade of the greatest aeronautical engineer of the twentieth century. This book sets out to prove that point, while also casting light on the forgotten heroes of the Supermarine workforce, without whom there would have been no Spitfire, no Battle of Britain victory and no ultimate victory. This is the story of a man who helped change the course of history – one of the great design leaders of the modern era.

The Supermarine S4 at Calshot, August 1925. Mitchell was an imaginative and innovative engineer with a flair for design, which resulted in aeroplanes that still look surprising today.

Prologue

Chesapeake Bay was unusually overcast even for October. It had been a cold night, and the autumn mists cleared to show that fall had come early to Baltimore. The beach, such as it was, was crowded with spectators. The contest they had come to see was simply the most exciting thing ever to hit Baltimore and a news-making event around the world. Racing seaplanes were the fastest man-made machines on the face of the earth.

Despite the autumnal chill, one young man was dressed for the occasion in a thick jacket over his swimming trunks as he stood looking out over the slightly choppy waters of the eastern American seaboard. Just thirty years old, muscular with a shock of sandy hair, his tall frame showed a lifetime of attention to its upkeep through tennis, cricket, swimming and golf, but his face showed lines of concern.

This was an important day for R. J. Mitchell, but it had not started well. In fact, the whole venture had a sense of foreboding. He was preparing for the greatest race of the year – the 1925 heat of the Schneider Trophy, the prize for the fastest flying boat or racing seaplane. At stake was a very European beautiful silver and bronze sculpture showing a classical zephyr skimming across the waves, set on a marble base with dominating beauty. The trophy – named in 1912 by its generous French originator, perhaps immodestly as the *Coupe d'Aviation Maritime Jacques Schneider* – was more than just a remarkable piece of art. It was the most coveted prize in the aviation world. This was a time when a million people would flock to watch the fastest men on Earth hurtle around a course and perhaps reach 250 mph. Only the very best aircraft designs were entered, and the costs of a team can be compared in order of magnitude to a NASA moon shot today.

At stake were the international reputations of nations keen to show their mastery of aeronautics and speed. It was also the place where the leading engineers and designers – often one and the same person – were testing new technologies, just as Monsieur Schneider had wished. This year Supermarine, Mitchell's company, was determined to win.

Mitchell was concerned because his brainchild had been damaged the night before and had needed repair in Baltimore. That brainchild was the Supermarine S4 – a radical new racing seaplane which looked like nothing that had come before.

Things were not going according to plan. The pilot, Henri Biard, had fallen on the ship's deck in the mid-Atlantic on the long journey from Southampton, and injured his wrist. Then the S4, Mitchell's pride and joy, had been damaged by a rigid pole of the ridiculous canvas hangars that the organisers had provided. Now it seemed that Biard had contracted influenza. Race day was just two days away and the S4 had not been tested after transit.

This day was the testing day, 23 October. There would be a navigation trial so that the competing pilots could orientate themselves with the course, but for the British team from Southampton, this was really to prove that the new creation would fly after being rebuilt following its transatlantic journey.

Flying a racing seaplane was about the only thing in aeronautics that Mitchell could not do himself. Everything else in the process of realising a design into a living and breathing high-speed machine was within his technical grasp. Today, he was asking another young man and a friend to risk his life to prove his engineering calculations were right and that his machine would fly.

Mitchell had told the pilot that if anything went wrong, he would strip off, dive in and rescue him. He was ready.

This race was unusual because aeronautical engineering had taken a giant step forward in the two years since the last competition at Cowes on the Isle of Wight. Agile seaplanes – designed with floats and a streamlined hull – had replaced flying boats as entrants. They were also increasingly monoplane – single winged – and no longer looked like antiques from the First World War. It was a brave new world.

Mitchell was only just out of his twenties and yet was already recognised as a radical aeronautical engineer. In his mind, gone was any reluctance to maintain the status quo. The design that he watched on this trial, from the slipway to the warm-up area, challenged the established norm; it was the most beautiful cantilever monoplane mid-wing two-plywood racing machine with a stressed-steel fuselage. It was a showpiece of technology, with its rigidity of structure made possible through the very nature of the steel, rather than relying on linen laid over wooden stringers and doped to tautness.

The Supermarine S4 was also fitted with the best aero engine available in Britain, and probably Europe, at the time. The Napier was streamlined to fit into a small fuselage – so small that the pilot had to get into the cockpit by facing to one side and only turning to face the controls when his shoulders were below the cockpit sill.

This brave pilot was born in Godalming, Surrey, of Channel Island and Norman-French ancestries evidenced by the first name he often used: Henri. But Biard was as English as they come and already a flying legend at thirty-three years old. He wanted to win, and influenza would not keep him in bed. To both designer and pilot, this race was important.

At Chesapeake, Mitchell would be forced to sit and watch the Americans show off their technical expertise. The American team, flying Curtiss racing seaplanes, had romped home at the last Schneider race at Cowes in 1923 after the French team had pulled out and Britain's entry, the Supermarine Sea Lion III, came third.

Standing ready on the picket boat, did Mitchell already have an inkling that this wasn't his year? Or did he shrug off the bad luck as the boat moved into position because everything was looking good? The repairs seemed to be holding, and he was happy that Biard had the machine under control as it took off.

Mitchell was hopeful until the fatal moment when the S4 completed its first run, turned and started a second. It suddenly lurched to one side and spun into the sea from 100 feet. The pilot and aeroplane had disappeared below the cold waters of Chesapeake Bay.

Mitchell urged the picket boat forward, but the engine stalled. It took forty minutes to reach the wreck site. Luckily, Biard had managed to wriggle out of the tiny cockpit and get to the surface. A fellow competitor, seeing that Biard had no life preserver, had landed close by and in a feat of valour taken off his own lifebelt and thrown it to him. Mitchell dived into the water to help get Biard to safety, all thoughts of victory gone.

What went wrong has never been explained. As with most aeroplane crashes, the Royal Aero Club, which had organised the British entry into the Schneider race, considered pilot error, some other human intervention or perhaps, as seems likely, there was a catastrophic mechanical or structural issue. Perhaps wing flutter?* The S4 was a revolutionary design without the usual structural support of braces, struts and wires seen in other types. Was it too radical for engineering and materiel sciences of the time?

Two days later, on race day, the British team was without its star machine and just had its other entrant, a biplane Gloster, to battle. The Americans were jubilant as they knew they would win now, as the only other competitors, the Italians, were having their own issues. The Americans won again, not just because the Curtiss was flying better than ever but because a new pilot, the then little-known James Doolittle,† had developed some tactics for the turns, where precious seconds could be saved.

---

* Wing flutter is when the mainplane or the control surfaces, like the ailerons, became unstable in the air flow and flutter.

† In 1942, Doolittle would become an American legend for leading the first counter-attack on the Japanese mainland after Pearl Harbor.

For many onlookers, it was shades of the America's Cup race between American and British yachts, except that the stakes were higher. Sailing super yachts demanded skill, water and wind knowledge but racing seaplanes required these attributes and all the planets of engineering, design and workmanship to be aligned.

The Schneider races were demanding on man and machine. In Chesapeake Bay, the Curtiss may have won, beating the British Gloster III and the Italian Macchi M33, but two other American contenders failed the course, and another Gloster III, plus Mitchell's S4 design, were unable to compete. Schneider racing was becoming serious, and it was clear that private entrants could not compete against the government entries of the USA and Italy. The day of the gifted amateur was over.

The technology used in the racing seaplanes would lead the way to military prowess in the air; sadly, Schneider himself thought it would aid the design and building of passenger machines but, even in 1925, the world was moving towards resolving the unfinished 'Great War'. The signs were there and clear. Germany was in turmoil, the rising power of Italy sought its place at the table and the highly energetic French, leaders of world aviation for a quarter of a century, were determined to win the peace and any future war. Schneider was convinced, despite his German ancestry, that France would be at the top of the aviation tree.

Each Schneider race had its value for Mitchell, who had learned to use failure as a stepping stone to success. Undaunted by the crash, he went back to his desk and pursued his design philosophy

– best possible by pushing the boundaries of technology – to iter-
ate, and reiterate, until he was designing the fastest seaplanes the
world had seen.

For Mitchell, this was just the beginning.

There are few, if any, pictures of a young Mitchell. But this view of him at work in his office at Southampton in the early 1930s shows keen concentration and the rolled-up-sleeves approach to his engineering.

1

In the Beginning

Reginald Joseph Mitchell, known later in life simply as R. J., was born into a lower-middle-class family on 20 May 1895 at 115 Congleton Road, Butt Lane, near Stoke-on-Trent. The Potteries in the English Midlands might not seem the most auspicious place for perhaps the greatest ever British aircraft designer and engineer to be born and brought up – this was a part of Britain that was renowned for its brick ovens, soot and grime. Yet, at the turn of the twentieth century, it also boasted a wealth of engineering expertise and a dedication to the railways, then the greatest high-tech business of the nation.

Life in Staffordshire before the First World War was good for the Mitchell family – three boys and two girls born to Herbert and Eliza Jane Mitchell (née Brain). Herbert hailed from Holmfirth in West Yorkshire, the *Last of the Summer Wine* village of television fame a century later. He was working towards having his own printing business, having started his professional life as a schoolmaster. In many ways, this was an archetypal Edwardian home with a live-in maid. They were secure in a Victorian house called

Victoria Cottage in a middle-class area of Stoke. The name was somewhat misleading: it was a substantial family home with spacious garden, lawns and coach houses in which Mitchell's father had created a playroom and then, as the boys grew, workshops where they practised their engineering skills.

The children were brought up with middle-class manners and outlets. Gordon tells us his grandfather demanded a 'certain high standard of behaviour' from the children, including respect, thoughtfulness and kindness.[1] These values may well have come from Herbert's Freemasonry, which he took very seriously as a 32nd degree Mason in the Jasper Lodge in Hanley. R. J. would later join the same lodge. Herbert also ensured that the family attended church regularly as he was a church warden at Normacot's Victorian Gothic Church of the Holy Evangelists, which was a good, solid Church of England establishment. The Mitchell family was imbued with the Protestant work ethic which obviously reflects in the last stages of R. J.'s life when he was battling cancer and yet had started some of his most exciting and forward-looking designs.

After a short spell of home education, in 1903 Mitchell was enrolled in Queensbury Road Higher Elementary School at the age of eight. This co-educational school in Normacot, the suburb where their home was situated, was famous in the area for its mathematics, for which Mitchell showed an early aptitude. He also excelled in billiards, golf, cricket and tennis at school, his hand/eye coordination being trained at a young age. In fact, throughout his life he loved sport of any kind and kept fit as a matter of course.

After selection at eleven, Mitchell went to Hanley Co-Educational Grammar School, known locally as the High School, to the north-east of Stoke. The suburb is shown in contemporary pre-First World War postcards as having both conical pottery kilns belching smoke and fumes, and parkland. By this time, he had already shown his abilities in engineering, which he probably inherited, along with his craft skills, from his father and his grandfather, who had been a millwright in Yorkshire. The aviation bug had also bitten early, and he secured funding for a lathe to make his own metal parts for model aeroplanes. It was in the coach house that he and his brothers built their models – without plans, according to R. J.'s son, Gordon Mitchell – from balsa wood and tissue coverings doped with cellulose for strength. To the north of Stoke, there were parks where it was possible to fly model aeroplanes – mainly gliders or powered by rubber bands.

When he was twelve, he even saved the life of his brother, Billy, after a gas lamp caused a fire in his younger brother's bedroom, running in through the smoke and pulling the boy free. Young Reg, as he was called, did not lack courage.

As Mitchell was growing up, aviation was new, exciting and highly dangerous. It was the cutting edge of technology and, for many, the place to be for smart young people. Up in Stoke, there was little aviation but publications like *Flight* and *The Aeroplane* were available, as well as access to *Jane's All the World's Flying Machines* in the public library. In his teens, Mitchell was an avid reader of newspapers and periodicals in technology. He read about how the American showman and aviator Samuel Cody had demonstrated his British Army Aeroplane No. 1 to astonished British Army generals on Laffan's Plain in Hampshire on 16 October 1908 and, the following summer, something even more astonishing: the news about the French aviation pioneer Louis Blériot crossing the Channel in a flimsy aeroplane in July 1909. He could hardly have missed the news because it was as amazing then as the first moon landing was in 1969. He was especially keen to read everything on aeronautics as he was also a devotee of aero-modelling. Some armchair experts in their comfortable club chairs on Pall Mall thought flying faster than 100 mph would cause the body to cave in with the air pressure – people had said the same about railway locomotives half a century earlier. But early aviation was not without risk. It cost lives, including that of Samuel Cody, who crashed and died five years later.

Mitchell's early upbringing created a young man with a passion for engineering and aviation, attention to detail by designing and making model flying aeroplanes, and a determination to succeed. In the pre-war period, those wanting a career in engineering rarely attended university but found apprenticeship opportunities in the great works of the day, many of whom specialised in railway loco-motives, steam turbines and ship systems. It was called 'serving time' in engineering, as the *Evening Sentinel*, a local newspaper in Staffordshire, reported on 27 September 1929: 'In his early career, Mr Mitchell almost became an architect in the Surveyor's depart-ment. There was no opening at the time and instead of pursuing a career in other channels, Mr Mitchell took up engineering and served his time with Messrs Kerr Stuart.'

Kerr, Stuart & Company was a relatively small firm with an excellent reputation for railway engineering reaching back to its foundation in Scotland in 1881. In 1892, the firm had started designing and building its own locomotives at the California Works in Fenton, Stoke-on-Trent. It developed a worldwide reputation for light railway locomotives and exported a number to Brazil and the Caribbean for sugar-estate haulage before the First World War.

The wider context is important. For much of the nineteenth century and into the twentieth, railways were transformational in Britain, and globally. These companies relied on innovation and cutting-edge technology, attracted the best minds, and helped shape the engineering skills of entire generations. The railway age also allowed small, independent firms, not tied to the big companies, to be commercially competitive. Kerr, Stuart & Company's other illustrious alumni include T. C. B. Coleman, the chief locomotive draughtsman of the London, Midland & Scottish Railway, the largest transportation organisation in the world in the 1920s; and L. T. C. Rolt, the pioneer of canal and railway preservation. In pre-war engineering, it was the railways that drove innovation. Mitchell absorbed that ethos and would go on to apply it to aeronautics.

It's possible to imagine Mitchell, up before dawn, having had a quick cold breakfast and filled his tea caddy, donning overalls and walking purposefully to the works to start a shift. Railway engineering apprenticeships may well have been the pinnacle of the Industrial Revolution, but they were still hard, dirty work and long hours. During those walks to and from the works, Mitchell must have dreamed of entering a cleaner branch of engineering.

Mitchell was lucky to have parents who could afford the Premium Apprenticeship, which provided additional study in evening classes in a local educational establishment, and he received an excellent practical and theoretical education at the Fenton works. The night school element at Fenton Technical School led to him being awarded the City & Guilds certificate, then a much-treasured indicator of a good grounding in the basics of engineering. It was followed by Mitchell's membership of the Institute of Mechanical Engineers in 1915, as prestigious then as it is today. Before Mitchell left Stoke, such was his potential that he was invited to lecture part time at Fenton and share his knowledge; this was a skill common to his time as an aircraft designer and engineer, when his teams would often benefit from his experience in engineering and problem solving. 'He would remain silent, thinking and considering, as a young engineer would bring him a problem and then after perhaps another minute or two, he would give his advice. Always sound. Always to be followed,' remembered one Supermariner.[*]

At this time aviation technology was developing rapidly. In 1912, the French banker and balloon enthusiast Jacques Schneider had launched his competition, aiming to set the conditions for manufacturers to improve technology, pilot skills and the overall reliability of aeroplanes. In addition to the trophy, Schneider offered a prize of £1,000 (equivalent to £97,000 in 2025) for the winner of a speed race with laps over a triangular course of 170 miles (increased to 220 miles in 1921). These were, in effect, time trials, with contestants being flagged off at fifteen-minute intervals, with the events carefully monitored by an international team of judges. This was real human endeavour. Each competition would be hosted by the previous winning country, and if a country won three times in a row, it would keep the trophy for ever.

Tommy Sopwith, one of the founding fathers of British aviation, had contested the 1914 race in Monaco with a small seaplane

---

[*] The name given to those who worked for Supermarine. From: supermariners. wordpress.com

named the Tabloid, the smallest and least powerful of the models that year. It was raced by Howard Pixton, a skilled aviator who won the Schneider Trophy for the British at the first attempt. He managed an average speed of almost 87 mph. In 1914, that was the fastest a seaplane had been. Mitchell would have read about the success and squirrelled away the contest in his brain as he prepared for his own career in aviation.

But first, there was an all-absorbing First World War. Mitchell was not conscripted, even though, it seems, he volunteered for the Royal Flying Corps. Like so many of his generation, he would have been profoundly shocked at the losses on the Flanders fields and would have wanted to do his bit with his fellow countrymen. However, he was in a reserved occupation as both a teacher at Fenton Technical School and an engineer, and therefore exempt from call-up under the Military Service Act.

Eric Mitchell, the middle child of Herbert and Eliza Jane Mitchell, did volunteer and served in the British Army in Egypt during the hostilities. Both served their country, but Reg was apparently far more valuable to the war effort as a trained engineer, as the Ministry of Munitions asserted in its 1916 refusal to release him for active service.

Mitchell's years of study and practical application had positioned him well for a career in engineering in almost any sector. He chose aeronautics, perhaps to the astonishment of his family back in Stoke-on-Trent. Why would he give up the opportunity of a secure career in the railway industry? Or even his father's printing business? Mitchell had other ideas, and that was certainly to the benefit of his nation.

Supermarine was founded by Noel Pemberton-Billing, seen here flying over Brooklands airfield in 1913, when he had just gained his aviator's certificate from the Royal Aero Club.

2

Super Marine

B efore the First World War, aeroplanes were scarce and flying them was an expensive pastime for a very few. But new technologies had started to sweep the country after the Wright Brothers first flew and the French had begun to lead Europe in the design of heavier-than-air flying machines. The military was a little slow to adopt aviation, with cries of 'It will frighten the horses' from cavalry generals, but the colourful American showman Samuel Cody had persuaded them that flying machines took reconnaissance into a new dimension with endless possibilities. Many entrepreneurs and visionaries saw that flying was a whole new arena to conquer. One of those men was Noel Pemberton-Billing, a figure who would be incredibly important to Mitchell's career.

Pemberton-Billing's life story is one of notoriety and controversy, but he was more far-sighted than popular culture would give him credit for. He was born Noel Billing in 1881 in north London, the son of an iron-founder, and educated in France, Ramsgate and London; he obviously didn't like his schooling much as he ran away from home at the age of thirteen, eventually ending up in South Africa. He added the name Pemberton to give himself a more exotic-sounding background, and joined the South African Mounted Police; he fought in the Second Anglo-Boer War (1899–1902) and was one of those who relieved the besieged town of Ladysmith in February 1900 in a major victory for the British. He was taken ill and invalided out of the police shortly afterwards, returning to London in 1903.

Back in Britain, Pemberton-Billing was keen for a way to get into aviation. He watched that other twentieth-century aviation legend, Frederick Handley Page, form a company and start to build gliders in 1909 at Barking Creek in Essex. Aeroplanes need airfields or at least flying strips. Initially, a well-drained flat piece of farmland close to a road or even a railway station was considered a good location. Proximity to London was important, which made Brooklands near Weybridge in Surrey a hub of aviation, including schools and workshops. There was also a motor-vehicle racing track – even today, it is possible to visit the heritage site and see how the junction of aeronautics and motor vehicles worked in developing basic engineering.

Pemberton-Billing tried opening an aerodrome at Fambridge in Essex, close enough to London to get interest from business and fun flyers; it failed probably because it was too ambitious for its time. Today, America is full of fixed-base operations (FBO) companies around major cities where there is everything needed for flying – an airfield, air traffic control, meteorology, restaurant, engineering support and fuel. In 1909, in Essex, Pemberton-Billing was a half century ahead of the curve. Yet, he kept the land and

sheds at Fambridge and started small-scale aircraft design, manufacture and repair instead.

Pemberton-Billing never seems to have been demoralised
by business failure. He was a man who could not be put down.
He qualified as a solicitor and started to think about making his
fortune another way. He considered luxury yachts, powered by
steam turbines, where he thought he could be a salesman; by 1912
he was operating from the River Itchen, across the water from
Southampton.

One of the prospective buyers was Handley Page. He was
active in the Royal Aeronautical Society and had exhibited his
own designs for aeroplanes at the British exhibition centre at
Olympia. He had been learning to fly* on one of them, called
Bluebird, which seems to have been unsuccessful. In 1913, when
the two men were discussing learning to fly, Pemberton-Billing
bet Handley Page £500 (worth around £49,000 today) that he
could do it in twenty-four hours. Pemberton-Billing won the bet
and gained Royal Aero Club certificate No. 683 in the process –
already there were nearly seven hundred people with the right to
fly a powered aeroplane in Britain.

That £500 was a godsend to Pemberton-Billing. With it he was
able to found what would become one of the most famous aviation
companies in the world – Supermarine.

---

* Geoffrey de Havilland, another great pioneer from whose company later would
come the Mosquito 'wooden wonder' and the Comet jet airliner, the world's
first, taught himself to fly. His first attempts to fly resulted in a crash but he built
another aeroplane, found a better engine from the Iris Motor Company and even
joined HM Balloon Factory as designer and test pilot – probably before he could
actually pilot an aeroplane.

The company was established in June 1914 as a result of a collaboration between Pemberton-Billing and the yacht designer Hubert ('Ginger' or 'Scotty', depending on the age of the friend) Scott-Paine. One of the most important business relationships in British aviation had started three years earlier through one of those coincidences that crop up frequently, it seems, in history. Pemberton-Billing had bumped into Scott-Paine near Shoreham station in Sussex, and the former asked for a loan of the latter's bike to catch the train to London.[1] Scott-Paine ended up working with Pemberton-Billing, delivering yachts and making his home aboard the yacht *Utopia* in the years immediately before the First World War. He was a squat, rugged individual with a mop of unruly ginger hair and an infectious laugh. In his youth a great traveller, he had earned the money to pay for the next leg of his journey by prize fighting. Scott-Paine was also a visionary, described as the Sir Richard Branson of his time, given his entrepreneurial flair and enthusiasm for aeroplanes, fast boats, publicity and setting records.

With his £500 from Handley Page, Pemberton-Billing acquired swamp land on the waterfront of the River Itchen at Oakbank Wharf and set up the Pemberton-Billing Company with an investor, Alfred de Broughton, who reportedly brought in £10,000. The shareholding was Pemberton-Billing 6,800 shares, de Broughton 3,700 and the electrical engineer, Lorenz Hans Herkomer, 500. Scott-Paine was not an immediate shareholder, but was Works Manager, and the final member of the management was draughtsman Carl Vasilesco, a Romanian, indicating the extraordinarily international band who settled into wooden shacks at Oakbank Wharf and the swamp behind it.

Pemberton-Billing used 'Supermarine' as his telegraphic address. The name's derivation is simple. If a submarine is a craft which goes under the surface of the sea, Pemberton-Billing reasoned, then a super-marine craft must travel above the surface – the seaplane or flying boat was therefore 'supermarine'.

The aviation industry was already taking off: British and Colonial Aeroplane Company (later Bristol Aeroplane), Handley Page, Short Brothers, Sopwith and Vickers were all in the game. Short Brothers at their Leysdown Works had offered an apprenticeship and received more than two hundred applications from suitably qualified young men. The result was so inspiring that in 1910 the Admiralty decided to build and furnish the world's first naval flying school at Eastchurch on the Isle of Sheppey on the Thames Estuary in Kent.

Government was catching up. As early as 1904, Lieutenant Colonel J. E. Capper of the Royal Engineers and Superintendent of His Majesty's Balloon Factory at Farnborough had visited the Wright Brothers in Dayton, Ohio, to see their experiments, which led to Cody's flight in 1908.* On 13 May 1912, the Royal Flying Corps had been established to support both the Royal Navy (Naval Wing) and the British Army in the field (Military Wing). There was a central Flying School, a Reserve cadre of officers initially, and the Balloon Factory became the Royal Aircraft Factory (RAF), which would go on to produce one of the greatest fighters of the First World War, the SE5a. The Balloon Factory's work

---

* It was probably the first beneficiary of a wind tunnel, although the War Office in London thought such devices were irrelevant to aeroplane design and that £2,500 was too expensive to continue its operation.

on aero-engines was also taken into the RAF, perhaps showing a better understanding of the potential of fixed-wing aeroplanes in wartime. In fact, the first armed aeroplanes in Britain were seen as early as 1912.

Pemberton-Billing wanted a slice of that aviation pie and thought his rudimentary knowledge of engineering would allow him to move into powered flight. Most British designers were struggling with propulsion, as engines, even for automobiles, were still very temperamental. That's OK on the road where it's possible to stop, but in the air it adds a whole new dimension to engine failure.

Pemberton-Billing worked hard on creating a viable flying machine at his simple shed in Essex. Balloons and airships still dominated the aeronautical scene, but he was more interested in heavier-than-air machines, and seaplanes especially.

The French were the front runners in flying training and aeroplane design, but the British were good at engineering and repair. This is why people like Pemberton-Billing adopted French designs and modified them, using the basic principles for their own. Many of the models that appeared at this time were not airworthy but development was picking up speed as engineers – often from non-aeronautical disciplines – grappled with thrust, drag, weight and other basic principles of flight.

Jumping on the bandwagon of aviation, Pemberton-Billing's PB1 single-seat flying boat fighter was shown off at the Aero and Motor Show in London's Olympia in March 1914. The PB1 had made use of the expertise of yacht hull designer Linton Hope, a man of loyalty and service, and soon to become the doyen of naval architecture in the Royal Naval Air Service (and later to be a confidant of Mitchell).* Early aviation, with its focus on seaplanes and flying boats, gained much from the south coast yachting industry, which was the world's leading design centre of the time.

The whole PB1 design was innovative, with a 50-hp French Gnome engine mounted between wings and fuselage which were made of spruce and mahogany, covered with doped linen to make them waterproof. Pemberton-Billing claimed it had flown when he showed it off at Olympia, but even with a centre of gravity change, it failed to fly at Southampton Water on 30 May 1914. Such claims and disappointments were typical of the flamboyant aeronautical entrepreneur. However, it appears the first signs that Supermarine would become a nationally recognised aero-company could be heard by the comments made at Olympia.

Into the rapid technological development of fixed-wing landplanes now stepped Pemberton-Billing with his simple PB9 design, which was carefully thought through for productionisation, also using a 50-hp Gnome. The prototype was built in eight days and was first flown in August 1914. The machine was successful, but was not ordered into production as a fighter. However, the prototype remained as a trainer for naval pilots. Pemberton-Billing was more successful a year later with the PB23E, later to enter production as the PB25. The designer had circumvented the issue of machine guns firing through propeller arcs and shredding them by mounting the engine at the rear, pushing the fighter along rather

---

* Macclesfield-born Hope represented Great Britain on the sailing team in the 1900 Olympics in France and won gold, so he knew a thing or two about hull forms.

than pulling it. It was ordered into service but never saw combat: a sad epitaph for such an innovative machine.

First World War aviation at sea was dominated by seaplanes and flying boats at which the company excelled, and which thrilled Pemberton-Billing, who had told his small design team that he wanted not aeroplanes which float but boats which fly. It was the way to speed and range. It was the way to profit, too, when this dreadful war was over, and the empire would need to be connected. In fact, it was an artform that at the time was as rarified as a spacecraft manufacturer would be considered half a century later.

However, Pemberton-Billing was already starting to look elsewhere for challenges. On the outbreak of war, he had volunteered for the Royal Naval Air Service which had just been set up on 1 July 1914 by the First Lord of the Admiralty, Winston Churchill. The day-to-day running of the firm was left in the hands of Scott-Paine, who had become the designated manager when Pemberton-Billing received Admiralty contracts to repair flying machines at Fambridge, on the site of his old airfield. Actually, Fambridge was just a flat field on the marshes with a couple of timber buildings to give shelter, but Their Lordships believed that Pemberton-Billing had the resources to effect repairs and they also needed a factory to design and build an anti-Zeppelin land-based flying machine to tackle the night raids by German airships. A contract for SuperMarine (the new styling of the name as a trading entity of Pemberton-Billing Limited) was agreed in December 1914 and Joseph Crabtree Taylor was hired to design the aeroplane, what would become the PB29. The basic specification, on a single sheet of paper, was for a machine that could fly for twelve hours at 10,000 feet; the altitude was a key user requirement, but the specification allowed for two hours' climb to height.

Pemberton-Billing was so convinced by the PB29 design that he personally financed the initial work to the tune of £6,000 (about £600,000 in today's equivalence) before the Admiralty sent the initial funding. To help, he brought in Cecil Richardson to run the Pemberton-Billing drawing office with a salary of £3 a week. The PB29 was an innovative design that featured a two-pilot crew, one to fly and the other to use the searchlight and Lewis machine guns.* The most radical design feature was the provision of four sets of wings – a quadruplane – presumed to give good endurance, and two 90-hp piston engines to create the power to get the flying machine to height. The design did not enter production but was test flown by Pemberton-Billing at Chingford, Essex. The issue for Pemberton-Billing Limited was that other companies had started to design, build and test single-seat fighters, which had better performance and, from the Admiralty's perspective, the advantage of a lower cost. Competition was fierce.

Pemberton-Billing was becoming more and more focused on politics so sold his shareholding and therefore the company to Scott-Paine in 1916. His aim was to stand for election to Parliament, which he achieved on the second attempt to represent the seat of Hertford, initially as an independent so he could

---

* It was probably the first British design with an enclosed cockpit for pilot and observer.

criticise the conduct of the war. He could be described as a right-winger with defined views on the role of women, the colonies (he founded *The Imperialist* magazine) and public housing, as well as the conduct of the war. He was a troublemaker in the House of Commons, refusing on one occasion in July 1918 to sit down when ordered by the Speaker and was therefore ejected from the House by the Serjeant at Arms and suspended. In the 1918 General Election he doubled his majority despite his antagonism to the prime minister, David Lloyd George, but resigned in 1921 and disappears from the aviation scene and this narrative. He eventually moved to Australia but returned to Britain on the outbreak of the Second World War. He died back in Essex in 1948.

When Pemberton-Billing sold his company on, the spirit of innovation and design adroitness seems to have followed. Scott-Paine had no political ambitions, but he was a shrewd businessman and took the opportunity to change the company's name to the more recognisable Supermarine Aviation Works Limited.* He completed the move out of Essex to the Oakbank Wharf which Pemberton-Billing had bought on the banks of the Itchen – his heart was on the water and not in the fields of Essex. He convinced the General Post Office that his telegraphic address could be simply 'Supermarin,† Southampton', and messages would be delivered promptly – Britain boasted a dozen daily deliveries. Those messages were often orders for seaplanes or requests for

---

* The name was officially changed in November 1916 with a nominal capital of £20,000 (£1.5 million in 2025 terms).

† Note the abbreviation for telegraphic purposes.

parts as a machine was on the water and unable to fly without that part.

The small team at Supermarine was now at Woolston and reor- ganised by Scott-Paine, who appointed F. J. Hargreaves as chief designer to also carry out the duties that a chief operation officer would perform in a small company today. Hargreaves remained at Supermarine for three years until he found a new post at Vosper in Portsmouth Harbour.*

By 1916, Admiralty policy was changing – to Supermarine's benefit. At the beginning of the First World War, the Royal Naval Air Service was the dominant air arm in Britain. The Naval Wing of the Royal Flying Corps had been spun off to create a naval service. The man behind this innovation was Winston Churchill, the First Lord of the Admiralty, a passionate advocate of new technology even though he seems rarely to have understood it – grasping its potential instead. He even tried learning to fly at Royal Naval Air Station Eastchurch, completing over a hun- dred hours of dual instruction with a Royal Marines major, but he failed to go solo. This did not stop Churchill from claiming the right to wear Royal Air Force wings on his Honorary Air Commodore's uniform when he was prime minister – who was going to stop the PM?†

---

* He was last heard of involved in pre-Second World War telescope develop- ments. Hargreaves' papers are lodged with the Science Museum in London. There has always been confusion between F. J. Hargreaves and W. A. Hargreaves at Supermarine.

† Churchill was awarded honorary wings by the Air Ministry on 1 April 1943; prior to this, he did not wear wings.

The Royal Navy had already developed seaplane carriers like HMS *Engadine*, a converted cross-Channel packet steamer, equipped with a crane to hoist seaplanes into and out of the water. *Engadine*'s seaplanes participated in the Cuxhaven Raid* of 1914, and she was a favourite of Churchill's. He understood the need for taking aviation to sea, but the technology of the day limited the application. Firms such as Supermarine and the Short Brothers in Kent knew that the flying boat was the immediate solution – boat hulled or on seaplane pontoons. For now, that was where their thoughts were moving, but they needed powerful and reliable engines to make them a reality.

In 1916, Their Lordships decided that the Royal Naval Air Service needed a range of flying boats, from a single-seat fighter to a large patrol bomber with both endurance and range. This was music to the ears of Supermarine. Before the war, the company had been facing financial ruin, but was saved by Admiralty contracts. It would go on to carry out essential war work by building the Norman Thompson NT2B training flying boat (a simple biplane that gave trainee aircrew the feel of a flying boat in the air and on the water), and was selected to be one of the sub-contractors to build the Short 184 flying boat (the standard naval seaplane of the period which mainly served the North Sea and Mediterranean) under licence for the Admiralty.

---

* The Cuxhaven Raid is considered the first strategic aerial bombing raid as it was designed to destabilise the German Zeppelin airship capabilities. It was an amazing feat of aviation.

The issue was how to make money – not a fortune, but enough to keep investing in the technology as it rapidly changed. Now, with an added injection of cash from various local Southampton businessmen, and a determination to pursue the flying boat, Supermarine was poised to expand – and the quality and skills of its people would be crucial. In 1916, Scott-Paine had advertised for new staff and one of the applicants was a recently qualified railway engineer from Stoke-on-Trent named Reginald Mitchell.

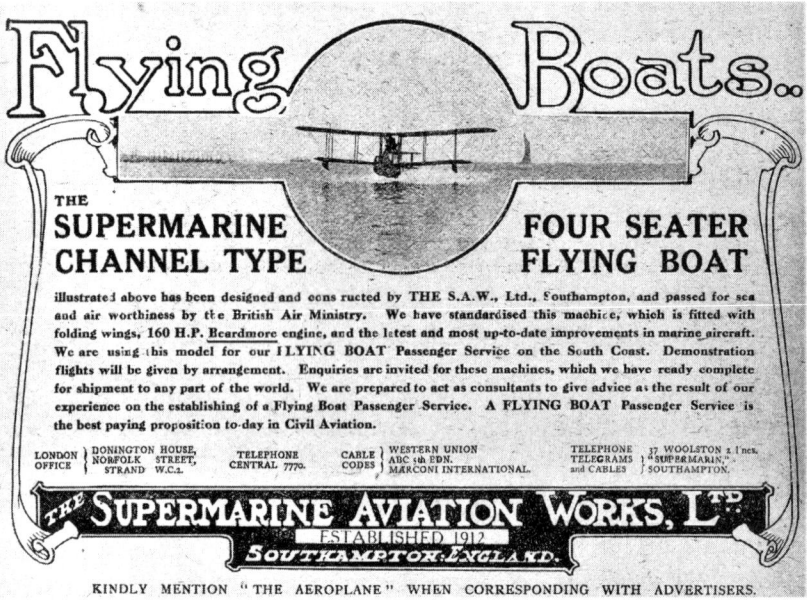

*The Supermarine Aviation Works fulfilled
government contracts in the First World War, but
had ambitions in post-war commercial aviation.*

3

Gateway to the Empire

Stepping off the railway service from Waterloo in the early evening of a summer day in 1916, Reginald Mitchell had entered a totally different world. Southampton's Terminus station immediately impressed with its feeling of openness and freedom. It was not just the smell of seaweed and the sea, with a hint of coal dust from ocean-going cargo ships in the nearby docks, but the lack of smoke in the air and the freshness of an onshore breeze. Southampton was so different from Staffordshire. There seemed to be much more light in the sky.

The journey from Stoke to London had been difficult. The train had been packed with soldiers mobilised for the third year of the First World War, most heading for the stalemate of the Western Front but perhaps a few continuing their journey to Southampton to embark on steamers for the Middle East. The city and its port had been designated No. 1 Military Embarkation Port earlier in the conflict, as, after all, Southampton prided itself on being the 'Gateway to the Empire', and the British Army was beginning to have some success in imperial Egypt and Palestine, driving Germany's allies, the Ottoman Turks, from the lands of Arabia.

Southampton was old, dating back to before the Saxons arrived in the British Isles over a thousand years previously. Historically vital to the maritime defence of Britain, it was also the departure point for the Pilgrim Fathers off to America in their sailing ship, *Mayflower*. It had withstood the unwanted attentions of French pirates after English troops had left there for Agincourt and now, five centuries later, it was still reeling from the sinking of the great ocean liner RMS *Titanic* just four years before. The loss of the ship and the more than five hundred local crew and passengers aboard had touched almost every street in Southampton, the home of the White Star Line, the owner of the 'unsinkable liner'. That had been followed by two years of war which had already taken the lives of many soldiers and sailors from the city, the neighbouring New Forest and the hinterland of what was once the County of Southampton, later simply Hampshire.

Taking the short walk from the station to the Itchen Ferry, which crossed the river from Southampton docks to almost right outside the main gates of the Pemberton-Billing Works, the history of the place must have flashed across the young engineer's mind. Southampton was a marine industrial centre, and the Itchen was its heart. Not only did Pemberton-Billing Ltd have its base there, but just downriver on the confluence with Southampton Water, less than a mile away, was the major naval shipbuilders of John I. Thornycroft & Company, makers of the Coastal Motor Boats and other fighting ships that were in daily action with the Royal Navy.

After meeting the team at the firm that would soon be known as Supermarine, Mitchell was a little shocked as, at the relatively young age of twenty-one, he had been offered a responsible position – assistant to Hubert Scott-Paine – in a company engaged in important war work. The firm was small, efficient and had a distinct liking for those educated in the exacting engineering of railways and steam. Pemberton-Billing and Scott-Paine seem to have had little difficulty in recruiting talent for the shop floor – people like Mitchell who were keen to get in on the ground floor of the new technologies. He was entering a new industry positioned even more at the leading edge of technology than the railways. It was a brave new world in more ways than one: new industry; new location; new lifestyle.

Woolston Works was rather ramshackle in appearance. The offices were floored with lino and the workshops were haphazard in layout, often in repurposed sheds from local shipyards. Because of the nature of the work – flying boats and amphibians – there were ramps and jetties, even mooring buoys out in the River Itchen. The smell of the salt water and seaweed would have been alien to Mitchell, but he would have soon become used to the odours. Less so, perhaps, the plumes of early oil refining at Fawley just a few miles to the south; when the wind was in the right direction, there was a distinctive tang in the air.

Immersing himself in the aviation trade, Mitchell set about working in every department of the small firm. He learned about the hull forms of flying boats and their building process, which had been developed from small sailing dinghies and used exotic materials – to Mitchell at least – of imported mahogany and cedarwood. There was also considerable use of cellulose dope on Irish linen to make the skins of the flying surfaces. Having started its life as a marine company, the firm was skilled in hull streamlining, radical propulsion and light but sturdy construction; and, as seaplanes and flying boats became the norm for Supermarine, the team developed engineering practices that had much in common with other forms of transport.

Mitchell was used to the smell and feel of a heavy machine shop: the noise of whirring lathes, the occasional thump of a heavy hammer on metal. But aeronautics was less metallic than Kerr, Stuart & Company in Fenton. He would have immediately sensed the order and calm of aeroplane construction, much of which was undertaken by craftsmen using woodworking tools. Supermarine, like most of the industry, was traditional, not dissimilar to yachts or pleasure boats: working in wood with fittings and joints made of turned or beaten metal, even then used sparingly for weight and cost reasons. He set to work straight away: surviving drawings for the Pemberton-Billing-designed Nighthawk* dated July 1916 bear the initials 'R. J. M.'

There was considerable talent in Supermarine's employ. The relationship between the customer – the Admiralty – and aircraft designers was necessarily close in the First World War. The Royal Naval Air Service was a prime mover of innovation under the leadership of Commodore Murray Sueter. He had taken command of

---

* The Nighthawk or PB31E was a serious weapons-carrying aeroplane with four wings. It was fitted, according to the drawings, with a Davis cannon to destroy Zeppelins and Lewis machine guns for self-defence. It even had power for a searchlight to illuminate its prey.

the Naval Air Department* in 1912 and is described by many as the father of the Royal Naval Air Service. In 1915, he was appointed superintendent of aircraft construction and sat for the Aeronautics Advisory Committee at the National Physical Laboratory (NPL) at Teddington. He brought several projects to fruition off the drawing board, including several with Supermarine, as well as with two other well-known but now historical aviation companies: Fairey and Parnall.

Until the end of the war, the Admiralty drafted in its own experts to design flying boats at Supermarine, known as the AD Boats (AD standing for Air Department of the Admiralty), intended as patrol aircraft to work alongside warships. The AD Boat, designed by Harold Yendall, Clifford Tinson and Harold Bolas – with a hull design by Lieutenant Linton Hope of the Royal Naval Air Service – had been built by Pemberton-Billing in 1916. In the Air Department, Harris Booth oversaw the design, while Bolas, Tinson and Yendall were seconded to Woolston.[1] Thus, in the design office, Mitchell was able to work with luminaries such as Bolas when still in his early twenties. Bolas would later be released on loan to Parnall & Sons, aspirant aeroplane makers, in 1917 to become chief designer there, where he would design the Parnall Panther machine-gun-armed biplane fighter.

Bolas can be credited with being an inspiration to Mitchell. After the AD Boats, Bolas next worked on a two-seat, two-cockpit

---

* The Naval Air Department would later move to Farnborough and become the world's leading naval aviation technology centre for half a century, with innovations like the aircraft carrier angled deck, the steam catapult, the hydraulic arrester wire and the mirror landing sight, without which the jet age would not have gone to sea.

biplane fighter called the AD Navyplane. Commodore Sueter passed design control to Mitchell at Woolston where he, with Bolas's help as it was his conception, finished the production designs in weeks rather than months, allowing Commander John Seddon to fly it for the first time in August 1916. It was a floatplane with the tail held in place by four tail booms. The crew nacelle, in front of the pusher engine, is thought to have been Mitchell's lead; it was fitted with a floor, spacious and lightweight – his railway engineering knowledge coming to the fore.

The AD Navyplane was actually proposed by Supermarine as a replacement for the Short 184 as it offered greater endurance and durability in moderate-to-high sea conditions, but the engine was not powerful enough for the task in hand and the project faltered. In the event, the Short 184 would fulfil the role because it had folding wings and could lift a torpedo. The AD Navyplane proved unsatisfactory from the Admiralty's point of view but the process was formative for Mitchell, who benefitted from the design experience, working with the Admiralty and Bolas, as well as understanding the need for power. Mitchell never forgot the lesson about the right engine for the right aerostructure.

In 1917 Supermarine started on the design for a single-seat naval fighter, powered by a 150-hp engine, meeting the Admiralty specification N1.B for 95 mph at 10,000 feet and having a service ceiling of 20,000 feet (in the days before oxygen*). It was specified by the Admiralty to counter the increasing number of

---

* Aviators were unaware of the effects of depleted oxygen in the body during the First World War. It led to the creation of the Institute of Aviation Medicine and aeroplanes carrying oxygen cylinders for aircrew as a matter of course.

Brandenberg fighter-seaplanes operating against the Home Fleet and the Dover Patrol off the German coast – and sometimes right up to Felixstowe and Great Yarmouth. (As Mitchell wrote in a letter to his brother Eric on 9 September 1917, 'Things are very dull here. We have to trust to an occasional air raid to liven things up a bit. They do it with aeroplanes now. The zepps have "done their bit".'[2]) The submission of what would come to be known as the Supermarine N1 'Baby' was designed by F. J. Hargreaves, the chief designer at Supermarine, based on the AD Boats. The Baby – the first British single-engined fighter flying boat* – was fast, but by the time the design was finished, and the first aeroplane was ready, the war had ended and the need had gone. In the early part of Mitchell's career, it is difficult at times to navigate the designs and his role in them. But the Baby design process was instrumental in Mitchell's thinking; his input has never been documented but is thought to have included work on the hull form. Its influence can clearly be seen in the design of the racing seaplanes that were to follow.

Mitchell also learned from the engineer and designer Cecil Richardson, but they crossed paths for only a short time as the latter left Supermarine Aviation in June 1918 with glowing references. He had seen the Baby fly and achieve its key user requirements but did not want to move to Woolston when the company relocated.

Throughout these early years, Scott-Paine would have seen the quiet strength, knowledge, skill and depth of thinking in Mitchell:

---

* A trend that would continue until the late 1940s and end with the jet-powered Saunders-Roe SRA/1 conceived for the Pacific War. When the Second World War ended, so did the need and such a concept was never taken up again.

a useful foil to his own exuberance, and a different accent to the Hampshire drawl of Southampton and the New Forest. Mitchell, with a slight stammer that initially made him appear shy, would have been content working with the more outgoing Scott-Paine, watching the businessman do deals, keep the team working hard and rewarding successes – it was wartime, but there was always room for a few small treats in the close-knit group at Supermarine, even if work was sometimes all-consuming. As Mitchell wrote to Eric on 9 September, 'I have been trying to get away from Southampton, but have not succeeded. The restrictions on munitions workers are rather exacting at present. We are turning out machines in large quantities now. I wonder if you see any of them over there. How should you like to go in for flying? . . . I wish I could.'[3]

Fitting into the Supermarine team, Mitchell had good prospects, as they would say at the time, and therefore was able to propose marriage to his sweetheart Florence Dayson. She was eleven years older than Mitchell and already headmistress of Dresden Infants' School back in Stoke-on-Trent. After Flo had resigned from the school board, they were married on 22 July 1918 at St Peter's Church, Caverswall, in Staffordshire. As one historian wrote, 'One can only wonder what qualities the young R. J. Mitchell must have had for Florence to give up her job and marry a man only a year out of his apprenticeship.'[4]

In a family pre-wedding picture, Mitchell is shown ready to go to church in a tailored three-piece suit with fob watch. He wears a straight tie with a high pin under a stiff white collar, which must have been uncomfortable. His brown hair has a right-hand parting and the rest a curled quiff of 'thatch'.

The new family home was in Bullar Road, Bitterne Park, described at the time as an up-and-coming suburb of Southampton. It was the first taste of life together. The couple settled in, acquiring a motorcycle combination as their family transport, and Flo quickly made friends in the neighbourhood while Mitchell was away, often for long hours, at the Woolston drawing office. Mitchell's work was never far from his mind. Flo later told a reporter that he 'loved snooker, but even in the middle of a game he'd suddenly put down his cue and out would come an old envelope or a scrap of paper and, as he began to draw, he would give me a rapid explanation of the diagrams he was making'.[5] His hard work was paying off as he was promoted to assistant works manager in 1918.

The end of war came quickly. With the cessation of hostilities on the Western Front in November 1918, there was general rejoicing that the 'war to end all wars' was over. Southampton had not seen the air raids of the East Coast and London, but the celebrations and commemorations were widespread.

The new Royal Air Force, amalgamating the Royal Naval Air Service (Admiralty) and the Royal Flying Corps (War Office), was greatly reduced in size and manpower but had surplus wartime machines, so new designs were not needed. There was commercial concern when Air Ministry* contracts were immediately put on hold as the British government wanted to reduce its deficit. For Supermarine, the end of the war had three consequences: first, the cancellation of orders; second, a pool of skilled aeroplane

---

* The formation of the Royal Air Force on 1 April 1918 meant that official control of design and contracts passed to the newly created Air Ministry, with many of the naval and military staffs coming over to the new body to maintain continuity.

technicians became available; and third – and this is where Scott-Paine and Mitchell were firmly allied – the opportunity to buy back airframes at knock-down prices. For Scott-Paine, it was about the dawn of commercial aviation and for Mitchell it was about developing new machines.

Southampton had been a focal point for troop movements to France and the Mediterranean but now had to redefine itself as a commercial port. To Scott-Paine, who was more interested in commercial designs than war machines, Southampton was a place of opportunity. He would need a new business model, but that was his forte and he rose to the challenge. Mitchell was pleased to join him.

The Air Ministry declared over 5,000 aeroplanes surplus to requirements, including over a hundred seaplanes and flying boats. Within a year, commercial flights were departing Croydon, south of London, to Paris-Le Bourget, and the Air Ministry created a Department of Civil Aviation to oversee the regulation, governance and exploitation of commercial aviation.

Never short of ideas, Scott-Paine and his new 'bright-eyed boy' Mitchell came up with a plan to buy back a number of the AD Boats and convert them for this new era of commercial aviation. Supermarine bought ten ADs for conversion in 1919, and their Certificates of Airworthiness were issued between July 1919 and May 1920. None had seen active service, having been delivered after November 1918.

The original plan seems to have been air taxi or ad hoc charters, but then some bright spark suggested that if the 200-hp Hispano-Suiza engine could be replaced by a lighter, more fuel-efficient 160-hp Beardmore, it would still be possible to add an additional cockpit area for three people in total and make the new machine, to be named the Supermarine Channel,* into a training flying boat. It only took a bit more woodwork to create room for four people and, lo and behold, what Supermarine claimed was the world's first international flying boat service had been created (there is debate among historians as to whether the Supermarine Channel was the first airliner as such; several other companies with wartime surplus airframes, like Handley Page and Vickers, might have a different view).

Suddenly, Mitchell found himself on the cusp of a new era in aviation, leading the engineering effort in a fast-moving, innovative company where his voice mattered and where individual initiative was valued. Aviation has been the same for a century. Mitchell's quiet manner and ability seemingly to pluck technical solutions out of the air speak volumes of both his brain and his apprenticeship back in Stoke-on-Trent. Early photographs of the tight-knit team show a group of people, no more than twenty strong, working on the early post-war modifications to the AD Boat including the seniors in suit and jacket, the other men in shirt sleeve order – braces and ties even.

Keen to recoup his expenditure and set an example of flying-boat air travel in the Southampton area, Scott-Paine hired some former Royal Naval Air Service pilots and started a passenger service from Southampton's Royal Pier at the Town Quay to Bournemouth, where a launch was used to ferry passengers ashore.

---

* First registered as a name on 14 February 1920.

On 16 August 1919, the Southampton–Isle of Wight service began, and even boat services could rely upon the Channel flying boat to deliver fuel when the surface craft ran out. In the first air-taxi service, passengers could board a flying boat if they missed the Isle of Wight ferry. Mitchell was delighted with usage of the three Supermarine Channels available at any one time; the others were kept as fleet reserves or were in maintenance, as reliability would be a keynote of Supermarine and Mitchell's engineering skills.

Not content with the local area, Supermarine wanted to start a cross-Channel service to Cherbourg, Le Havre and St Malo, with Bournemouth seemingly the most advantageous departure point on the south coast, presumably because of the market there for travelling to France and the excellent rail connection with London via Basingstoke and Southampton.* This time, for scheduled services, a pontoon had been constructed on Bournemouth Pier. Scott-Paine appointed Henri Biard, a former squadron commander in the Royal Naval Air Service, and now using the title 'Captain' to demonstrate his civilian air transport credentials, as the first pilot of the cross-Channel airways. These were definitely flights for the wealthy and adventurous – today's private-jet travellers face the same costs but rarely need to glide to the shore when their aircraft runs out of fuel, as happened on the maiden flight of the service. Not averse to strike breaking, Supermarine's Channels were also used to fly first-class passengers and newspapers when

---

* Supermarine claimed to have coined the phrase 'airport' for its Southampton base for trans-Channel and local seaplane services.

both the railways and the Channel Steam Packets that crossed to France went on strike.

In August 1919, the annual Cowes Regatta demonstrated the utility of a commercial flying boat for air taxi and sightseeing work. Since 1826, the Cowes Regatta on the Solent has been a highlight of the social calendar, sandwiched between Glorious Goodwood horse racing across the water in Sussex and the opening of the grouse-shooting season. From the beginning it had royal patronage and so attracted the rich and famous; many of the larger yachts were owned by City gents who had professional skippers to race them for them. In the days before television, the eight days of yacht racing attracted tens of thousands of spectators who went by ferry, steamer and motor launch to the Isle of Wight. Scott-Paine saw the opportunity and, always with an eye on publicity, took a Channel flying boat to the regatta as prelude to opening a Channel Islands service. It attracted public attention, with people pointing out what an amazing machine it was, which in turn attracted the media.

By 1919, Supermarine was becoming the British company with the greatest expertise in flying boats and seaplanes. And so it was a natural choice for a Schneider Trophy entry. Although the First World War had put a temporary halt to the races, the post-war aviation scene was vibrant and the victorious powers of France, Italy and Great Britain were keen to re-establish the contest. In Britain, there was a real passion for racing seaplanes that had started before the First World War and continued through the conflict with the development of some innovative war machines; now, in peacetime, the need for speed and reaching the 200 mph 'barrier' became almost an obsession.

The performance of the Baby was such that the machine showed enough promise for the Royal Aero Club, which chose Britain's entries, to take an interest. The Club, responsible for the governance of British sport flying, promoted the Baby as an entrant in the Schneider Trophy race of 1919 at Bournemouth.

Three prototypes of the Baby had been built or were under construction on 11 November 1918 and the first two, serial numbers N59 and N60, were in Admiralty, later Air Ministry, hands. The third aeroplane, N61, had been modified by Hargreaves to have a larger fin and rudder and was probably the airframe that was designated Sea Lion, Supermarine's Schneider entry. Mitchell's first real design work was on the engineering modifications to compete in the races.

Yet, despite the preparation and redesign, the Royal Aero Club thought an Avro design and two modified landplanes on floats from Fairey and Sopwith would be faster. By the time race day came around, the Sea Lion was fielded by the Club, but Mitchell was in two minds, as the foggy weather was not compatible with the competition. He was right, as the French entrants did not complete the course and the other British entrants retired. Squadron Leader B. D. Hobbs, a distinguished anti-Zeppelin fighter pilot, crashed in the Sea Lion (not distinguished by a mark number) and so also didn't finish the course. The Italian pilot did complete the course, but was disqualified.

Mitchell was not impressed, but took note – not least when Scott-Paine decided to show off the Channel by flying down to the start of the competition on 10 September. However, despite Scott-Paine's best efforts, the airline business began to stall. There were too many initial weak links in the chain to make it really successful in Britain – weather, lack of heating, need for a friendly boatman, refuelling issues. The primitive conditions for passengers, especially after the summer, proved disappointing even though the first signs of Southampton–Le Havre had been promising. The Franco-British air link closed down after about a month through lack of interest from the fare-paying public.

Growth in scheduled commercial aviation might have temporarily slowed down but the Channel was in demand around the world, albeit in small numbers. The first customer was the Royal Norwegian Naval Air Service, which used a Channel Mk I flying boat for training prior to acquiring the Mk II variant with a more powerful Siddeley Puma engine for a coastal air service. Orders from the Royal Swedish Navy and the Imperial Japanese Navy followed on quickly; the Japanese were impressed by the Channel's ability to deal with crosswinds and high-swell conditions after a round-the-island flight from Woolston. The most exotic was an order from Venezuela for a Channel Mk II to survey the upstream areas of the Orinoco River.*

Later New Zealand and, in 1922, Chile joined the customer list, making eighteen airframes in all. Ideas for air services in Florida, the Caribbean and the North Sea popped up with regularity, but the aeronautical industry was not yet ready for guaranteed and robust schedules. Nevertheless, there were commercial opportunities to use flying boats for the security of the new oil exploration rigs off Trinidad.

---

* 436 tributaries were discovered or surveyed by the Channel flying boat.

Supermarine's elaborate post-war stationery says that the company was a contractor to the navies of Great Britain, Imperial Japan, Sweden, Norway, Portugal and 'other foreign governments' as well as the Admiralty and the new Air Ministry – designers and constructors of Supermarine flying boats and amphibian flying boats. Great ambition, perhaps, but justified.

Meanwhile, Mitchell remained at his drawing board, building on the experience of the Channel conversions and the need to carry more passengers if a service was to be profitable. He was learning fast and maturing as a person and as an engineer – and he had a clear vision of his future.

Following his promotion to chief engineer in 1920, Mitchell started modifying wartime aeroplanes, while also developing a folding-wing amphibian for dual use. This Sea Eagle is pictured about to alight on Southampton Water.

4

First Designs

Appointed chief designer of Supermarine Aviation Works Ltd in 1919 following the departure of F. J. Hargreaves, Mitchell moved up to a management role from the important but second-tier job of assistant works manager. Industry in the inter-war period was very hierarchical, and job titles mattered for not just salaries but also social standing. Mitchell was only twenty-four years old, yet was already proving himself with his hard work and innovative thinking about the future of flying boats and high-speed flight. He was already finding his trademark ability to bring a design into development and then hand over the detail to others in the team to take the project to production. But there was more to come: Mitchell's additional appointment as chief engineer in 1920 is considered by many to be the most important accolade. It recognised his skills and training in an industry that was at the heart of technical innovation, far outstripping railways, shipbuilding and even motor transport.

He set to work on building up the Supermarine business in

a new era in which the wartime aero manufacturers now had to adjust to the peace.

The First World War, like most conflicts, had seen an explosion of technology, especially in aviation. In 1914, most military flying machines were unarmed for reconnaissance; by the Armistice, they were quite sophisticated. The Bristol Fighter of 1917 served with the Royal Air Force until nearly 1932 – but somehow military development in the 1920s ceased and it took the threat of another war in Europe to get it moving again.

Germany, Britain's pre-war and wartime aeronautical rival, was barred from meaningful aviation by the Versailles Treaty in 1919 – although that didn't stop the Weimar Republic later teaming with Soviet Russia on flying training, nor the German glider industry developing much better wing forms, which would come into play in the 1930s. Italy, a victor in 1918, poured funding into aviation; America, too, was developing aeronautics with state aid, having been embarrassed by having no competent aeroplane to cover its men in the trenches from 1917–18.

In Britain, however, the gentleman amateur still reigned supreme and the state stood back – there was little interest in the new science of aeronautics in Whitehall, where rebuilding an economy ravaged by conflict naturally had the priority.

The European scene was divided between those nations favouring transport and commercial flight, such as the Netherlands, or fast aeroplanes and flying boats, such as Italy, or all-round capabilities spawned from the war, such as France and the UK. Britain had a number of really innovative companies that would become household names for another half century.

After the war, the Royal Air Force took control of all military aviation in Britain. It provided aeroplanes to the Fleet for the new aircraft carrier concept and supported the British Army in the field, especially in the outreaches of the empire where the government preferred air power to boots on the ground. The budget was small and aeroplanes from the war were repurposed and sent overseas.

Ministers like Churchill saw air power as cost effective in a period of European history that many thought would be peaceful for a century. Against the background of austerity as Britain tried to rebuild its revenue streams, the defence budget was drastically cut, yet technology was moving at such a pace that new orders were forthcoming. The Air Ministry spent a considerable amount of time in direct talks with the aeroplane industry to find common ground for the future equipment plan. For Supermarine, this initially meant flying boats for the Royal Navy, used as 'Fleet spotters' to see over the horizon in the days before radar allowed long-range surveillance; long-range patrol requirements were yet to come.

Supermarine had a vision of using flying boats for both commercial passenger flights and for connecting the military outposts of the empire. With a quarter of the globe under nominal British control, air power was the only conceivable way of keeping control. The flying boat was the immediate answer to both Supermarine's growth markets, because of the lack of runways and the fact that so much of the world's surface is water – not just seas and lakes, but wide rivers as well. Supermarine was however a niche player and taking redundant airframes was a way for the company to keep in business.

Mitchell flew to Paris-Le Bourget for the first aeronautical exhibition since the Armistice in December 1919 to see what developments in aero-engines and passenger aeroplanes were on show. The French were centre stage with the Blériot Mammoth, a twenty-eight-seater, and Vickers was there with the Vimy Commercial, converted from a bomber. Supermarine was not represented but that was not the point; Mitchell wanted to see the engines.

Mitchell, the youngest chief designer in the British industry, knew he needed to be innovative, so he hired people to help him develop the company and its products. Working all hours to ensure that Supermarine's products were marketable, he set about creating a team to work on new ventures in seaplane and flying-boat development.[1]

He built on Supermarine's previous work, pushing the concepts forward. The Supermarine family of early flying boats all owe their gestation to First World War designs from the pencils of several different teams. As Mitchell developed his skill as an aeronautical engineer, because that was his first calling, he developed his design talents as well. It can be argued that design was subordinate to engineering in these early days of flight; it was possible to 'design a rib and turn to the engineering department and say: "I'll have twenty just like these" and it would work,' says the pilot and engineer Alfred Southwell.* The basic aerodynamics

---

* Heritage aviation pilot and Bristol University graduate aeronautical engineer who has studied early wing design.

of wing and fuselage structures were almost taken as a given with the Linton Hope float designs that came from yachting.

Supermarine was keen to develop the flying-boat concept from the First World War anti-submarine-warfare naval aircraft, aiming to provide the new Royal Air Force with a single-seat flying-boat fighter. The Sea King owes its lineage to the Supermarine Baby and the Sea Lion, which sank after the 1919 Schneider Trophy race at Bournemouth. Mitchell may have been considering the concept from his first days at Supermarine, but it was the public launch of a model at the Aero Show at Olympia in West London in 1920 that brought the Sea King I design to the world's attention. Scott-Paine loved the publicity; according to Eric Lovell-Cooper, the metal expert who Mitchell employed in 1924, the boss used every attempt to court attention, even contacting the local newspaper, the *Southern Daily Echo*, whenever he or Mitchell had an idea. The latter was always solid and Scott-Paine often a little showy.

Details are hard to find but it appears that Supermarine bought back the second N1 Baby – serial N60 – which Mitchell, by now the chief designer, modified for the exhibition. Supermarine corporate strategy was to claim a stake in the fighter flying-boat market and its tactic was to use the Baby basic design and modify it until a superior machine could be made.

For the Sea King II, Mitchell stipulated, it seems, a larger fin and rudder than the original Admiralty design for the Baby from which there are real signs of antecedence. The Sea King II was offered to the Air Ministry as a high-performance scout – fighter – with a fixed Lewis gun, and which could operate from the main gun turrets of battleships, battlecruisers and heavy cruisers.

The Royal Navy too was wrestling with design concepts for taking aeroplanes to sea. By working together – and because Mitchell was a good engineer with a flair for design – Supermarine won several important contracts that kept the company afloat when other aero manufacturers were forced to diversify into automobiles, or merge.

Mitchell excelled himself with the Sea King II in that his redesigns greatly improved its performance. The tail unit was described by Supermarine in press handouts as a 'fin and rudder of ample dimensions and a monoplane tail plane with reversed camber', which helped with seakeeping on the water, and there was a steerable tail wheel combined with a water rudder. Innovative stuff for 1921.

Mitchell was also busy with other forward-looking designs.

In September 1920 the government in London offered prize money for an effective commercial amphibian aeroplane as water runways were far more accessible than those on land. Most major cities in Britain and its empire were seaside or riverside locations, so that added to the need for a seaplane. So was born the Supermarine Commercial Amphibian, a biplane with a Linton Hope hull and Mitchell's favoured large tail and water rudder. Along with Fairey and Vickers, Supermarine had a flying machine ready for trials at Martlesham Heath* within ten weeks, thanks

---

* The Aeroplane and Armament Experimental Establishment (A&AEE) was a government scientific establishment which functioned for nearly 100 years at several locations to ensure that the latest developments in aircraft and armaments were tested thoroughly before entering service. The last incarnation was at Boscombe Down during the Second World War, where it remained until 1996.

to Mitchell's hard work and long hours. The design would inform many of Supermarine's later models.

The company was then commissioned to design a three-seater spotter amphibian, which would go on to be called both Seal II and Seagull II. Nomenclature of the Supermarine flying boats in the 1920s is confusing now and probably was then. The Seal/Seagull is a classic dilemma in evidence of that naming issue. Many historians believe that the Seal I was actually the Commercial Amphibian. That aside, the Seal II design was revolutionary in its own way as it featured a retractable undercarriage and an improved hull shape to prevent spray. The Air Ministry wanted the lowest possible landing speed so that medium sea states, or landing on the small, short flight decks of the first aircraft carriers, could be attempted.

The first Seal II was handed over at Woolston on 2 June 1921, just seven months after the Air Ministry specification was issued, and was flown straight to trials on the waters at the Isle of Grain in the Thames Estuary. For the first time, Mitchell had to understand the exacting world of aircraft carrier aviation, a new branch of aeronautical engineering. That meant low landing speeds, a robust structure and the provision of folding wings so that the amphibian could be struck down into a hangar below the flight deck.

To quote Supermarine's press handout, 'the hull is of the well-known Supermarine circular construction, combining in a high degree the requisites of strength, lightness and resiliency.' No doubt this release was approved by Mitchell as chief designer.

Internationally, only Japan showed an interest in the Seal II in 1921, buying one for intelligence purposes. On 4 July 1922, the

Seal II was renamed the Seagull to avoid confusion with the commercial variant, and a single naval Seagull II was exported to the Imperial Japanese Navy at Kasumigaura, the operating site of the Yokohama naval base.

Despite the lack of commercial success, the design was a stepping stone, and could be said to be the father of Supermarine's highly successful and versatile Walrus a decade later.

Even before a design was built and flew, Mitchell was keen to harness any recent innovations and requirements from Whitehall. To take a case in point, Mitchell worked on the closely related Scylla and Swan designs of 1921 and 1922 respectively. The former was in response to an Air Ministry requirement; the latter was aimed at the developing civil transport market as the Twin-Engined Commercial Flying Boat, which first appears in a planning drawing of July 1922. An artist's impression of the design was used in Supermarine press advertisements during 1922 and 1923 and this attracted the attention of Imperial Airways, the international airline founded in 1924.

Supermarine would claim that the Swan, which first flew in March 1924, was the world's first twin-engined amphibious flying boat; this was important because there were a growing number of airports with runways. The Swan has a direct line from the Commercial Amphibian, retaining the best features and yet being enlarged to carry twelve passengers. A simple examination of the schematic drawings shows that Mitchell was progressing his own ideas for overwing fuel tanks and gravity feed to the engines and relative comfort for the passengers. It was impressive for the time: Supermarine was keen to show its forward thinking for commercial aeroplanes on trade routes and its ability to design a long-range military reconnaissance aircraft. This was less than a decade since Mitchell had been taken on by Scott-Paine.

Mitchell realised that a large open crew compartment, although relatively simple to engineer, was a major issue with the performance of the Swan because of the drag induced. He found that he could maintain centre of gravity, important for the flying boat to take off without the tendency to *porpoise*,* and fly in a smooth way so as not to make the journey uncomfortable for the passengers. Other modifications showed that Mitchell understood production engineering required simplicity, such as square windows rather than oval-shaped ones and that if the two wings could be aligned then that made building simpler. A newly configured Swan flew on 9 June 1926 with wicker chairs for the passengers – on the first flight these included eight women from the design and tracing offices plus the Imperial Airways representative. Regulation and governance were a little different in the 1920s.

The Sea Eagle design, signed off on 27 March 1922, was a further step in a bid by British companies to enter into the commercial flying-boat market. The Sea Eagle was a pusher biplane passenger amphibian, which Mitchell laboured to perfect in the early 1920s. In an effort to reduce drag and increase lift, he designed in staggered wings. The simplicity of the approach, and his experience with hull forms, led to an aeroplane that the media called 'the boat which flies', as Pemberton-Billing had dreamt – or, as *Flight* put it, 'a seaworthy amphibian'. Rolls-Royce had also designed and

---

* When the power, sea and hull are not in alignment.

tested a more reliable engine called the Eagle IX, which Mitchell decided to use. The Sea Eagle has the appearance of a boat, with its forward fuselage reminiscent of a cabin cruiser for passenger comfort with triple, sliding windows, and yet the pilot was seated in the open just in front of the wings – so presumably protected somewhat from the spray of take-off and landing.

The Sea Eagle's public debut was the King's Cup Air Race of 1923, coming just two days after the granting of the type's airworthiness certificate. The design attracted attention at Cowes Week and carried the director of civil aviation, Sir Sefton Brancker, sightseeing above the famous regatta. Brancker also flew in a Sea Eagle to the Isle of Wight with Lord Apsley, the local MP, who was so impressed that he told Parliament: 'Seaplane travel will be one of the first methods of aerial locomotion' to gain popularity. That prophecy held good for four decades until post-war land-based airliners overtook their flying-boat colleagues, making use of hundreds of airfields created for the Second World War.

The flying-boat business was not exactly mass production because the Air Ministry had reduced budgets following the Armistice. So for Supermarine, it was a matter of keeping afloat rather than prospering as a commercial enterprise. By 1922, the design staff had grown to a dozen. Luckily, two things kept the company going – Mitchell's determination to succeed and a senior Royal Air Force officer, Sir Geoffrey Salmond,* ensuring that there was progress in aeronautics. Salmond wrote a letter to confirm that the company could anticipate orders but without

---

* Air member for supply and research, later Chief of the Air Staff.

making any formal promise. It was enough to keep the creditors off Supermarine's back and could be used with HM Treasury as some form of leverage.

Mitchell set to work with the knowledge that Salmond was suggesting that eighteen flying boats from the aircraft industry would be required in the period ending on 31 March 1924, the end of the government financial year. Such decisions and promises in the military and commercial aviation sectors allowed firms such as Avro, Hawker and Supermarine to keep staff and progress technology that would lead to the Lancaster, Hurricane and Spitfire in less than fifteen years.

Mitchell was the youngest of the great aeronautical engineers who turned to design work in the 1920s. His counterparts were older, some by a few years, but others by a decade or more. Mitchell designed to Air Ministry specifications and requirements because that's where the money lay, but he also ventured into his own products for a perceived market that might be just around the corner. He was a firm believer in flying boats as the commercial future of Supermarine, at least for passenger carriage and military reconnaissance purposes.

He first modified the designs of others and kept the best features, then gradually used that experience to branch out and create his own ideas, perhaps building on proven concepts from people like Linton Hope to bring his ideas to fruition. He wasn't alone in the schematic approach. Mitchell grew in confidence as his work succeeded.

Now he had his sights set on the ultimate prize: the Schneider Trophy.

After Pemberton-Billing's departure, Hubert Scott-Paine (far right) took the helm at Supermarine as Mitchell (second right) developed his skills. The aeroplane is the Sea Lion II Schneider Trophy contender.

5

Schneider 1922 and 1923

In every engineer's career there must be one or more pivotal moments. For Mitchell, the first was starting work at Supermarine and moving from railways to aeroplanes; the second was winning the Schneider Trophy at Naples in 1922.

Monaco had been the venue for the first Schneider Trophy race in 1913; this had sparked the imaginations of both Pemberton-Billing and Scott-Paine. It could be the way to instant success – or, at least, publicity. The first seeds of the desire to design and build a racing seaplane had been planted when both men read the press reports from Monaco. The First World War had interrupted that thought pattern, but Scott-Paine was now keen to continue. To gain recognition in the media and politics, he wanted to win a Schneider Trophy heat.

The Italians had come first in the 1919 event at Bournemouth, but were disqualified. They then managed to win again in 1920 and 1921, causing the British aircraft industry to sit up and realise that something had to be done to stop the trophy being permanently held in Italy.

Scott-Paine was determined to win in 1922, and, in effect, funded the Supermarine entry. He asked Mitchell to look at previous designs to come up with a potential winner. Mitchell felt that there were two areas where the Baby could be improved so that it stood a good chance in the Schneider races. He modified the tail to be larger, almost rectangular, to give better directional control in the air, and gave it a sizeable water rudder, finalising the design as late as 1921. He also modified the forward fuselage – how easy it would have been to rebuild the wooden frame and covering – to make it streamlined in the air and better able to take the swell on landing and during taxi. Hargreaves in the Sea Lion I had been concerned with spray coming over the bow into the cockpit, but Mitchell wanted the new model to have a curvy hull to aerodynamically direct any spray past the cockpit. His design was called the Sea Lion II.

In Naples, Mitchell watched with growing excitement – well, as much excitement as a lad from Staffordshire can muster in Italian climes – as Henri Biard, Supermarine's test pilot, took the Sea Lion II around the 200-mile course, following the hydrogen-filled balloon markers in a triangle from the city to a point almost due south, then turning across the bay to the village of Torre del Greco (in the shadow of Vesuvius). It was becoming clear to Mitchell, Scott-Paine, the Italians (with their state sponsorship) and perhaps even the crowd of several hundreds of thousands (for whom the race was a holiday) that the Macchi racing seaplanes were, surprisingly, no match for the biplane from England with its ancestry stretching back to the Admiralty seaplanes of the First World War. Through clever engineering, Mitchell had been able to reduce drag and improve the control surfaces so that Biard would not lose time on the turns. Mitchell had been confident that the Sea Lion II would go well after the team had retuned the 450-hp Napier Lion engine. The short-sleeved Biard reached an average of 145.7 mph – an almost unheard-of speed – and won.

It is perhaps sad that the Sea Lion II was highly successful but, in the event, nobody ordered the military version, which was a major aim of the entry from Scott-Paine's perspective. Britain had dramatically scaled back the order of battle to a little over 350 aeroplanes, with no fresh orders in the offing, and commercial aviation was still not yet off the ground.

Winning was nonetheless a huge achievement – but it wasn't enough for Supermarine. Mitchell and Scott-Paine already had their eye on next year's race. In September 1923, there was an air of expectation around the Solent for the next Schneider contest. Could Britain pull off a second win in a row – and would the man to pull the rabbit out of the hat be Mitchell? The British expected the French to come back strongly with state support. The US government was rumoured to have funded Curtiss to develop a winner; it was America's first outing, and US pride was at stake. Suddenly it emerged that the Italians, in political turmoil back home after Mussolini had taken power the previous year, would rely on last year's contender.

Blackburn, Hawker and Supermarine, the British entrants, were using re-modelled First World War airframes for their bids: very much make-do solutions for a limited budget. For Supermarine, the Sea Lion II was now past its sell-by date, and the only financially viable alternative was to re-engine the basic airframe with something more powerful. But Mitchell was still struggling with the design of the Sea Lion III. It needed to have less drag and cope with a more powerful engine, the Napier Lion III, and he needed to make it streamlined. The result was an almost jet-engine look, with the air intake and radiator completely cowled and a pusher four-bladed propeller. The key to the future of racing sea-planes was the frontal cross-section – today everyone talks about radar cross-section for stealth, but then it was all about drag: less drag, more speed. The development of engines, fuel systems and, above all, propeller shape was beginning to tell. If a flying boat was going to lift from the suction of the water, it needed a design that allowed it to 'unstick', but the key to that was getting the power, speed and design right so that the flying boat only left the water at flying speed – not a moment before or after. This was especially true when Mitchell was looking for optimum performance with the Sea Lion III design.

The aeroplane, painted to look like a sea lion, had a tiny cockpit for Henri Biard to again show his amazing skills as a flying-boat pilot. But it wasn't enough.

The race saw the contenders on a slipway provided by S. E. Saunders & Company (which would later become Saunders-Roe, also known as Saro) at Cowes, with huge gatherings on the shores of the Solent near Calshot, Lee-on-Solent and Portsmouth, and fewer spectators on the Isle of Wight. Special trains were again run from London. There was some tension in the air. After all, it was a world-news-making sporting event that was also filled with danger; more than one person attended to see a spill on the water.

However, the seventh Schneider Trophy contest at Cowes was a foregone conclusion, with the Americans obviously outpacing the Supermarine Sea Lion III – the US came first and second, with speeds 20 mph in excess of Biard. Mitchell immediately saw what the Americans had, but the Supermarine team had yet to acquire: in-line engines, rather than the radial ones that the British were still clinging to (in other words, the cylinders in a line rather than in a Catherine-wheel shape). The racing seaplane and not the racing flying boat was where the Schneider would be going next: for Mitchell, it would be new engines and a new way forward.

This defeat was enough for Scott-Paine. There had been tension at the top of Supermarine for some time: a distinct breakdown in relations between the directors, which caused a crisis for the company. It was one which Mitchell was pleased to avoid, although he would have seen the board-room wrangles. Every organisation has its personality clashes and the challenges of managing people usually needs considerable experience. Mitchell was young and inexperienced when he was made chief designer at Supermarine so he had much to learn in all fields.

In 1919, Scott-Paine had invited Squadron Commander James Bird, a marine architect and government contracts supervisor who had also been a Royal Naval Air Service pilot during the First World War, to invest in the company and join as a director. Bird set about making the company pay its way. Scott-Paine wanted to take the company towards commercial aviation and make the bedrock of an airline along the south coast and cross-Channel. He wanted commercial, passenger-carrying machines. Bird was a pragmatist; he knew commercial air transport was a little way off – there was still not enough reliability, endurance or passenger comfort. He also knew the economic position in which Britain found itself after borrowing from the Americans and the dominions during the war. Supermarine needed to design and build bread-and-butter flying boats, seaplanes and amphibians to stay afloat.

What's more, Scott-Paine was frequently absent with other interests: running his own airline business and making fast boats. The airline, British Marine Air Navigation Company, would, it was hoped, establish routes for which it would acquire passenger flying boats from Supermarine in a form of virtuous cycle. The fleet was initially made up of Sea Eagles: regular commercial services started on 25 September 1923 linking the first 'airport' at Southampton town pier with Guernsey in the Channel Islands. (The firm merged with three other airlines to form Imperial Airways in 1924, but this service established something of a record by operating on most days for the next five years.)

By November 1923, Bird had had enough of Scott-Paine's absences and preoccupation with the airline. It was inevitable that the Board would divide, and the only solution was for Bird to buy out Scott-Paine if the company was to survive. He was able to attract sufficient backers to fund a takeover and offered Scott-Paine £192,000 for his shares. Scott-Paine accepted and departed the company. It was agreed that Mitchell, already recognised as a major talent, would receive a salary of £1,200 per annum initially, rising to £1,300 and no less than £1,400 for the following eight years; and he would be made technical director in 1927. Bird then set about recapitalising the company, reduced staff and expanded the business with a listing on the London Stock

Exchange in 1925. Mitchell was one of those who bought shares and watched his investment go from strength to strength. The capitalisation rose from £13,500 to £250,000 in a year.

There is no doubt that Scott-Paine was visionary. Unlike Pemberton-Billing, he was interested in the physical rather than the theoretical and theatrical. He had inspired the company's leadership in flying-boat design. He also saw the flying boat's potential as an airliner for linking countries without the need for expensive runways and airports – parallel thinking to Juan Trippe in Florida, who created Pan American Airlines using flying boats. In 1927, Scott-Paine's new company, British Power Boats, pioneered custom-built tenders for flying boats and its clientele included Imperial Airways. He was also associated with T. E. Lawrence,* then an airman under an assumed name in the Royal Air Force with a passion for fast boats. Lawrence and Scott-Paine shared a love of speed on the water, although it is reported that the latter found the former 'tiresome'. Scott-Paine would go on to hold the world speed record for a watercraft with *Miss Britain III* at 110 mph in 1934.

Back at Supermarine, the firm was going from strength to strength. By the time Scott-Paine left, it had a serious following of London supporters, including members of the Air Council such as the Duke of Sutherland (Under Secretary of State for Air), Brigadier-General Ralph Bagnall-Wild (formerly president of the Royal Aeronautical Society and then director of research for

---

* Lawrence of Arabia had become a household name after the highly successful guerilla operation he had led in the Arabian Desert in the First World War.

the Air Ministry) and Air Vice-Marshal Sir Vyell Vyvyan (a former head of coastal area defence*). In Parliament, there were then, as there are now, supporters of aeronautical technology such as Sir Warden Chilcott MP, a former Royal Naval Air Service officer who represented Liverpool (Walton). These worthies were much taken with Mitchell's work on a series of flying boats, including the Seagull II, and they had visited Woolston on 23 February 1923 to see production and presumably to check on the investment of taxpayers' money.

The following year, on 27 June 1924, HRH the Prince of Wales (the future King Edward VIII) spent time in Southampton looking at the Supermarine Aviation works and its products, just two days after the modified Swan first flew. Another supporter was born!

Mitchell was also making strong local connections. By 1923, he and Flo were members of the Woolston Tennis Club, which gave access to 'society' in Southampton including the local Member of Parliament for Southampton, Lord Apsley, who became a friend. In 1924 he started the Apsley League, a competition for local tennis clubs, and was keen to promote the game as much as build social contacts. One can easily imagine the tall, athletically fit young Mitchell in his Artex shirt, white flannels and a tweed jacket, lovingly spinning his Slazenger racket in hand, waiting for his turn on the grass. All the time, eyeing up the competition.

Born Allen Bathurst, the son of Seymour Bathurst, 7th Earl Bathurst, and Lilias Margaret Frances Borthwick in the same year

---

* RAF Coastal Command was not formed until 1936.

as Mitchell, Lord Apsley was a distinguished soldier with gallantry awards and long service in the Territorial Army; he fought in the First World War in the Middle East as a Royal Gloucestershire Hussar. Both age and war record would have attracted Mitchell even though Apsley resided in Gloucestershire for much of the remainder of his life. He held the seat of Southampton (Itchen) from 1922 until 1929 and was elected for Bristol (Central) in 1931 and sat in the Commons until his death in 1942.

From 1925, about the time he befriended Mitchell, he took a keen interest in aviation. From Mitchell's perspective, the Apsley friendship was beneficial to Supermarine as he was parliamentary private secretary (PPS)* to the undersecretary for Overseas Trade 1922–24 and then PPS to the Minister for Transport 1925–29 and later to the Minister for the Coordination of Defence in 1936. In addition, Apsley was a huge fan of aviation: he became president of the UK Pilots' Association in 1925 and understood the airline business as a board member of Western Airways and Western Air Transport.

Despite all of this attention, Supermarine was still a small operation, even though Mitchell, on becoming chief designer and chief engineer, had started recruitment for the design team. The manufacturing side was divided into the people who maintained the jigs, presses and lathes and those who actually cut wood and metal for manufacture. There was a certain amount of class distinction.

---

* The Member of Parliament responsible for explaining the relevant minister's actions and policies to other MPs.

Sadly, no organogram of the company appears to have survived and, anyway, it was not the vogue then to make hierarchies. Everyone knew their job and relative position, and worked hard accordingly. Finding good people was not difficult as the culture was to advance by changing companies and learning new skills; Southampton was the home of several aeronautical enterprises so there was a rich pool of skilled men and women. In pre-computer days, drafting with pencil and ink was an artform developed from a science. All engineers had to draw and their final work was traced by a team of women whose concentration and attention to detail surpassed the men. The women were as vital to the team as the young men that Mitchell had started to employ.

A long-serving member of the technical team, Eric Lovell-Cooper, has left a pen-picture of life in the design office, the very heart of the business. Lovell-Cooper moved from Norwich and joined Supermarine from the aircraft manufacturer Boulton Paul in 1924. Another valuable team member – Supermarine might have been small, but it was not short of talent.

'Mitchell took me on because he knew wood was going out. He wanted somebody that knew about metalwork,' Lovell-Cooper recalled. He didn't meet Mitchell until the Wednesday or Thursday of his first week, and initially he had second thoughts about the move; he considered staying until only Friday or Saturday (there was Saturday working in those days) before handing in his notice. His description is a fascinating picture of Woolston at the time:

I thought, what have I let myself in for! It was a row of derelict houses with a gateway. The house next door had an empty room full of derelict bicycles, that's what it looked like through the window. They weren't broken, they'd just been left there by the people at Supermarine's [sic] who rode to work. Above were the offices where all the girls worked. The bedrooms of the houses, you see.

The drawing office was lit half by gas and half by electricity, and some of the gas was just jets, open fish-tail jets. Mitchell's office wasn't as big as this room. I thought, what the hell have I let myself in for? Is it worthwhile staying here?[1]

Lovell-Cooper did stay and became a valuable member of Mitchell's team through the Schneider Trophy developments and into the Spitfire work. In 1937, he was promoted to chief draughtsman, a key member of the management team that took the Spitfire through its seventy-two variants and into history.

Before any thought of a fighter aeroplane had entered Mitchell's mind, though, there was a large military flying boat to design.

*If there had been no Schneider Trophy or Spitfire,
the Southampton flying boat would have secured
Mitchell's reputation for innovation. This robust design
proved itself with a cruise to the Far East in 1927–28.*

6

Southampton: the Game Changer

There is one design of the 1920s that would have guaranteed Mitchell's name in the halls of fame even without the racing seaplanes and the iconic Spitfire: the Southampton military flying boat. It was ahead of its time, surpassed all expectations and deserves better recognition.

Between the wars, the British Empire stretched from Canada to Hong Kong, Australia to Egypt. Long-range flying boats would be needed because there was very little spare cash available in the Treasury for seaplane carriers, flying-boat tenders or even aircraft carriers. Flat-decked aircraft carriers had been pioneered by the Royal Navy at the end of the First World War and this meant wheeled-undercarriage aircraft could go to sea to protect the Fleet and project power. The issue was that they were small and of limited range. Flying boats like Mitchell's magnificent Southampton, which could easily reach Bordeaux, about 420 nautical miles south of Plymouth, filled that gap in the British inventory – power projection at range.

The Southampton flying boat was, for the next five years, that main capability in the air and one of the most successful ever used by the Royal Air Force. With a reputation for reliability, its service life of eleven years was surpassed only by that of the Sunderland. It was designed by Mitchell to Air Ministry Specification R18/24 and owes much to the Swan, its immediate predecessor. By the mid-1920s, it was clear that Mitchell's civilian Swan flying boat could be a contender to replace the Felixstowe F5 flying boats – the standard flying boats used by the Royal Air Force – from the end of the First World War. The innovation in design shown by Supermarine proved an immediate success, being ordered straight from the drawing board, establishing Mitchell as a name known in the corridors of power in Whitehall. It also brought Supermarine into the front ranks of aeronautical companies alongside Avro and Short.

The Southampton 'embodied all the experience that the Supermarine organisation had accumulated', according to the standard reference on the Supermarine designs.[1] It's true that the engineering for this design had been in the making for a decade. For the Southampton, Mitchell was able to harness all his experience with the Swan and earlier boats to produce a design that combined elegance with efficiency, and yet required craftsmen to shape and render the hull form.

Mitchell was innovative in the internal structure, with a double bottom running from stem to stern, allowing for various watertight compartments (in fact, the Mk I variant had ten watertight areas for the carriage equipment and personnel, and to allow for the safety of the boat in rough water conditions). The basic wooden construction included marine ply for the decking for ease of main-tenance and for movement of personnel in flight. Mitchell chose to mount the engines on pylons, in such a fashion that the ground crew found maintenance – even changes of powerplant – easy.

Defensive armament for the long sea patrol included two offset cupolas for two rear gunners who might double as the radio oper-ator and the navigator. Unusually for large aeroplanes of the time, either rear gunner had a good field of fire behind and below. The canted tail section allowed sight of any enemy aeroplane creeping up behind (although, as far as is known, no enemy was encoun-tered in the inter-war period in which the Southampton served in Royal Air Force colours). The other crew members were a pilot and, seated to his right, a co-pilot, both capable of operating the aeroplane singularly but both required for the demanding take-off and landing phases of flight. Crew conditions were good for the time, despite the pilots' cockpit being exposed to the elements, including the spray on take-off and alighting back on the water.

The Air Ministry had been so confident that Mitchell could develop the Southampton from the existing Swan that specifi-cation R18/24 was issued around the simple design and a first contract for six aircraft arrived on Mitchell's desk without wood being worked. Part of the confidence was that the design would be a classic flying boat rather than an amphibian, which made devel-opment and production easier, and, to a certain extent, cheaper.

A few days later came a contract for a further Southampton to be used purely for experimental flying at the Marine Aircraft Experimental Establishment (MAES). The Royal Naval Air Service base had been the centre of British seaplane design and development for almost a decade but was formalised just months after the Royal Air Force was created from army and naval aviation. Flying-boat and seaplane trials had been the province of the Admiralty during the First World War. New types were developed and new war-fighting techniques honed at the Isle of Grain on the Kent coast of the Thames Estuary at the MAES from October 1918. These flying machines included seaplanes, flying boats, amphibians, naval fighters and torpedo bombers as well as balloons and airships. The MAES was the first of its kind in the world when it was created by the First Lord of the Admiralty, Sir Eric Geddes MP. It was clear within a few years that it needed investment. On 16 March 1920, the MAES was renamed the Marine and Armament Experimental Establishment (MAEE) to bring in the evaluation of aerial weapons. In another reorganisation, the base was renamed the Marine Aircraft Experimental Establishment on 1 March 1924, and it was moved to the Suffolk coast at Felixstowe where there was already the infrastructure of the Seaplane Experimental Station.

Throughout the 1920s, the MAEE carried out acceptance trials for maritime aircraft, and manufacturers would deliver new types almost immediately after the first flight at their respective factories.* However, Mitchell's Southampton was ordered off the

---

* The MAEE itself continued to the end of the Second World War to be subordinate to the Ministry of Supply, but when the Royal Air Force stopped flying-boat development in 1953, it was reduced to marine craft and survival equipment. By March 1956, it was surplus to requirements and wound into the Aeroplane and Armament Experimental Establishment at Boscombe Down, with some of it going to the Royal Aircraft Establishment at Farnborough. It was a golden age of flying-boat development – in half a century going from flimsy machines which

drawing board in 1924 because the previous design, the Swan, had been so successful; the Royal Air Force may also have needed to replace its Felixstowe flying fleet with a better design as soon as possible. For a while, Felixstowe referred to the Southampton as the Swan Conversion, indicating that it was a proven concept. In all, Supermarine delivered two batches of eighteen flying boats within a year. It was an amazing feat of good organisation by Mitchell's design team and the production team.

The Air Ministry was enthused by the Supermarine attitude, which included weekly reports with photographs. The Felixstowe team who evaluated the sea worthiness of the Southampton were equally enthusiastic, finding the aeroplane lived up to expectations. MAEE received the first Southampton Mk I after it was first flown at Southampton by Henri Biard on 10 March 1925. Biard apparently reported no real vices except for a wing-tip float that was damaged on landing, probably due to heavy swell in Southampton Water. Mitchell re-examined the floats, which allowed balance on the water, and decided to change the design to improve the incidence of the float on contact with the water. It took only four days from the first flight to the completion of manufacturer's trials, and the prototype was delivered to Felixstowe by Biard. En route he practised feathering one engine and still maintained height, a feat that was remarked upon in the final Air Ministry report, which found no significant changes were needed.

---

could only be flown in calm sea conditions to the monster four-engined patrol flying boat of the Battle of the Atlantic.

First deliveries were literally just down the road – or just down Southampton Water – to the Royal Air Force station at Calshot, located on a sand promontory that divides the Solent from the waterway to Southampton and Hamble. The service debut was only weeks after the first flight, with No. 480 Coastal Reconnaissance Flight taking the first Southampton Mk I on charge at moorings on the lee side of the base. Visitors to the Calshot water-sports venue can still see the giant hangars that housed flying boats (which were hauled out of the water on trolleys), amphibians (which could taxi up a ramp) and, a few years after the Southampton arrived, the racing seaplanes for the Schneider events.

Woolston Works built the first six Southampton flying boats with ease, but the forecast of a further order from the Air Ministry would mean severe congestion on the Itchen. Commander Bird consulted with Mitchell, and they decided that the only space available and useful would be a waterside boatyard at Hythe on the New Forest side of Southampton Water. A series of water taxis were laid on to deliver components from Woolston to Hythe. The Supermarine building would become the focus of much finishing work into the 1930s; the structure is still virtually intact. It was close to the British Power Boats factory of Scott-Paine, who saw a host of Seagull and Southampton aeroplanes complete assembly and be test flown from Hythe rather than the Itchen at Woolston.

The Southampton was the iconic large British military aeroplane of its day: the Vulcan V-Bomber or Nimrod maritime reconnaissance aircraft. It was known to even non-aviation specialists and, of course, the City of Southampton basked in the glory that the name brought as the flying boat started a series of 'cruises', first around the British Isles and then on the 'empire routes' to British bases in Africa and Asia. These flights helped pioneer trade routes for Imperial Airways. (A few years later this seemed like timely reconnaissance; in 1939, Britain needed the deployment of a new generation of flying boats east and south as the country went to war with the Axis nations of Germany, Italy and Japan.)

The first excursion in September 1925 was a twenty-day trip covering 10,000 miles around the coast of the British Isles. A century ago this was no mean feat and demonstrated both the maturity of the Mitchell design and the support facilities of the Royal Air Force in seemingly every place where there was water. The flying boats could not go above the weather as they never flew above 11,000 feet, so the crew members had to wear rugged insulated Sidcot or seal-skin suits, and passengers (senior officers) were accommodated in the gunners' cupolas aft of the wings – a wet place to be on take-off and recovery to the water.

The first demonstration was when four Southampton flying boats left Calshot, formed up over the Solent and flew to conduct Fleet exercises with the Royal Navy in the Irish Sea. The opportunity was taken to show off Mitchell's latest creation at coastal towns and resorts where there were still holidaymakers on the beaches, fishermen inshore and people going about their everyday business. To see four large flying boats in formation cruise by at a few thousand feet must have been magical. The formation made landfall in Northern Ireland – showing the flag shortly after the creation of the Free State when there were deep concerns about the Union – and in Galloway and other parts of south-west Scotland.

The Air Ministry put out a communiqué – as a press release was then called – on 8 October 1925, which said that the cruise had seen the Southampton flying boats 'function successfully quite separately and independently of their land bases'. This was possible because Mitchell's design allowed for refuelling to be undertaken in ports and small harbours, using tankers to pump the aviation gasoline to the flying boats – this was made simple by the marine ply decking on the fuselage. When Mitchell was briefed on the success of this cruise, he must have thought that the future of long-range travel and military expeditionary deployments lay in the flying boat: rugged, straightforward designs with simple access for engineering maintenance. Mitchell certainly knew that if the Southampton's success continued then the Supermarine company would be on a stable financial footing.

Separately, a single Felixstowe-based Southampton flying boat also undertook a national tour of England, Wales, Northern Ireland and Scotland that autumn. The first leg carried the Coastal Area Commanders in the gunners' cupolas from the Suffolk coast to the Mount Batten flying-boat station in Plymouth Sound, around North Foreland and down the Channel, overflying Calshot on the way. After night-stopping at Plymouth, the Southampton flew on around Cornwall and operated with the Royal Navy in the western approaches. It then went north up the Bristol Channel. The plan was to reach Carrickfergus in Belfast Lough by nightfall. Again, the leg was successfully completed, and the flying boat was refuelled before laying at anchor by the ancient castle overnight. In the evening light, it attracted the attention of crowds for whom a large flying boat was a marvel.

The great cruise for the Southampton continued to Oban, with its large expanse of sheltered waters, before it turned northeast up the Great Glen to Cromarty near Inverness. It then went around Banff and down the east coast past Montrose to the Firth of Forth, alighting at Rosyth. The final leg was down the east coast of England to return triumphant to Felixstowe.

Keen to show off the Southampton to the political leadership of the country as well as the taxpayers, in 1926 Calshot-based flying boats were also deployed to Cromer on the Norfolk coast. It was the holiday season, and the beachgoers were rewarded with majestic flying boats cruising by at a thousand feet with engines roaring. A rare sight and, for many, a first glimpse of a flying boat. The Secretary of State for Air, Sir Samuel Hoare,* took the opportunity to don a Sidcot suit and travel from Cromer to Great Yarmouth in the forward gunners' cupola of one of the flying boats. Hoare was impressed and, reportedly, wrote to Mitchell to tell him so, as well as suggesting that flying boats should be a regular feature of the air pageants at RAF Hendon. This they became and for many were a major attraction.

For the Royal Air Force, the advent of the Southampton as a dependable flying machine with range, endurance and relative crew comfort meant there was a clear means of what today would be called 'defence diplomacy' and 'effective at range' – in other words, showing the British flag and the reach of the Royal Air Force. As a result of the confidence placed in the reliability of the

---

* Hoare, successively Foreign Secretary and British Ambassador to Madrid during the Second World War, was a sometimes controversial character but shares credit with Winston Churchill for keeping Spain out of the Second World War.

Supermarine design, two airframes were selected to fly around the Mediterranean Sea to the British mandate of Egypt. This Mediterranean cruise needs to be seen against the background of what was happening in an area that was vital to British interests, with bases at Gibraltar, Malta, Cyprus, Alexandria (Egypt) and Haifa (British Mandate of Palestine) guarding the Suez Canal route to India. In 1922, Benito Mussolini had marched his fascists to Rome and taken over the government with promises of making the Mediterranean an Italian lake, joining Italy with its North African territorial ambitions. The British government was keen to show it had mastery of the air and sea and could reinforce the bases within days if tension rose. So the Southampton was ideal to project strategic power and was armed sufficiently to deter a modest assault from enemy fighters.

Led by Russian Civil War and Jutland veteran Squadron Leader Gerald Livock, the boats departed RAF Cattewater in Plymouth Sound for Aboukir in Egypt on 1 July 1926. The route took them to Hourtin near Bordeaux and Istres in the south of France before an ocean crossing to Naples, then Valletta (Malta) and on to the North African coast at Benghazi. A short hop to Sollum brought them to Egypt before completing the outward leg at Aboukir on 10 July. Mitchell was keen to have the progress reports, to assess the serviceability and whether there were radical changes needed, as the Air Ministry was considering another batch of Southampton flying boats. The return trip took in Haifa, Famagusta in Cyprus, then Suda Bay and Corfu in Greece, before Valletta and courtesy calls in Italy and France for fuel and supplies. In all, 6,000 nautical miles were covered without incident, proving that extended-range operations were possible for flying boats operating independently.

The Air Ministry issued a report on the cruise and took the unusual step of declassifying it, not only because it was seriously impressed with the Southampton, but also because it wanted to help Supermarine sell the flying boats to allies such as Argentina and Australia. So important was the Southampton to Supermarine that it commissioned a small run of reproductions of the report. One of these special bulletins is kept in the RAF Museum archive at Hendon – where the Southampton was often the star of the air pageant in the mid-1920s.

The report says that the cruise was 'undertaken as an ordinary service exercise to a set time-table'. The 'machine miles flown' were 12,000 nautical miles, indicating that there was considerable flying at bases en route. The boats flew down the Garonne from Bordeaux Hourtin to reach Marseille Berre where the Southampton was shown off to the French navy. The communiqué adds a remarkable testimony to Supermarine Southampton: 'No trouble whatsoever was experienced, either with the aircraft or with the Napier Lion engines.'

The success of the cruise was a positive result not just for the Royal Air Force but for Supermarine as well. These flights attracted the attention of Argentina, Japan and Turkey, all countries with long coastlines to patrol and protect, which saw the validity of the Mitchell design, giving the Southampton export potential not in the original specification.

It was clear, however, that a wooden hull was not durable for long-range and sustained operations; one of the most important results of the cruise was the realisation that wooden-hulled flying boats like the Southampton would absorb nearly 500 lb of water in a few months. This led Mitchell to consider using metal instead, which would also give more internal space and perhaps, Mitchell thought, a longer life to the hull. He was right. So Mitchell undertook discussions with Saunders, based locally on the Isle of Wight, where there was expertise in working sheet metal. (A decade later, Supermarine would face the problem of working metal again, when the production of the Spitfire ground to a halt through a lack of skills inside the company and needed reliable sub-contractors.)

Mitchell's team worked hard to understand the benefits of the Duralumin hull. In the end, it was found that the anodised metal saved weight both in structural terms and because of the watertight integrity. The Mk II variant of the Southampton therefore had more room in the hull which in turn provided clean lines. Mitchell and his team were leading the world in metal skin structures for aeroplanes at this time and were also innovative. The beaching gear needed to take a flying boat onto land and the shock absorbers needed to cope with extreme moments of stress to the airframe required some special care in design to prevent undue wear. Mitchell arranged for the maximum load location to be engineered with pneumatic tyres to absorb the moment, thus ensuring that the stress travelled to the strongest part of the fuselage. To quote Denis Le Penn Webb,* it was 'a simple practical

---

* Denis Webb joined as chief storeman in 1935 and was head of the sub-contracts department at Supermarine 1942–47; a vital role, as the Spitfire, for example, was built as a result of more than 150 sub-contractors contributing key assemblies and parts. https://spitfiremakers.org.uk/

solution to the problem typical of R. J. Mitchell'.[2] Mitchell's innovative spirit is a constant factor through the narratives and memoirs of Supermarine staff.

Mitchell was also interested in the Air Ministry's plans for installing better wireless telegraphy – high-frequency radios that used Morse code rather than voices. This meant that the maritime headquarters at Mount Batten on Plymouth Sound could keep in touch with flying boats well away from line-of-sight radio networks, and that the flying boat could gain up-to-date weather reports from coastal stations.

To prove the Southampton Mk II hull and the other modifications, including more practical fuel-tank construction, the Air Ministry authorised the most ambitious flight yet. The Royal Air Force formed the Far East Flight and announced a cruise to Australia. The formal Air Ministry requirements were: to open the air route to Australia and the East; to select landing sites; to see how far flying boats and their crews were capable of operating away from fixed bases and under widely varying climatic conditions; to show the flag.

The Far East Flight was epic. The mammoth undertaking of flying four Southampton Mk IIs on a journey of 27,000 nautical miles over fourteen months would be hard to contemplate today. At the time, 1927–28, it was front-page news, and many thought it couldn't be done. The Far East Flight was led by Group Captain Henry Cave-Browne-Cave who had recently been deputy director of technical development at the Air Ministry, and whose pedigree included having been commissioned as an engineering officer in the Royal Naval Air Service and selected to train as a seaplane pilot. Cave-Browne-Cave, from a powerful clan dating back to the English Civil War, would become a strong supporter of Mitchell and Supermarine.

The aeroplanes were fully prepared for the Far East Flight, with Squadron Leader Livock as second-in-command, bringing all his Mediterranean cruise experience. The nine officers and supporting aircrew departed Calshot for Plymouth, and then to Bordeaux and across Europe to India and Singapore. The flight was so successful that the Air Ministry agreed to extend it to Hong Kong and to circumnavigate Australia anticlockwise.

The four flying boats spent much of the southern summer of 1927–28 in Far East waters. The airframes did not return to Britain but were kept in Singapore to form No. 205 Squadron, based at RAF Seletar. To create RAF Seletar, three officers and twenty-three airmen had been sent to assist with maintenance and to carry out the major inspections mandated by Supermarine and the Air Ministry. Being an engineer, Cave-Browne-Cave was able to liaise with Supermarine on various modifications to the flying boats, including replacement rivets, and working through ideas for preventing barnacles on the hull. Mitchell had incorporated beaching chassis gear into his design for the Southampton to allow the flying boat to be brought out of the water for periodic servicing.

RAF Seletar in February 1928 was still under construction, the area having been a patch of mangrove and sandbars just three years earlier. The accommodation was limited: the flight office was a small attap dwelling on stilts over the water and the airmen lived in buildings made of matting. The nearest Royal Air Force station was Karachi in Imperial India – that's nearly halfway back to England. The Seletar base was fully developed just in time for the Imperial Japanese Navy to take it over in 1942!

Everywhere they went, the Southamptons fired up the public imagination, especially in Seletar and in Australia, where a great show of welcome was hosted in Melbourne. The Royal Australian Air Force also took interest in the Southampton following the successful circumnavigation of the continent.

Mitchell never doubted that it could be done, but the cruise was a huge advertisement for Supermarine's engineering prowess. In July 1928, the Southampton was exhibited at the Olympia Aero Show. The publicity for the show called it 'The Greatest Formation Flight in the History of Post-War Aviation', adding that it demonstrated 'the durability, high efficiency, sea and air worthiness of "Supermarine" construction'. We can thank Victor Paine, in charge of publicity for Mitchell, for those fine words. The Southampton was also inspected by Prince Albert, Duke of York (later King George VI), who was also a pilot and apparently remarked on its spacious cockpit.

The Royal Air Force was keen to do more. In September 1930, No. 201 Squadron at Calshot was tasked to fly around the Baltic Sea coasts of Denmark, Estonia, Finland, Latvia, Norway and Sweden, including a stop at Stockholm. The Swedes were keen on improving their reconnaissance of the archipelago and the approaches to the naval bases on the south coast. It was another highly successful venture of 3,330 nautical miles. The Royal Danish Navy acquired a single Southampton as a result (a modified design that would be known as the Nanok), and, although further orders were not forthcoming, the potential of flying boats was not lost on the Scandinavian countries.

Nor was it lost on Argentina, which has rich fishing grounds, merchant ships to protect, and disputed exclusive economic zones as well as national sea borders to patrol.

Comando de la Aviación Naval Argentina* (COAN) had been formed in October 1919 and gradually developed from using cast-off Argentine Air Force flying machines to having its own budget and requirements staff. Supermarine came to the attention of the great naval moderniser Manuel Domecq García who, despite being born in Paraguay, was a dominating figure in Argentina until his death in 1951. He read the reports of the Southampton flying boat cruises and immediately knew that the range and reliability of the design would be ideal for the over 3,000 miles that needed to be patrolled. Almirante (Admiral) García made the Southampton flying boat the central plank of his strategy for modernisation.

The order, when it came in 1929, was for a total of eight flying boats – five Mk I with wooden hulls – and support to get them into service. The COAN took a close interest in the construction, with two officers being posted to Britain to oversee the work. Supermarine even sent out Brian Powell, a technical representative, to supervise the reassembly on site at Puerta Belgrano in August 1930. This set the scene for close cooperation which lasted until the socialist-fascist Juan Domingo Perón came to power; it was rejuvenated in the 1960s and 1970s when Argentina briefly

---

* Argentina Naval Aviation.

returned to democracy, including the acquisition of Type 42 destroyers and an aircraft carrier.

The Southampton was replaced by the American Catalina amphibious flying boat in 1948 but the British design continued to train pilots for another decade. In between service entry and retirement, one Southampton carried out royal duties. In 1931, Mitchell was highly delighted when news reached him that the Prince of Wales, the future King Edward VIII, and his younger brother, Prince Albert (later King George VI), were transported across the estuary of the River Plate between Argentina and Montevideo in a COAN Southampton Mk II. Both donned thick flying suits for the open cockpit crossing, which took about two hours. The occasion for the visit was the British Empire Exhibition in Buenos Aires and a subsequent courtesy visit to Britain's other great ally in South America, Uruguay. Mitchell, in true form, received a note from the Foreign Office, smiled and got back to work.

But the Southampton wasn't the only Supermarine success in the 1920s – Mitchell was already starting to become known as a global leader in all types of seaplane, including the fastest in the world.

*A rare photograph of Mitchell (left) at RAF Calshot with
the S5 – Mitchell's contender for the 1927 Schneider Trophy,
which Supermarine won for Great Britain.*

7

Need for Speed

Mitchell's success with flying boats brought Supermarine international recognition, but it was his pioneering work on racing seaplanes that would make him famous. While he was developing the Southampton, he was also working on radical ideas for pushing the boundaries of speed. By the time the next Schneider Trophy heat came around in 1925, Mitchell was ready.

He had learned from his defeat in 1923. He knew that the modified flying-boat designs of the past would not be enough for future competitions, especially while Italy and the USA had state monies involved. Supermarine was no novice in this contest, but the British contestants suffered from the lack of official state sponsorship. In Italy, the Italian socialist-turned-fascist dictator Benito Mussolini had come to power in 1922 to make Italy great again. He started a technological revolution (without thinking of the costs to the nation, which was still one of the poorest in Europe), sponsoring the aeronautical industry which was predominantly in the north of the country where the great lakes of Como and

Garda are to be found. These lakes provided the runways for the development of racing seaplanes and a training ground for some of the greatest racing pilots of the age.

So, lacking that level of government support, Mitchell started from scratch; he brought in a few of his newly developing team and started on a racing seaplane idea: the S4.*

The radical S4 is perhaps the first time we see Mitchell really stretch his talents at an early stage of his career. His innovative aim was to create a low-drag monoplane with a semi-monocoque rear fuselage and thin cantilever wings. The floats were developed at the NPL and manufactured by Short Brothers at Rochester. Even today it looks futuristic, so it must have been little less than revolutionary to behold when it was rolled out at Woolston. Alan Clifton, head of the technical office at Supermarine, later wrote of its 'breathtakingly clean lines, which caused a sensation when photos were released'.[1]

In two short years, Mitchell had gone from the Sea Lion III – an aerodynamically dirty, pusher biplane which was reminiscent of a bygone age of flying – to a sleek speed racer. In 1925, the S4 was way ahead of its time with its one-piece monoplane wing without bracing wires, and powered by a specially developed 700-hp Napier engine. Only the Italian Macchi M33 monoplane air racer flying boat came close in pure aesthetics, but it was still a flying boat, having the penalty of carrying around a boat hull, whereas for the S4 Mitchell had gone for pontoons (as floats were then called). *Flight* magazine enthusiastically commented, 'It is little short of

---

* Supermarine S1, S2 and S3 designs were the Sea Lion I, II and III respectively.

astonishing that he should have been able to break away from the types with which he had been connected.'[2]

Ultimately, however, the S4 was not the success for which Mitchell had hoped, even if it was the most beautiful of the designs for which he can take credit.

To reduce the entry costs, the development funding was divided equally between Napier and Supermarine, with the Air Ministry agreeing to underwrite a successful project. (In the end, the Air Ministry bought the S4 and allocated a military serial, even though it was never worn.) The design team worked around the clock, led by Mitchell, to bring the project from conception to first flight, on 24 August 1925, in just five months.

Mitchell had compromised on the design in several places. The rear-positioned cockpit was there for centre of gravity reasons but to the pilot, Henri Biard, it was very badly sited because of his lack of visibility. It created a blind spot in which even large ocean liners like RMS *Majestic* disappeared, as Biard found when he nearly collided with the ship off Calshot on his first take-off run – which was much longer than envisaged. The S4 was the fastest British aeroplane so far and Biard was the fastest human – for a while – as he did manage to capture a British air speed record at 226.75 mph but, alas, there was no time for any handling trial before the aeroplane was dismantled and shipped to America by sea for the 1925 Schneider event at Bay Shore Park in Baltimore.

The American population had not seen such an event as the Schneider Trophy before. The traditional US sports of football and baseball were played in stadia and welcomed tens of thousands of fans. But seaplane racing was something new and very exciting.

However, unlike Venice or the Solent, the Baltimore course did not present many locations for the vast crowds that followed the trophy race heats in Europe. The bad weather, too, was less than helpful. However, the crowds still came.

As discussed (*see* the Prologue), the S4 looked like a winner, but it was not to be. The cause of the crash has never been determined but modern analysis shows that there appears to have been wing flutter or a control issue. Biard, injured with broken ribs, was pulled from the water, and the S4 was out of the race.

As a designer and a thoroughly nice human being, Mitchell cared deeply about the health, welfare and safety of his people, especially 'his' pilots, as he saw them. Supermarine's safety record was second to none in an age when air accidents were so frequent as to be almost commonplace. As Supermarine stalwart Eric Lovell-Cooper said, the need for speed created machines that could fly at 'speeds that were suicidal then'.[3]

Mitchell continued his personal campaign – although he would not have seen it as such – for a more scientific approach to high-speed flight. He wanted the government to become involved to reduce the financial risk and improve technological progress. He went on to speak publicly to the Royal Aeronautical Society in 1927 about the joint development of high-speed flight with aero constructors and engine manufacturers being teamed rather than operating independently.

The Air Ministry was already listening. The main supporter was Air Marshal Sir John Salmond (later Chief of the Air Staff) and he was followed in December 1926 by Air Marshal Jack Higgins, as the Air Member for Supply and Research. The main development was the requirement for wind-tunnel testing and the purchase of prototype development aircraft. Salmond obtained the initial funding to acquire high-speed racing machines from Gloster and Supermarine. Short Brothers was consulted about float design, as well as a flying machine, and the Royal Aero Club coordinated work on engines from Bristol and Napier.

But it wasn't just engineering that would win the Schneider. It was the aircrew. Formed at Felixstowe in December 1926, the Royal Air Force High Speed Flight – known simply as 'The Flight' – was created on a temporary basis to ensure that racing seaplane pilots were well trained, fit and could compete directly with the Americans and the Italians, as both nations saw winning the Schneider outright after three races as being of national importance.

Getting approval for the creation of the Royal Air Force High Speed Flight wasn't easy. Air Vice-Marshal Geoffrey Salmond,* the previous Air Member for Supply and Research, was one of two brothers to lead the Royal Air Force and was a strong advocate of levelling the playing field with the Italians and Americans. Salmond carried out an investigation after the calamity at Chesapeake Bay, and wrote to Sir Hugh Trenchard, the Chief of the Air Staff, on 27 November 1925: 'However good our material may be, all efforts in this direction will be wasted unless the pilots, personnel and ground organization is of the highest efficiency . . . I would, therefore, suggest that the Royal Air Force should take the responsibility of providing the pilots and personnel required.'[4]

---

* Brother of John.

Trenchard was apt to be forthright and 'old school' about mixing his beloved Royal Air Force with the private sector. He saw himself as the customer of the aeroplane industry, not as the partner. He was also worried about reputational risk, as he told the Secretary of State for Air, Sir Samuel Hoare, just what he thought on 29 December: 'We should not enter for private races either Service machines or Service pilots. Every principle can be broken bearing in mind the fact – is the occasion worth it? If we break the principle, it would be justified if we succeed, but it would not if we failed.'[5]

It seems that the Chief of the Air Staff was concerned about setting a precedent, although his argument on others coming for assistance was misplaced, as the Schneider Trophy was so important in terms of national prestige, and the support it would give to an industry that would need to export in the future. No fool, Trenchard also saw the writing on the wall and added, 'they must do the whole thing and be completely responsible in every way'. Hoare's response was: 'I am convinced that to win the Cup would do real good to British aviation.'

Despite the obvious pre-eminence of British military pilots flying state-of-the-art high-speed aeroplanes, there was not at this time any thought that Europe would go to war again. Everyone was relying on the League of Nations and the diplomatic skills of both Britain and France. Even Winston Churchill seemed to be content with trusting the empire and dominions to run themselves (it was only later with the rise of Hitler that he became more concerned about peace in Europe).

Luckily for Mitchell, the contender companies (Gloster, Shorts and Supermarine) and the country, on this one occasion, would work together. Sir Samuel Hoare agreed; he said the Schneider Trophy was a special case but that the Treasury – led by Winston Churchill – would need to be handled carefully. Public opinion – and that meant the media – was also needed to get behind the race, which would certainly bring Churchill into line. Churchill supported aeronautical innovation but not at any cost.

And so the High Speed Flight was formed. Mitchell and the Supermarine team were delighted.

The 1926 Schneider event in Hampton Roads in America was contested only by Italy and the USA and saw an Italian victory, the Italians having been told by Mussolini to win at all costs, keeping the competition open. The Air Ministry plan was now to take on all comers in the 1927 competition in Venice, and show the world a British winner again. The Royal Aero Club, the Royal Air Force, Supermarine and, most especially, Mitchell, were all determined to win; it was Britain on show to Italy.

Mitchell's response was to create the Supermarine S5: a low-wing monoplane with braced wings and floats, constructed of Duralumin and plate with a light alloy. The S4 racer was per-haps Mitchell's first truly imaginative design, but it wasn't perfect; so Mitchell adjusted his ideas to ensure the S5 was more conserva-tive and perhaps safer in concept, design and build. The monocoque construction was a technique that would give the Spitfire an edge over the Hawker Hurricane a decade later. Mitchell accepted research from the NPL at Teddington to reduce the frontal area of the floats to minimise drag, and modified the engine radiators. Streamlining the airframe and reducing weight created an even better design. The S5 first took to the air on 14 June 1927. It showed great promise in trials.

As soon as they were ready, the recently ordered machines from Shorts, Gloster and Supermarine were tested. Mitchell sent three S5s: two racing entrants and a spare. The key, he urged, was understanding the flight envelope* of each racing seaplane – even if two were identical in theory, they would be different in the air at high speed.

To see the contestants, a number of experienced seaplane and high-speed test pilots gathered at Calshot on 9 August 1927, including veteran combat pilots like Flying Officer Harry Schofield, Flight Lieutenants Oswald Worsley, Sidney Webster and Samuel Kinkead,[†] and Squadron Leader Leonard Slatter; the latter two knew each other from First World War flying a decade before. A few weeks later came the final agreement to fund the Royal Air Force contribution to the 1927 competition to the tune of £2,500. The volume of loose minutes, reports and other 'bumf' can be seen today in Britain's National Archives, underlining that the smaller the issue, the more entrenched are the senior officers.

Mitchell had been aware of the ministry wranglings but was far too busy to take much notice as he was hard at work preparing the S5. The Air Ministry and Supermarine took care to restrict

---

* The flight envelope is the limit to which an airframe can operate. It is proved by testing and flying rather than from a drawing-board calculation.

† 'Kink' distinguished himself in the Russian Civil War leading B Flight of No. 47 Squadron on the Russian steppes; the author's great uncle was one of his fitters and supernumerary aircrew.

information flow about the aeroplane (and the Shorts and Gloster entries), not wishing to give the Italians in particular a heads-up on the engine power and estimated speeds. However, on 9 August, the ministry released some fascinating details about how advanced was the Mitchell design and engineering. The emphasis was very much on Mitchell as the chief engineer of the Supermarine Aviation Works; there was no mention of a designer. The press release also drew attention to the powerplant by calling the racing seaplane the Supermarine-Napier S5. There were, the Air Ministry said, many novel features in the design, including:

- All the fuel is carried in the starboard to balance the engine torque of the Napier engine; the floats were both constructed of the then new material called Duralumin (which the Spitfire would later make famous)
- The wing surfaces hold the cooling radiators for the Napier engine and because they are flush, present very little if any drag to the airframe
- The fuselage is metal, with the skin 'taking practically all the stresses' of the design (again, a Spitfire feature a decade later)
- The improved Napier engine is mounted on a cantilevered extension of the fuselage
- The wing itself is made of wood with a laminate covering
- Oil for the engine is cooled by passing along both sides of the fuselage
- The propeller is all-metal and signed by Fairey with the optimum pitch for racing

Perhaps most interesting of all was Mitchell's attention to the fuselage cross-section which made the selection of pilots for the High Speed Flight one of stature and weight as well as flying prowess. The press release said: 'The fuselage is probably smaller in cross-sectional area than any fuselage previously designed, and the pilots have had to be specially fitted with the machines . . . the area of the maximum section is only just over half that of the S4.'

It wasn't all plain sailing for Mitchell. The S5, perhaps because of its advanced technology, was proving difficult to fabricate and would only just be ready for release to the Royal Air Force before the race in September. Mitchell had asked the production team – he never seems to have 'instructed' people at Supermarine – to make the second S5 more streamlined and to flush the rivet head wherever possible. There were also problems with carbon monoxide fumes from the Napier, even though the cockpit was open. This says something about the exhaust plume and volume of gases being passed aft from the engine. Without bone-dome flying helmets and just leather, there was also a possibility in the small cockpit that the pilot would be knocked unconscious if the airframe buffeted too much. This was a risky business, and everyone knew the perils, including Mitchell, who always fretted about the test pilots.

The initial trials at Calshot indicated that if the conditions were right, the S5 could win and embarrass the Italian dictator Mussolini, who was going to be present at Venice.

It was clear that the machines and pilots were closely matched. As the *Morning Post* newspaper reported, 'for almost the first time in the history of the Schneider Cup [sic] the nearer the race approaches the more difficult it is to spot the winner'.[6] There was even the threat of sabotage in what was otherwise a carnival atmosphere with 250,000 spectators crowding the start/finish line at Porto I Lido, which would not have to been to Mitchell's liking.

The S5 triumphed; it was a significant victory for Britain and for all involved, not least Mitchell. The *Southern Daily Echo* reported that he 'witnessed the victory of his creation from the shores of the Lido, and while the plaudits of the crowd were handed out to the pilot, the praise of everyone intimately connected with the technical side of the achievement was also bestowed upon Mr Mitchell as he stood with his wife to see the result posted on the board.'[7]

For many, it was vindication of the idea that high-profile air races and similar events needed total government funding and official sponsorship. On 19 October 1927, Mitchell made this point in a speech in Stoke-on-Trent, saying,

> I speak from experience when I say that a great deal of knowledge is gained from the designing and construction of such craft, and this knowledge is applicable to the improvement of other types of aircraft such as are used in the Royal Air Force. The design of these Service craft, in fact, has been very much improved as a result of these contests. For this reason alone these sporting contests are worth continuing.[8]

Trenchard did not agree. He saw no benefit in his pilots being involved. Perhaps he anticipated the death of Kinkead on 12 March 1928, when the S5 he was flying crashed into the Solent off Calshot during a world record attempt. Mitchell was devastated, especially when Henri Biard, who had witnessed the event alongside him, took the view that something had gone wrong with the seaplane as it dived vertically into the sea. Perhaps it was aileron flutter, which had been attributed to the Biard crash off Baltimore in the S4. The Board of Inquiry thought it might have been an error in judging the height above the sea caused by the glassy water conditions of the day – flat calm makes landing a seaplane hazardous because depth perception is missing. The inquiry eventually was unable to determine the cause.

After Kinkead's death, there were those, Mitchell probably among them, who wondered whether the endless search for more speed was really necessary. After all, hadn't Churchill recently said that there would be no war for a decade or more?

In 1928, the world's largest engineering firm, Vickers-Armstrong, rode into Supermarine's headquarters as a white knight, saving the Southampton company from bankruptcy. Mitchell was key to the takeover, as his 'golden handcuffs' agreement testifies.

8

Vickers Takeover

In 1927, at just thirty-two years old, the boy from the Potteries was appointed technical director of Supermarine, also retaining the titles of chief designer and chief engineer. He had already developed a reputation that had brought him to the attention of the senior executives of the British aviation industry. Now, thanks to the success of the S5 and the Southampton, he was really on their radar.

Although he had left his grease-stained blue overalls behind in Staffordshire, Mitchell never forgot his apprenticeship training in the railway industry, and often employed young men from a similar background. Mitchell also adopted his father's costume for work, always wearing a tie and usually a suit. He encouraged the drawing-office team to be smartly dressed as it grew. However, it seems that Mitchell seldom returned to his roots, such was the pressure of work at Supermarine and the pace of the innovation that he implemented.

Before the First World War, there was a definite class distinction between blue-collar workers and white-collar office employees. Engineering was one area where the movement of skilled people from the shop floor to the management offices was encouraged and supported. Mitchell was not the only talented young man to rise up and take charge. But to make the ladder and climb it, the person needed determination and skill. In engineering, a regional accent was not a hindrance to the intelligent and trained employee.

What set Mitchell apart from most other designers was his ability to create a team for a project from the pool of talent at Supermarine, or to attract talent from elsewhere in what was now becoming a very competitive market. By the late 1920s, he had built a team of young, enthusiastic and well-qualified engineers with diverse backgrounds and skills. Mitchell was always good at bringing his people along with praise and constructive criticism, ensuring that the right people were given the right experience and encouragement.

Back in 1921, a young man who had served an apprenticeship at the Austin Motor Company had been taken on at Supermarine. Joe Smith was a rather withdrawn, even bashful, young draughts-man with 'a steady hand and clear lines' who would go on to take a leading role in the firm, rising to chief draughtsman to Mitchell and later becoming chief designer himself in 1941. 'We owe a lot to Smith,' said the chief naval test pilot, Captain Eric (Winkle) Brown.[1] 'He was a driving force behind the Seafire, the naval Spitfire, and I could always count on him coming with the Royal Aircraft Establishment to see progress during the War – we had a naval mess with pink gin.'

When Alan Clifton joined Supermarine in 1923, he hoped but could not be sure that he would move up in the company, but progress he did, getting a thorough grounding in stress and other calculations, which several of the Supermariners interviewed in the 1990s recalled 'were almost done in his head'. Clifton went on to be Smith's principal assistant and eventually his successor as chief designer.

Another stalwart was Ernest Mansbridge, who joined in 1924. Unusually for the time, he was a graduate engineer and by 1929 he was in charge of all aerodynamics, meeting performance requirements, weights and flight testing of Supermarine products. His mathematical skills in performance and flight testing later made him indispensable for the Type 224 and then the Type 300. So much was Mansbridge a member of the Supermarine family that most of his children went on to work for the company.

By 1925, Mitchell also needed a metallurgist and appointed Arthur Black to lead the development of metal – first fittings, then cladding and eventually construction. Many on Mitchell's team were old hands, like Arthur Shirvall, who went from apprentice in 1918 to running flying-boat hull design in a decade.

In 1926, the workload had become such that Mitchell needed an assistant and, following the time-honoured practice in the aviation industry, the chief draughtsman, Frank Holroyd, stepped up into the newly created job. Holroyd was a likeable character and supported Mitchell through the Schneider Trophy work.

These were just some of the trusted team members Mitchell had put in place when, in 1928, Supermarine entered an entirely new phase.

The shop-floor workers at Woolston were craftsmen, and in the drawing office were men and women who knew their tasks, but given the high cost of research and development, without investment and proper management the company was doomed to failure. In 1928, Vickers-Armstrong rode in as the white knight to save Supermarine and buy its obvious expertise and customer base, seeing the potential of the small team led by Mitchell.

For a century and a half, Vickers was the name most closely associated with heavy industry in Britain and its empire. The company was founded in 1828 as a Sheffield steel foundry and after 'going public' it branched out into military equipment (such as the Vickers machine gun, which was developed after the Maxim company was acquired in 1896) and shipbuilding, with a huge shipyard at Barrow-in-Furness, which still builds submarines for the Royal Navy. In fact, the Royal Navy's first submarine, *Holland 1*, was built by Vickers in 1901.

Across the world, Vickers' name is synonymous with heavy industry, innovation and precision, especially in its marine department which led the world in propeller shafts for large warships and passenger liners. It built motors after acquiring Wolseley and torpedoes after buying Whitehead & Company. It also held a small stake in S. E. Saunders & Company of Cowes on the nearby Isle of Wight, renowned for its hull designs, which had been incorporated in the Channel commercial flying-boat design. Later, Saunders-Roe, or Saro as it was better known, would work closely with Supermarine during the development of large reconnaissance flying boats in the 1930s.

The main heavy industry of the time was the railways, and Vickers was not slow in building and maintaining steam locomotives through the acquisition of Metropolitan to create Metropolitan-Vickers, a household name at the turn of the twentieth century. Vickers was also an early pioneer of aviation in Britain. The company opened a flying school at Brooklands (the airfield next to the Weybridge head office) in 1911 and started the manufacture of aeronautical components.

After merging with the large British engineering firm Armstrong Whitworth in 1927, the Board saw further potential in aeronautics and the company had the funding to break into the industry from its base at Weybridge. So the industrial giant bought the Supermarine cottage industry lock, stock and barrel. Vickers was world famous, and it would invest in the people and plant at Supermarine to make it world famous too.

Sir Robert McLean, the charismatic and well-connected executive chairman, set about sorting out Supermarine. He wanted a strong leadership, modern working practices and to inject cash to take the designs international. He was also keen that Supermarine would still function as a separate company, and so he kept it on a long lead. He knew there was a real gem in the senior management: young Reginald Mitchell. The strength of the team he had built demonstrated to McLean that Mitchell was the right man to lead the newly acquired Supermarine Aviation Works (Vickers) Ltd. He was indeed the right man. McLean made it a contractual condition that Mitchell should be given 'golden handcuffs' for a further five years to ensure his continued commitment to the company.

Commander Bird* announced the takeover by Vickers to the Supermarine staff in a letter to each of them, accompanied by a hundred cigarettes, probably Players Navy Cut, which was considered a fine gesture at a time when everybody smoked. Everyone also received a colourised picture of the Southampton flying boats in the Far East, stressing the success of the design and the fact that, as Denis Le Penn Webb suggested, the large open-water flying boat was not only a world-beater but was also the saviour of Supermarine until the Vickers buy-out.[2]

Almost unconcerned about the takeover, Mitchell was developing the Supermarine seaplane range for both speed and endurance. However, there was some disruption to come. On the completion of the sale, Vickers' management, especially McLean, wanted some drastic changes to the way in which Supermarine did business. This was the beginning of turning the cottage industry into an international aerospace company.

Trevor Westbrook was Vickers' man put in to supervise the reorganisation of the Woolston Works in 1928. Westbrook was only twenty-eight years old when he was appointed to the position of supervisor, a role that meant he had the day-to-day running of the Woolston and Hythe facilities. He was considered by many to be too inexperienced, especially when handling the workforce, but he did streamline many procedures and removed several

---

* Bird remained on the Board of Supermarine after the sale, then returned as general manager in 1941 and gave over part of his home, Park Place near Wickham in Hampshire, which was used by the Women's Voluntary Service as a base for the sorting of rivets for Spitfire production.

'Spanish'* practices. The general manager is the oil that makes the cogs turn smoothly in a great engineering company. Those cogs needed to be perfect because there was strong competition from equally determined companies. Sometimes that meant being unpopular and pushing the workforce hard even in the factory holiday period. Westbrook was not universally liked but he did get things moving. He was direct and forthright, he knew what he wanted to achieve, and he had Mitchell's support. His achievements included the rebuilding of the design office and the drawing office, a proper stores system and the rationalisation of work. Without Westbrook, Supermarine would not have been able later to design, develop and build not just the Spitfire but the amphibious flying boat the Walrus, to which many a downed pilot owes his life. His role with the later Schneider Trophy work would also be pivotal.

The integration of Supermarine into Vickers was not all plain sailing. In January 1930, returning from a minor operation in hospital and some convalescence, Mitchell was appalled to find Barnes Wallis, a young engineer who would later leap to public acclaim with his Second World War bomb designs, sitting at the chief designer's desk, feet on the work surface and leafing through key documents relating to the Supermarine products under design or build.

Wallis had been sent to Southampton because McLean was intent on shaping his career. Wallis had been working on airships at Howden in Yorkshire, but McLean felt they were not the way

---

* A form of working to rule that delayed the production of airframes – for example, the view that painters could only paint.

forward for Vickers. The choices for Wallis were Weybridge – the main Vickers aeroplane design house – or the newly acquired Supermarine at Southampton.

McLean had issued a head-office instruction that month: 'With immediate effect, Mr Wallis is appointed Deputy Chief Designer to the Supermarine Aviation Works, to be in charge, in the first instance of the detail drawing office and all detail design . . . He will be responsible generally to Mr Mitchell, whose general ideas are not to be departed from without his concurrence.'[3] McLean had committed the cardinal management sin of being too general in his instructions, trying to keep both sides happy and giving no demarcation lines between general and detail.

'McLean promised Wallis a free hand, with authority to restructure the [design] department, hire and fire,' according to Richard Morris in his biography of Wallis.[4] In the mind of the Vickers boss, the clean-out and restructuring would take about a year. Then, he reckoned, he could bring Wallis back to Weybridge to develop his career into airframes, aerostructures and perhaps even weapons. Barnes and Molly Wallis thought about renting a house near Portsmouth from where it was an easy commute to Woolston. It fell through – and just as well.

Mitchell did not take kindly to the Vickers plans for Wallis. He felt that he had the upper hand at Supermarine, given his 'golden handcuffs' and the fact that Wallis would be a temporary embuggerance. Mitchell was determined that Wallis's tenure would be even shorter than twelve months. And what of Mitchell's team? They supported R. J.; they knew he would be growing the business now that Vickers had opened a line of credit.

Mitchell's immediate tactic was to create a new drawing office and take the best people, including Frank Holroyd, with him to another part of the Supermarine works. Mitchell was playing the long game, but Wallis wasn't finished. He went to the Vickers head office in London and tried character assassination through his report, apparently read from a notebook: 'Mitchell was a bad leader, a poor timekeeper and had an imperfect grasp of structural design'.[5] This is all rubbish, of course. It could be argued that Wallis knew nothing about flying boats. McLean understood Wallis's frustration but knew that Mitchell was more valuable at Supermarine than Wallis could ever be. According to Richard Morris, Vickers had bought Supermarine to capture the talents of Mitchell[6] – some might say not as a plaything for Barnes Wallis. Mitchell had outplayed Wallis – and sooner than he had hoped. By 30 January 1930, Mitchell was the master of Supermarine again.

Vickers did get another man in place. In 1931, Harold Payn – always known as 'Agony' or 'Ag' – was posted in from Vickers at Weybridge to be Mitchell's technical assistant, but far from being a placeman, he integrated into the culture well and became a trusted friend to Mitchell. As a former Royal Flying Corps and then Royal Air Force pilot, he was a production test pilot at Woolston and effectively the go-to man on technical issues.*

---

* Payn was one of the small group around Mitchell on 5 March 1936 when the Type 300, which became the Spitfire, flew for the first time. Payn remained in day-to-day charge of the Design Department as he moved up in the hierarchy after Mitchell's untimely death until 1940 when the Security Service, MI5, took an interest in Payn's German wife and decided he was a security risk with his proximity to the Spitfire; he sadly committed suicide.

Throughout the 1920s, Mitchell had shown himself to be both pragmatic and determined; he was not to be cowed, and he held an unshakeable belief in the strength of the team at Supermarine. Mitchell hated public speaking – even to his own employees – but he persevered, making himself a force within Supermarine. He did not suffer fools but would not shout at them like many of the senior managers in industry at the time. Instead, he was quiet and said not a word: far more devastating than being the martinet. He was a good listener, according to those who worked closely with him in the design office or the technical office. Advice was always welcomed even if it wasn't always used. He liked to think through a problem of design undisturbed. His people appreciated the fact that he took full responsibility for a project and for the work of his juniors, many of whom were actually older than him. His focus was intense, and he had high expectations of his team. Vera Cross, his personal assistant who joined Supermarine in 1927, remembered, 'You soon got used to his moods and learnt to keep out of his way when he was concentrating on a problem . . . He was a great driving force and once his mind was made up he went all out to achieve his end. Normal working hours did not interest him, and if he was engaged on some important project he would work until quite late in the evenings and expect his staff to do the same.'[7]

He was, however, very popular and relished time spent with the team. Joe Smith recalled,

If you were away on a business visit with him and the day's work was over, there was always the possibility of some prank developing. He was literally the life and soul of the party on such occasions as the annual drawing office dinner, when with no thought of dignity, he became the ringleader in any sort of fun and games, usually aided and abetted by the firm's test pilots.[8]

For Mitchell, work was his primary ethic, but he was not above being playful and initiating practical jokes, making his personality much more rounded than some official histories of Supermarine or the British aircraft industry at the time would have us believe. He was certainly brought up in a relatively strict Edwardian household, but he loved jokes and had what today might be called a schoolboy sense of humour. He was not averse to flouting petty bureaucracy, such as the time in Paris for an aviation exhibition in 1930 when he visited the Folies-Bergère but lost his cloakroom ticket, and the attendant refused to return his overcoat. Mitchell was accompanied by an Air Ministry colleague who distracted the cloakroom attendant long enough for Mitchell to vault the counter, retrieve his coat and both Englishmen to escape. Another occasion, undated, is when Mitchell and Arthur Shirvall, Supermarine's trusted float designer, were at the NPL at Teddington. The job required an overnight stay in a small hotel where both men shared a room. On retiring for the night, Mitchell's bed collapsed, and it was clear that Shirvall was the perpetrator when the latter ran in fits of almost girly giggles to the bathroom. On Shirvall's return, he leaped into bed only for it to collapse as well because Mitchell had removed the screws keeping the legs on. Both men dissolved into fits of laughter.

At home, Mitchell seems to have lost the slight stammer which had made him appear shy. His only son Gordon was born in 1920 and in 1927 they moved into a larger house fit for a family. This home, which Mitchell helped to design, was in Portswood, then a leafy suburb of Southampton, close to both the Woolston Works and Eastleigh airfield. The Mitchells employed a home help, a gardener and a live-in maid. Called Hazeldene, it had a fine garden and was a place for father and son to bond. The *Daily Echo*, a Southampton newspaper, reported in 2005 that 'as he moved into his teens in the early 1930s Gordon and [his father's] relationship developed, the pair spending treasured days together at air pageants while as a family they would play tennis and golf at Bramshaw.'[9] Gordon told the *Daily Echo* that for his father, 'His family life was an escape for him, and he valued that. He was a very affectionate father but very strict – he kept you on your toes. He also had a wicked sense of fun though.'*

His home was also often a place of work. Flo recalled that in the Mitchell house they 'lived aeroplanes. There were always people from Supermarine or pilots in our Southampton house, talking about their aircraft or the speeds at which they could fly, and they often sat up into the early hours of the morning.'[10]

---

* Gordon grew into a man with stark physical similarities to his father – 'the same strong jaw, angular features and receding hairline', according to the *Daily Echo*. But Gordon did not want to be an engineer; he chose veterinary science instead. Quite why his son did not follow in his father's footsteps is easy to understand, as Gordon knew if he did, fellow workers would have said that any advancement was down to nepotism. He finished school, went to work on a farm in Dorset and then undertook courses in biology at Reading University.

Mitchell had started driving on the road with a motorbike and sidecar but very quickly acquired a saloon car, possibly a Riley. It is perhaps surprising to a modern reader that he did not need to take a driving test. These were not introduced until 1934 – by which time, he was driving his second Rolls-Royce. Records are hard to find but it seems that the great engineer wanted the best automobile, and he knew the Rolls-Royce team, so his first was a 20-hp 1928 model, black with a snakeskin roof, known to the family as 'the Hearse'. (Next in 1932 he bought a 25-hp model, probably yellow, and eventually drove a 3.5-litre Bentley.) Gordon recalls the excitement in the house when Mitchell brought home his first Rolls-Royce, saying his father was 'as excited as a schoolboy'.[11]

Mitchell was by now well connected in local political and social circles in south Hampshire. He had joined his father's Masonic Lodge just before he left Stoke-on-Trent, and in Southampton was inducted into the Royal Gloucester Lodge, where he started to climb the ladder of local respectability. He was well established at the tennis club in Bitterne Park, where he was not only an excellent sportsman but made good friends who became important supporters of Supermarine. Lord Apsley undoubtedly helped the Schneider cause, prompted by Mitchell. Lord Apsley was also a director of the family's former newspaper, the *Morning Post* (which was sold to the *Daily Telegraph* in 1937, both papers supporting rearmament, having recognised that Adolf Hitler would become a tyrant). Sadly, he died in an air accident in Malta when the Halifax in which he was travelling suffered engine failure on take-off.

It is said that Mitchell even considered standing for Parliament himself. He was rarely vocal on his personal politics, but it is most likely that he was a natural Conservative. He aspired to live up to his middle-class roots with membership of the tennis club and by mixing with the influential people of the district. It was not just about growing the potential of Supermarine, but also about growing his own character, developing his network and being part of the local scene. He also favoured the status quo as good for business and trade, and therefore good for the country. Because he rarely wrote – or what he did write has been lost – we can only surmise. However, at one point, probably before the 1929 General Election, it is possible that Lord Apsley talked seriously about Mitchell replacing him as a candidate in Southampton. However, the pressure of work at Supermarine would have meant the company could ill afford to lose the technical director and chief designer/engineer.

Luckily for the nation, and perhaps Western civilisation, Mitchell decided against politics and stuck to his engineering career.

The game was afoot in 1929. The Supermarine S5 had won the Schneider Trophy in 1927 and now there was a real chance of a second consecutive win with the S6 racing seaplane.

9

Schneider 1929

The new structure and the backing of Vickers would prove crucial to Mitchell's next Schneider entries; Vickers was able to inject cash into research and development, and because it was so dominant, Supermarine was able to get good terms from its supply chain. Mitchell was now working hard on a new, improved racing seaplane: the S6. The key to its success would be horsepower.

The First World War had seen military aeroplanes on both sides – German and Allied – using mainly French-built or -designed aero-engines. The main feature was reliability. The engines of this period were adapted from motor-car designs, and built for the temperature gradients of flying – ambient temperature on the ground and freezing at 12,000 feet or more. Just as temperature and altitude took its toll on pilots, they did the same for mechanical systems.

Much of the following decade of peace saw the major manufacturers seeking reliable and more and more powerful engines.

Some aeroplane designers, such as Geoffrey de Havilland, decided to build their own engines but other, smaller companies, such as Supermarine, had to work with the designers at Napier and the motor-car manufacturer Rolls-Royce in Derby. Mitchell soon realised that to work hand-in-glove with the engine design teams would pay dividends.

D. Napier & Son was a well-established motor-industry name before the First World War with its roots in Scotland and later London, making precision parts for the sugar industry and the Royal Arsenal at Woolwich. When motoring became the vogue at the turn of the century, Napier moved into the business with some outstanding classic cars. Mitchell would have been well aware of the company's success, including in endurance racing, in these early years. The company appears to have built its own engines, gearboxes and drive shafts for domestic and export customers. It diversified into fast boats – hence was known to Scott-Paine as well. In the First World War, the company provided aero-engines to the Royal Aircraft Factory and later in the conflict built complete aeroplanes, such as the RE8 reconnaissance biplane, which was highly regarded and trusted by its operators.

After the war, motor cars and engines dominated the Napier product list. Mitchell found that the Lion engine series worked well for him, and used it in lighter flying boats such as the Seagull, which would enter service with the Royal Air Force and the newly formed Royal Australian Air Force. But, even though the Lion V with 492 hp was a significantly powerful engine for the time, it seems the Napier was not exactly what Supermarine wanted for the S6. For much of the 1920s, Mitchell had been wedded to Napier more than anyone else, but he was concerned about reliability when it came to racing seaplanes. Supermarine needed peak performance even if the engine would be 'blown' at the end of the race. Mitchell was determined to win and needed the best.

Despite his heavy engineering apprenticeship, Mitchell knew that he could not master every aspect of the fast-developing technologies in the aeronautical industry. He brought in people like Lovell-Cooper, who was a metals specialist; and he sought advice from the aero-engine producers, including Armstrong Siddeley and Bristol, but especially made use of his fast-growing relationship with Sir Henry Royce, a fellow trainee from the railway industry. To this day, while most of us abbreviate Rolls-Royce to 'Rolls', those at Derby and Filton refer to the company as 'Royce's'. Rolls-Royce was a household name before the First World War and its motor products were synonymous with everything that was good in engineering. A Rolls-Royce solution meant it was the best. It was here that Supermarine benefitted the most.

Turning to a leading authority of aero-engineering, Mitchell met with Major George Bulman, director of engine development at the Air Ministry, who offered advice on the risks of using the new R-type engine, which Royce had authorised to be developed with the profits from the Silver Ghost motor car. Typical of Mitchell, he was not satisfied with one visit to London, but sought Bulman's advice three times running, and in the end it was Bulman's faith in the Derby team that made Mitchell leave Napier on the quayside in favour of Rolls-Royce. The response of Napier to being ditched from the racing seaplanes is not recorded, but just over a decade later the company was bought by English Electric in

Lancashire, which went on to develop the first British jet bomber, the Canberra, and that rocket of a fighter aeroplane, the Lightning.

It is fascinating to understand now that Rolls-Royce had avoided racing its motor cars in the same way as Bentley and Napier, who liked to test their designs to the limit. The Derby team had only been in aero-engine design, development and manufacturing since about 1914, so the sector was relatively new and risky. It took a Whitehall meeting to convince the company that racing seaplanes would be of benefit for development and for future markets. Royce himself was less concerned as he knew the Eagle engine, which Mitchell had used in the Sea Eagle, was reliable. Royce was the master; in the words of his biographer, Peter Reese, he was a designer with a 'deep interest in the materials used and the need to maximise their performance'.[1] He was fixated on saving weight – so important in an aero-engine – as well as maintaining quality when needed, but also on finding simple fixes for problems instead of being too 'Rolls-Royce about the solution', as Ministry of Defence officials are wont to say in the twenty-first century.

Royce and Mitchell were in constant communication, although most of those letters no longer exist. It was the personal rapport and frequent visits to West Wittering for Mitchell, and to Woolston for Royce, that sealed the relationship.

Royce promised an engine, adapted from the Rolls-Royce Buzzard, of at least 1,900 hp, and his team created a prototype spirit engine that could develop 1,850 hp on the test bench. Mitchell went to Derby to witness a couple of runs and to discuss the engineering for engines that would be used for one race only.

In six months, Royce would galvanise his company to produce a world-class – world-beating – aero-engine that, according to the Air Ministry, would have taken another enterprise about five years to develop. The R-type would develop into the Merlin, then the Griffon, which both provided war-winning power for the front-line aeroplanes of the Royal Navy and the Royal Air Force. (Until the end, only Marshal of the Royal Air Force Lord Trenchard would not come round to believing that the Schneider races had directly contributed to the fighter aircraft performance that had won the Battle of Britain.)

Chief test pilot of Supermarine Jeffrey Quill later wrote that 'throughout his career Mitchell showed an extraordinary capacity for making the right decision at the right moment, which is one of the most elusive characteristics necessary to a successful designer.'[2] This is Mitchell approaching the pinnacle of his design and engineering career. The intellectual powerhouse was ready for the challenge of this Schneider Trophy.

Mitchell's plans were taking shape. However, during the late 1920s, various senior members of the Air Council and the Air Staff expressed concerns about the resources going into the Schneider, so it wasn't all plain sailing. Mitchell isolated himself from the Whitehall debates, but he had an ally in the wings. Probably unbeknownst to Mitchell, T. E. Lawrence, who had been serving in the Royal Air Force under the assumed name of Aircraftsman Shaw in 1925–26, was a strong supporter and not without political influence. He was a friend of the Salmond brothers; the Italians liked him, and he seems to have lobbied for a Schneider Committee to be formed with military-aviation as well as political membership. It helped that the then chancellor of the exchequer, Winston Churchill, was a huge supporter of aviation. However, as is typical for government, support waxed and waned: at one stage, after the 1927 race in Venice, the High Speed Flight had been disbanded, but it was now back in business for the future races after political intervention.

A Treasury note was circulated on 28 December 1928: 'Their Lordships agree that on this occasion a suitable British team can be provided only by the Royal Air Force and They therefore sanction the expenditure involved by this course. They trust however that the Air Council will be careful not to commit themselves to competing in any contest which may be held in the future.'

In 1929, Lawrence was able to witness the Schneider contest first-hand. After being posted to the North-West Frontier, he seems to have been offered a choice of posting, and chose RAF Cattewater on Plymouth Sound, the south-west approaches' flying-boat station. There he could indulge his interest in high-speed water craft. He wrote to a friend and said: 'I'm a cross between clerk and deck-hand on a RAF Motor Boat.'[3] It is not every aircraftsman that is personally posted by the Chief of the Air Staff, but such was the relationship between Lawrence and Trenchard. Suddenly, Lawrence found himself involved in the preparations for the Calshot race event of 1929.

The last race, in which the Supermarine S5 had taken first and second prizes, had been held at Venice in 1927. The cost of annual competitions was making a worthwhile event difficult to achieve so the aero clubs of the competing nations got together and agreed to hold the event every two years instead. A biennial event would seem to be fairer and allow more time for development as aeroplane technology was now moving at a pace. Metal construction was replacing the traditional seasoned spruce, which was in short supply after the building boom of the First World War.

At the RAF Calshot flying-boat base in 1929, the competition would be Italy versus the United Kingdom. The two new French designs were not ready in time and the Americans did not enter. The competitors were allotted hangar space and all the facilities necessary to race. Railways allocated special trains from Waterloo station to the south coast, bringing spectators keen to witness a second British victory. Mitchell was determined that they would not be disappointed.

The Supermarine S6 with the Rolls-Royce R engine had been tested and Mitchell hoped that the new combination of airframe and powerplant would be sufficient – but as power increased so did the opportunity for error.

Calshot was ready by early September 1929. The Italian team had aeroplane issues and had asked for a postponement, but this was not agreed, as the year was progressing and the competition was already costing a small fortune. Mitchell was always tense before a contest. Writing in the *Manchester Guardian*, Major F. A. de Vere Robinson noted that Mitchell had told him 'in his quiet, convincing manner, for he is a man of few words, that he was always on tenterhooks when his machines were in the air'.[4] Nearly a million people turned out on the Hampshire shore and the Isle of Wight to witness the greatest spectacular of the year.

The winner was the Supermarine S6 flown by Flight Lieutenant Dick Waghorn, a fighter pilot and flying instructor from the

RAF Central Flying School. Waghorn's skill took the S6 to an average speed of 328.63 mph, setting a new world record for seaplanes. The Macchi M52R came second; a modified Supermarine S5, victor two years earlier, came in third. In the event, the new Italian Macchi M67s failed to finish. Flight Lieutenant Richard Atcherley, in another S6, also claimed a new world record, and would have taken second place if he had not been disqualified for turning inside a marker buoy.* Both Waghorn and Atcherley reported that the R engine was prone to overheating, but the new Duralumin radiators on the wing surfaces and floats, an innovation by Mitchell, had kept the temperatures manageable.

Britain had achieved a second consecutive win. Just one more was needed to permanently secure the trophy.

It was an important win for Mitchell, though he remained modest as always. Atcherley later recalled that Mitchell 'was always keen to listen to pilots' opinions and never pressed his own views against theirs . . . He set his sights deliberately high, for he had little use for "second-bests". Yet he was the most unpompous man I ever met.'[5]

The Prince of Wales attended the event and spoke with Mitchell afterwards. According to the *Southern Daily Echo*, 'The Prince said he regarded the British victory as a magnificent performance. Nothing had given him greater pleasure. He also discussed with

---

* Sadly, Waghorn died testing a new aeroplane and engine combination at the Royal Aircraft Establishment in 1931; Atcherley continued to serve in the Royal Air Force after the Schneider races, commanding fighters in the Western Desert and post-war training appointments. On retirement, thirty years after he became the fastest man on earth, he joined Folland Aircraft, makers of the Gnat of Red Arrows fame. He died in 1970.

Mr. Mitchell the planes and various details of their construction as well as their flying qualities and speeds . . . The Prince was deeply interested and impressed.'[6] Also present were the prime minister, the dour Scot Ramsay MacDonald, T. E. Lawrence, Hubert Scott-Paine and various diplomats from London. Lawrence was again masquerading as a very junior airman, driving one of Scott-Paine's high-speed launches around the Solent and acting as the administration clerk for the enterprise – as well as being invited to parties with diplomats all keen to meet him. Interestingly, Lawrence is quite circumspect about racing seaplanes. Throughout his correspondence of the period, he seems to be more concerned about how much work was involved, how tiring it all was, and what a relief it was when it was finally over. There was, no doubt, personal and professional pride and satisfaction in a job well done – Lawrence later told Lord Trenchard: 'The Schneider show ran like clockwork: a great relief, after all the months everybody spent on it. It tired me out, anyway'.[7]

Did Lawrence celebrate the victory that day? Historian Pieter Shipster writes that:

> Lawrence's letters reveal no sentiments of overt or jingois-
> tic pride in Britain's victory. This is perhaps not surprising
> given Lawrence's lifelong dislike for competitive contests,
> but it is surprising that Lawrence with his professed love
> of flying and his passion for speed and mechanical per-
> fection did not make any comment – at least in his
> correspondence – on the beautiful Schneider Cup [sic] air-
> craft that were at the cutting edge of aviation technology

and high speed flight that he saw being flown day after day while at Calshot.[8]

Perhaps Lawrence did take note when, five days after the Schneider contest, Squadron Leader Orlebar,* commanding offi-cer of the High Speed Flight, flew an S6 airframe to a new world absolute air-speed record of 357.7 mph. It was another triumph for Mitchell, Supermarine and all those who had supported the Schneider entries.

At Southampton, aboard the steward ship SS *Orford*, Ramsay MacDonald pledged his support and that of the government, including the Air Ministry and Royal Air Force, to defending this second successive win with a view to gaining the Schneider Trophy permanently. It would take a mere two months to change that pledge.

Following the Wall Street Crash in October 1929, and with a worsening world economic outlook, the government of Ramsay MacDonald withdrew funding and direct support for a third and final bid to win the Schneider Trophy outright in the 1931 contest at Cowes. In a surprise announcement, the government blamed the move away from Schneider's original intentions (it was not lost on Mitchell that Jacques Schneider had wanted his competition to help the development of commercial rather than military aviation), and saying that sufficient high-speed flight data had been collected and further official support was no longer needed. The wording of

---

* After the Schneider Trophy contest Orlebar went on to command RAF Northolt as the Hawker Hurricane came into service, then No 10 Group and finally was Deputy Commander of Combined Operations.

the official announcement has all the hallmarks of the best civil service scraping-the-barrel-of-excuses, and naivety of socialist forward thinking. The government was broke, and thought private enterprise was capable of funding the contest. The decision shows a lack of ambition.

So there would be no state development money for the 1931 contest, and no allocation of the world's most experienced high-speed pilots from the Royal Air Force. Had it not been for the timely intervention of Colonel the Master of Sempill, a veteran aviator with his eyes on flying over Mount Everest, there might not have been a third win. But Sempill sorted out a wealthy donor.

Cometh the crisis, cometh the heroine. The government had not reckoned with seventy-three-year-old Fanny Lucy Houston DBE, a former suffragette and a lady with very determined views.

*Public interest in the Schneider contest rose to a fever pitch in 1931;
anyone who doubts the draw of the races just needs to look at this crowd
at Cowes on the Isle of Wight as the S6b crosses the finishing line.*

10

Leave It to Lucy

Britain has often been blessed with extraordinary people will-ing to stand up and be counted. One such figure, supreme in the Schneider and Spitfire story, was Lucy Houston, an ultra-nationalist and philanthropist.

Lucy Houston was born Fanny Radmall, a draper's daughter from Lambeth, south-east London, who first came to fame as a chorus girl in London's West End and by sixteen years old was the mistress of Freddy Gretton, the owner of Bass Brewery. When Gretton died in 1882, he left her a legacy of £6,000 a year, worth over £600,000 in current value. She was made. She had a business head on her and invested in her own career on the stage, leaving the footlights for 'proper' acting. A lady in a hurry, she eloped with Theodore Brinckman, a wealthy aristocrat, in 1883, only to ask for a divorce twelve years later. The settlement added to her wealth and she was then able to court and marry 'confirmed bachelor' the 9th Baron Byron in 1901.

London's political scene at the turn of the century was charged with the Entente with the French abroad and votes for women at home. Lucy, as she now styled herself, jumped into the fray by bank-rolling the suffragette cause and standing bail for Emmeline Pankhurst, the de facto leader of Votes for Women. When the First World War came along, Lucy was at the forefront of charity work – slogans included 'Give Him Socks' and 'A Match for Our Matchless Troops from Lady Byron'. She also created the Bluebirds' Nest Rest Home on Hampstead Heath so nurses from the Western Front in Flanders had somewhere in London to rest and recuperate. It was for this selfless deed that she was made a Dame of the British Empire.

Lord Byron died in 1917. It then took Lucy seven years to snare and marry Sir Robert Houston, whose friends even called him 'hard, ruthless and [an] unpleasant bachelor'.[1] This did not deter the good Lady Houston, as she now became, and they were married on 12 December 1924. It was aboard his luxury yacht *Liberty* that Robert died only sixteen months into the marriage, leaving Lucy five times what he said he would when they married. In fact, Lucy started life again with £5.5 million (about £300 million today) and the real risk of death duties. She took the bull by the horns and approached the Chancellor of the Exchequer, Winston Churchill, with the offer of an *ex gratia* payment of £1.6 million as a settlement with no liability admitted. He accepted the offer, which would be worth around £83 million in current value.

Invested well, Lucy's wealth grew and within a few years she had taken up the cause of British aviation and the politics of the

Conservative Party. Churchill liked aviation, and he was a crusading Conservative with a distinct pro-empire standpoint, which mirrored that of the widowed Lady Houston. The two appear to have formed an association that allowed Churchill to enlist Lucy's support when it came to promoting his Conservative ideals, which included rearmament and the need for modern technology to take Britain into the new age of aviation.

Following the government's withdrawal of support for the 1931 Schneider competition, the industry had continued to lobby for funds. However, on 15 January 1931, on the advice of Air Chief Marshal Sir Hugh Trenchard, the recently retired Chief of the Air Staff about to take up the reins of being Commissioner of the Metropolitan Police, the announcement was made. Trenchard had said that there was no advantage to the government, the Air Ministry or the Royal Air Force in having a competitor in the race, as aeronautical innovation and aircraft development would continue whether or not Britain competed. Also on 15 January 1931 – in the fastest confirmation of policy ever – the Air Ministry wrote to Vickers, Supermarine and the Royal Aero Club, the British governing body for the race, to withdraw all official backing to what the Cabinet called a sporting event. This government withdrawal included the use of pilots and engineers from the Royal Navy and the Royal Air Force; it also meant no use of the winning 1929 Supermarine S6 racing seaplanes, and that the Solent would not be policed so that the race could be staged. Mitchell and his team, as well as Rolls-Royce, knew that providing a new race-winning airframe would not be possible. Action was needed.

Lucy was ready. Her political and media campaign shocked the government. She questioned Trenchard's technical knowledge and added her own fervent imperial ideals, saying that Britain needed to win the race in 1931 and to permanently have the trophy because the nation needed the success. Lucy's words initially carried less weight than those of Trenchard, but the Royal Aero Club, led by the irrepressible Sir Philip Sassoon as its chairman, immediately started lobbying newspapers and establishment friends to find a way of changing MacDonald's mind. This started with a letter from the Royal Aero Club to the Cabinet offering to raise £100,000 (about £6 million today), estimated to be half the funds needed to get Mitchell into a position to field a racing seaplane. The government, Sassoon argued, could make the aeroplanes, pilots and the policing available if it simply rescinded its ban. Mitchell had already decided to start work on the changes he thought that the 1929 winning S6 would need to clinch victory in the 1931 race.

At the prompting of Lucy, a national newspaper sent a telegram to MacDonald at No. 10 Downing Street: 'To prevent the socialist government being spoilsports, Lady Houston will be responsible for all the extra expenses beyond what Sir Philip Sassoon says can now be found, so that Great Britain can take part in the race for the Schneider Trophy.'[2]

Lord Rothermere, owner of the *Daily Mail*, now worked with Lucy and gave her opportunities to move the government and an opposition that he saw as being too soft. Lucy rose to the occasion and thundered: 'Every true Briton would rather sell his last shirt than admit England could not afford to defend herself'.[3]

She thereby cleverly conflated the Schneider Trophy and Mitchell's designs with the defence of the nation, tugging at the heartstrings and natural pride in the country that existed at the time. Sassoon, later to become Under-Secretary for Air in the new Conservative government, the *Daily Mail* and Lady Houston won the day for Mitchell to continue work and the RAF High Speed Flight to be available for the Schneider Trophy race. It would be touch and go for the British team, but Supermarine's people worked day and night. Mitchell was up for it.

However, the on-off-on nature of the race sponsorship caused considerable upheaval in the design teams at Supermarine and Rolls-Royce. This was perhaps the greatest meeting of aeronautical engineering minds of the pre-war period and Jeffrey Quill is full of praise for the teamwork:

All this [political procrastination] had caused a great and nearly fatal delay as far as designers and developers were concerned and the competitive threat from the Italian aircraft was very great – especially from the Macchi M72 with the Fiat tandem engine. Rolls-Royce embarked urgently upon a programme to extract yet more power from the R Type engine and Supermarine laid down two modified S6s, to be called S6b, capable of taking the more powerful engine. These aircraft had to be built in [a] tremendous hurry and it was due to the Herculean efforts of Trevor Westbrook, the young, forceful and extremely energetic general manager of Supermarine, as well as, of course, of Mitchell's design team, that they were ready on time.[4]

For the modified S6 engine, what Mitchell really wanted was more than 2,200 hp, and he was delighted when Rolls-Royce was able to achieve 2,350 hp. The only downside (besides the engine's weight, which would require redesigning the float struts), was that spirit engines demanded fuel at a rate of around three to four gallons a nautical mile, and additional tankage would be needed. Fuel developed for the R-type was the beginning of high-octane aviation fuel at British refineries at Rotterdam, on the Thames and the Mersey, and would lead to the 100-octane combat fuel for the Spitfires and Hurricanes of the Battle of Britain.* The S6b would be fuelled by a mixture of benzol, Romanian naphthalene gasoline and a small amount of lead to aid combustion.

In 1931, hopeful of stopping the triumphant British bid to win the Schneider Trophy outright with a third victory, the Italian government entered two Macchi MC72 racing seaplanes, and the French entered a Bernard HV220 and a Nieuport Delage. Again, the Americans were absent with no competitive racing seaplane. But both Italy and France had their hopes dashed by not being able to pass the scrutiny at RAF Calshot, the race headquarters on Southampton Water; all racing entrants were required to follow a detailed series of rules and were checked prior to being allowed to enter the competition. The Italians were just not ready – but they later proved what a threat they would have been to the

---

* Thankfully two large oil tankers loaded with 100-octane were said to be the last ships to leave Rotterdam when the Germans invaded in May 1940. Another historical aside is that the Schneider spirit was developed into the classic maritime powerplant which propelled the *Blue Bird* to a world land-speed record in September 1935. The need for speed was not just in the air.

Supermarine design when, in 1933 and again in October 1934, Francesco Agello* flew a re-engined Macchi on Lake Garda, reaching a staggering 440.68 mph, a record that still stands for seaplanes.

Development of the S6 was not without its problems. This high-end racing was dangerous and demanding. Mitchell had also upgraded two 1929 S6 airframes (known now as S6a) with the new Rolls-Royce engine in 1931. One of these aircraft suffered a freak accident when Flight Lieutenant Linton Hope[†] hit a surface ship's wash and the machine he was flying cartwheeled; although the airframe was recovered, it was not immediately available for racing. Linton Hope was replaced by Lieutenant Jerry Brinton RN who crashed shortly afterwards on 18 August 1931 in an accident put down to losing control on the take-off run; sadly he died. As Denis Le Penn Webb explained, 'Opening the throttle too wide and too quickly on an S6 or S6b could produce sufficient torque reaction to capsize them.'[5]

However, on race day, the crowds would not be disappointed. On 13 September 1931, the British competitors were the only ones to complete the course over the Solent but did so to an estimated crowd of over a million. Special trains and buses had been laid on to bring the adoring public to the greatest exhibition of high-speed flight ever seen in Britain. Newspapers and newsreels were positioned along the route and over Calshot in specially chartered

---

* Agello (1902–42) was a celebrated Italian test pilot who died testing a Macchi fighter in the Second World War.

† Hope senior died in December 1920 and his aviation-minded son, Group Captain Linton Hope FRAeS, was killed in action in 1941.

boats. It is said that one of the turning pylons for the course was situated within sight of Henry Royce's house at Wittering where he was living out his final days of retirement.

Flight Lieutenant John Boothman flew the S6b at an average speed of 340.08 mph, which demonstrated the remarkable power that the R-type engine could produce: 2,350 hp, an unheard-of figure in 1931. His teammates from the RAF High Speed Flight, Leonard Snaith and Frank Long, flew the reserve S6b and the S6a, also completing the course and electrifying the patriotic spirit of the crowd. The trophy was Britain's, but perhaps more importantly the technical achievement was not missed by the British government, nor by representatives of France and Italy.

Keen to exploit the most from the Flight and the machines available at Calshot, Flight Lieutenant George Stainforth went on to take the world record of 407.5 mph a fortnight later, flying the S6b that had its engine tweaked to deliver more than 2,350 hp for the attempt (though it was not as much as Mitchell had hoped). He was the fastest man on earth, having broken the 400-mph speed barrier, which had fixated designers for a decade; Mitchell was delighted.

There was, however, some disagreement about the validity of such speed records. After the success of the 1929 race, there had been considerable debate, which Mitchell watched with interest but into which he did not plunge. Major J. S. Buchanan of the Royal Aeronautical Society hosted a dinner at St Ermin's Hotel in London on 15 November 1929 and invited the great and the good, including the Officer Commanding RAF Mount Batten, Wing Commander Sydney Smith. In his correspondence, carefully preserved at the RAF Museum, is the dinner invitation which invited guests to debate, along the lines of an Oxford Union motion, the statement: 'The present rules for the Schneider Trophy Race and the High Speed Record are not consistent with the proper development of high-speed aircraft.' This was because landplanes were now surpassing seaplanes as the future of aeronautics.

Alas, no record of the debate can be found but it is clear that there was growing discord in the London establishment – the Royal Aero Club, the Royal Aeronautical Society and even the Air Ministry – about rules and regulations.

Even after Britain had won the Schneider Trophy outright, there was still concern about the American attitude to the speed record, with the National Aeronautic Association deliberately downgrading the British record by a conversion error between kilometres per hour (the international record measure) and miles per hour. The 655 km/h was translated by the Americans as 406 mph not 407, giving them a chance to lodge a claim with a Curtiss racing seaplane. The Royal Aero Club was livid when, on 2 April 1932, the NAA issued a certificate for the L. S. Thompson Speed Trophy,* delivered by Senator Hiram Bingham to the British Ambassador in Washington DC, with the incorrect speed. The club's secretary wrote to various luminaries on 19 April 1932: 'To my mind the Certificate of the National Aeronautic Association is a piece of gross American impertinence.'

---

* Now held at the RAF Academy at Cranwell.

Nevertheless, the award to Squadron Leader Stainforth, then at the Royal Aircraft Establishment, was well received by members of the High Speed Flight (by now disbanded), with Stainforth replying with profuse thanks on 16 April. It seemed that the Americans were trying to take the world speed record by claiming a speed that was less than the 5 km/h needed by the international convention. Then everyone had to sit up and take note. Mitchell, as always, concentrated on the next project, not looking back in case he tripped over.

For his leadership during the Schneider races, Mitchell would be awarded a serious state honour in 1932: the CBE (Commander of the Order of the British Empire) – what the military call a 'neck decoration'. It was well deserved but, with typical modesty, Mitchell declared it was one for the team. He attended Buckingham Palace in full court dress including sword. According to his son Gordon, Mitchell was not keen on dressing up to this extent but Flo persuaded him. The formal picture seems to indicate some reluctance to dress with lace and even carry a sword.

Mitchell's achievement was remarkable – he had pushed the boundaries of technology and produced three unbeatable aeroplanes. But there was more to come.

It has been suggested that the S6b led directly to the Spitfire. It is clear by simple observation, of course, that this cannot be true. The streamlined use of the in-line Rolls-Royce engine with which Mitchell had reduced the airframe drag in the S6b was important; but the wing structure and layout, engine cooling, fuselage construction and cockpit arrangements were simply technology demonstrators. There is no linear development line between the S6b and the Spitfire. However, it is also true that the Schneider racers were crucial to the technical development of the Spitfire, and probably to other aeroplanes: the lessons learned from construction, engine mounting and configuration were vital to the design of the iconic fighter. Without the Supermarine racing seaplanes, there would have been no Spitfire.

*Famous for its rugged dependability, a Mitchell trait, the
Walrus amphibian biplane was still in production in 1943.
Here it is seen launching from an aircraft carrier.*

11

Back to Business

With the national, even international, fame of the Schneider Trophy win, Mitchell became a household name and a celebrity, not just in the Southampton area. But it was straight back to work.

Vickers was keen to maintain the development of flying boats, which were still the prime business of Supermarine. The global financial crisis that started in 1929 had taken many businesses to an early and unjustified grave. But not Supermarine. The cottage industry might have struggled to fit the model of big business that was Vickers but, in the end, Sir Robert McLean had to agree that it was one of the few companies that had weathered the recession through good business sense, based on sound designs and embracing technology to reduce costs. In other words, the bottom line remained black.

The Southampton flying boat was one of the key designs keeping Supermarine afloat. As one reader of the *Southampton Evening Echo* wrote in a letter to the paper:

This was the time of the Depression and the General Strike, when a machine was finished, there was an order for another one. With a steady wage and the prospect of another bonus, the workforce was fortunate and happy. This air of well-being, stimulated by the success of the Schneider Trophy Races, made the firm, and Woolston generally, a vigorous and attractive area.[1]

Meanwhile, Mitchell's expert team continued to grow.

On 7 July 1930, he had recruited an outstanding engineer with a wealth of experience, including war service and time in the drawing office at Parnall, a stalwart of the British aeronautical industry at the time. Alfred Faddy – he was always known as Alf, from the shop floor to the board room – was to become pivotal in the last seven years of Mitchell's life, as the chief designer relied upon him more and more. He was later described as 'a man of few words, a sturdy independence of spirit and a quiet and rather philosophical sense of humour'.[2] Faddy's apprenticeship at C. A. Parsons & Company of Newcastle, then the world's leading steam turbine technology provider, was to be a cornerstone of the excellence that Mitchell wanted to achieve. In 1986, Eric 'Jack' Davis, a pre-war Supermariner, commented at a Royal Aeronautical Society lecture that Faddy 'was meticulous to the extreme and was not satisfied with anything less than the best', which put him firmly in the same category as Mitchell, adding he 'drew with the pencil and designed with the rubber' – an observation that many Supermariners also made about Mitchell.[3] Davis also recalled that Faddy was a perfectionist and determined character that had junior draughtsmen living in fear. He was 'never satisfied with what you did and would say "don't you think you ought to try. . ." and then tear up and get them to redo their work, often two or three times on paper to reduce weight and refine it to the simplest design.' He believed that it was cheaper to design with care than 'building a machine which needed everything to be changed to make it good'.[4]

It is also at this time that the Canadian engineer Beverley Shenstone appeared on the scene. It seems Shenstone was brought into Supermarine at the suggestion of Faddy. Initially, Faddy found he had to work hard to convince Mitchell that a university-educated engineer would be an asset to Supermarine. He argued that Shenstone possessed vital skills that nobody else in Supermarine had because of his academic approach to wing design following his studies in Germany at the University of Berlin, and that he was fully conversant with monoplane design after his time at Junkers, the leading German design house at Wasserkuppe. As wings create the bulk of the lift in an aeroplane, an aerodynamicist would be vital for both racing seaplanes and monoplane fighters. In the end, Mitchell saw the validity of Faddy's case. Again, Mitchell was bringing into Supermarine people who understood technology, even in a different field of engineering. He knew that he needed to harness everything from materials science to flow mechanics. He was not alone; the other great aircraft companies in Britain were doing the same, especially Gloster and Hawker.

It seems Shenstone may have been placed at Junkers by Group Captain Christie, the British Air Attaché in Berlin, after they met when the Canadian was studying at Berlin University. Although Shenstone had wanted to work on flying-boat stability at Dornier, Junkers was offering the opportunity to examine all-metal monoplane and tailless aeroplane development. In early 1931, Shenstone met Air Commodore John Chamier,* a former deputy director of operations and intelligence at the Air Ministry, now a director of Vickers-Armstrong, who was talent-scouting in Germany. At Junkers, Shenstone acted as his translator. When Chamier heard that Shenstone had been tutored by Alexander Lippisch, the European wing expert, and Ludwig Prandtl, the famed physicist and aerodynamicist, he said, 'Come to work at Vickers.' Shenstone came over to Britain and first tried his luck at Hawker, where chief designer Sydney Camm turned him down, before joining Supermarine.

In his interview with Mitchell he offered his experience on monoplane stability, including the elliptical wing. He also told Mitchell in no uncertain terms that the traditional Supermarine method of flying-boat construction was wasteful and out-of-date – too many ill-fitting sheets and fittings interrupting the air flow. Mitchell suggested a two-month trial on a giant flying boat that had been envisioned but not yet built; Shenstone succeeded in reducing the weight by about half a tonne and improving the lift generation in association with aileron flutter. Shenstone worked

---

* Credited with the formation of the Air Training Corps in February 1941.

with Mitchell for the next half decade, including on the real issue of aileron flutter, which had probably caused two racing seaplanes to crash.

Supermarine was riding high after the Schneider successes. However, the firm did produce several unsuccessful designs during these years.

The Air Yacht was designed and developed in some secrecy, even though its original purpose was as a replacement for the Southampton Mk II as an armed reconnaissance flying boat (to specification R5/27, which shows that it began in 1927). When the military contract was not forthcoming, Supermarine entered discussions with the Guinness brewing family. This wasn't the first time they had bought a flying boat from Supermarine. Denmark had shown interest in torpedo-carrying flying boats in 1926 and had specified the carriage of anti-ship torpedoes under the wing. Mitchell's design, called the Nanok, was basically a three-engined version of the Southampton, but it was not successful, and was converted into an air yacht for the Guinness family and renamed the Solent. These new discussions with the Guinness family resulted in a second Air Yacht with a luxury interior, which was first flown by Henri Biard in February 1930. However, Ernest Guinness changed his mind, even though the certificate of airworthiness had been granted on 22 December 1931. The design had been re-engined with three 525-hp Armstrong Siddeley Panther engines, but rather than giving more power, these only served to create more weight as the struts and bracings needed to support the high wing 'imposed too much drag for any hope of success', said Denis Le Penn Webb.[5]

In the event, the Air Yacht languished in the Hythe hangar until October 1932 when a wealthy American lady saw it and fell in love. The cabins with hot and cold air supplies, comfortable beds, small bath and toilet facilities, a lounge with sofas and full cooking facilities were a great draw for those rich enough to afford the Air Yacht. Mitchell, despite his engineering and provincial background, knew his market. There was even a telescopic wireless mast which could be erected when afloat, allowing the passengers to send and receive telegrams.

Mrs June James bought the flying boat on sight and was off to the Mediterranean. Alas, ill fortune followed the Air Yacht, named *Windward III*, and it crashed into the sea off Capri on 25 January 1933. It was wrecked, and only the Panther engines were recovered to Hythe. There were mercifully no fatalities, but it can be assumed that Mitchell was not unhappy to see the end of the Air Yacht.

There was another interesting development at this time: a monoplane flying boat with more than a little German influence.

The Treaty of Versailles had limited the German capability and capacity of waging war, especially in aeronautics. Having an air force, training military pilots and designing aeroplanes for combat were all banned. Germany, of course, even before Hitler came to power in 1933, found ways around the ban imposed by the Allied powers. For example, development of aero-engines and the training of pilots, specialist navigators and engineers were undertaken in the Soviet Union. At home, many of the pre-eminent German designers worked on gliders and sailplanes, developing the world's leading capability in aerodynamics before any university in the British Empire could offer doctoral courses.

One enterprising company, Dornier,* circumvented the Treaty's limits on power, speed and size by setting up a factory on the opposite side of Lake Constance (Bodensee) on German-Swiss territory. Dornier wanted to create not a war machine but a 100-passenger airliner that could fly to America. At that time, the only way forward was still a flying boat – or flying ship, as the Germans called it. Funded by the German government through the transport fund, the Dornier Do X was conceived in 1924 and built by 1929. It was huge. It weighed 56 tonnes and had twelve Bristol Jupiter engines built under licence by Siemens with both tractor and pusher propellers. It was really aimed at the American market, but it was fraught with problems – the problems of a trailblazer, including design issues with the tail structure.

One person who took note was Mitchell. Vickers had an eye on the international, long-range passenger market for flying boats which did away with the need for expensive aerodromes along the empire routes. Mitchell realised that flying boats could also change destinations as long as there was an expanse of water on which to land – although they did need to be calm and sheltered and equipped with fuel. Mitchell liked the notion of a large flying boat for commercial travel, and Supermarine's enquiries had shown

---

* Dornier went on to build many interesting flying-boat designs in the 1930s including the Do 24 three-engined reconnaissance and rescue flying boat, of which 279 were built. The German military appreciated the flying boat as much as the British, despite not having an empire to connect, but rather wanted to exert control of the Baltic Sea approaches and the North Sea.

that there was a market opening up to the empire – Australia, Singapore, Cape Town and colonial stations in between. The design and build of a large flying boat were not out of the question, even for a small company like Supermarine. After all, at the Hythe Works the Southampton was now being built for Argentina's naval air service.

During Barnes Wallis's short time at Supermarine, Mitchell seems to have been content with Wallis looking at the Guinness Air Yacht design, which had its teething problems, and some initial work on the Air Ministry requirement for a long-range patrol flying boat. Wallis was also keen to look at giant flying boats, and to understand the issues with broad chord and long wings, such as those used on the Dornier Do X. The design and experimental work would require all the expertise at Vickers, but especially the key figures in the Supermarine drawing office and technical department such as Alf Faddy, Joe Smith and the works manager, Trevor Westbrook.

The Type 179, nicknamed 'the Giant' at Supermarine, was a design to rival the Dornier Do X as a forty-seat, all-metal passenger-carrying flying-boat airliner with six Rolls-Royce Buzzard engines and a triple tail arrangement. The Type 179 was also known as the Mediterranean Flying Boat, as the design, if it had been built, would have operated there with Imperial Airways. Mitchell hoped it would beat the Dornier on the UK to Portugal route.

When Henri Biard took the controls of a Dornier over the Bay of Biscay sometime in the summer of 1930, he was a little dismayed by the fact it was flying no more than 20 feet above the water because, the Germans told him, it could add 20 knots to the ground speed that way. He said he was light on the controls and the enclosed cockpit reduced noise to just background level.

Vickers gave the go-ahead for the keel to be laid in May 1931 and construction of the hull – 'plating' in flying-boat parlance – began in the autumn. But by January 1932, the financial impact of the Depression had reached even Vickers, and the project was shelved. Perhaps Mitchell took heart that only three Do X were actually built as well.

According to Denis Le Penn Webb, Frank Holroyd fell foul of the government's cancellation of the Type 179 project and was dismissed;[6] Vickers had a totally different attitude to success and failure. It seems that the big projects like the Giant were always destined to fail, whereas the smaller and medium-size flying boats and racing seaplanes were record breakers and successes. That was due to the nature of Supermarine as a cottage industry rather than the engineering skills of Mitchell.*

In 1931, following the Schneider success and using data from the float design of the S6 series, there was a chance of an engineering step forward that Mitchell was keen to follow. He applied himself to perfecting, as he saw it, the Southampton.

---

* In 1931, there was a brief sideshow at Woolston. Vickers had won an order for the Viastra high-wing luxury twelve-passenger aeroplanes including one, ordered in 1933, for the Prince of Wales, the future Edward VIII, a stalwart aviation enthusiast. Weybridge apparently had no space, so three of the single-engine design were built at Woolston, but the design was so versatile that it was built in two and three-engined configurations for the Australian market. Mitchell rather thought the Viastra was a sideshow for Supermarine, and useful perhaps only for keeping in with the parent company.

Britain was slow to rearm in the 1930s. The government of the day, like almost every government, wanted to spend money on public support that would generate votes rather than on defence projects that might never be needed. The Admiralty, War Office and the Air Ministry were all fighting their corners for a contingent defence when other government departments were spending money for the 'public good'.

Britain, though, was not a continental power with contiguous land borders; it was a maritime trading power with a far-flung empire. Granted the Royal Navy was the largest and best equipped in the world in 1930, but the speed of reaction required meant more air power was needed.

With a lack of suitable airfields, the flying boat was still the platform of choice in 1930. The Southampton long-range cruises to the Far East and Mediterranean indicated that, for the time being, the flying boat was the way to project power. Flying-boat technology was improving quickly and Mitchell's team were working to ensure that Supermarine stayed in front of the rival Bristol and Short Brothers aeroplanes. The designs coming from the technical department and drawing office were capturing the latest Air Ministry requirements as well as the developments which Mitchell could envisage.

The Royal Air Force, often developing naval bases and anchorages, had established a chain of bunkering facilities and bases across the empire and friendly treaty states in the Middle East. So operating to Hong Kong or Australia, even to South Africa via the River Nile and the Great Lakes of Central Africa, was relatively straightforward. The key areas of interest remained the route to

India – the Jewel in the Crown – and the tension spots where the Italians, for example, were flexing muscles. There was always the risk of uprisings; Churchill had been one who proposed that the Royal Air Force 'policed the empire' from the air.

Flying boats then were the power projection of the moment, and Supermarine was well placed to build on the success of the Southampton. Mitchell had already struggled with an advanced Southampton design known as the X: a stainless-steel-hulled, three-engined version, which was jointly created by Vickers and the Woolston-based team in 1929. Mitchell allowed the Southampton X superstructure to be designed and built by Weybridge. But the Armstrong Siddeley Jaguar engines used in this model were not powerful enough, even with three mounted between the wings. The test pilot for the initial trials in March 1930 was Captain Joseph 'Mutt' Summers, the Vickers chief test pilot, who would go on to take the Type 300 into the air six years later. All agreed, Mitchell included, that just enlarging, revamping or stretching a proven design was not the best way forward. Closely spaced frames holding the alloy skin of the flying boat in place were not enough; and the fact that the X was two tonnes over design weight, and therefore slower, didn't help. The hull had external stringers, allowing more space inside.

As Denis Le Penn Webb wrote: 'The aircraft was overweight and aerodynamically dirty and was not a success.'[7] It could be argued that Mitchell was distracted by the Schneider racers and didn't always oversee every project, so this was perhaps his downfall with the X. He went back to smaller flying boats with less weight in the structure.

After seeing that three-engined machines did not offer any real improvement in performance for the significant increase in weight and cost of manufacture, Vickers and Mitchell returned to two-engined updates to the Southampton with models that were more modern, easier to build, easier to support and maintain, and better operationally. In the archives held at Solent Sky Museum, there is a Supermarine report that states: 'A change of policy in 1931, favouring twin-engined flying boats in place of the somewhat unsuccessful three-engined boats recently produced, rendered it obvious that our best course was to revert to the Southampton Mk II . . . and to use it for the development of a new design.'*

Technology was progressing and Mitchell was never slow to pick up the trail. Rolls-Royce was moving ahead with in-line engines derived from the R-type. Modifications included the provision of an enclosed cockpit for operations in salty conditions, such as the Arabian Gulf. Mitchell worked on steel designs, often corresponding with Henry Cave-Browne-Cave and with Ernie Mansbridge, the bright young engineer. He again sought to interest Imperial Airways in passenger-carrying flying boats now that the long-range capability had been proved and the empire routes scouted.

The Scapa flying boat was designed to replace the Southampton series, incorporating all the lessons identified from the operations of the flying boats in Europe, Asia and Australia.

---

* Written by Arthur Shirvall, Supermarine's hydrodynamics specialist at Woolston.

The key to a successful flying boat remained the hull design, both on the water and in the air. Designing the shape and construction should have involved not just aerodynamic mathematics – never Mitchell's strong suit, apparently – but physical testing of a craftsman's model in a tank, probably at the NPL. The same Supermarine report says, 'since no tank testing was conducted on models of the Mk II until after the machine was built the success of the hull must be attributed to pure chance'. Or good judgement?

Vickers offered the Air Ministry the opportunity to have a development flying boat built at the end of the last Southampton Mk II production line. It was christened initially the Mk IV, and was later renamed the Scapa by the ministry. It looks the part, with a hull superstructure designed to take an enclosed cockpit, yet maintaining the tried and tested biplane wings.

It had design refinements of course; Mitchell was always good at using the eraser as well as the pencil. The hull shape is finer, and tests of a model proved the improvements, leading the Air Ministry to issue specification R20/31 in November. The real key to the speed and endurance figures, though, was the Rolls-Royce water-cooled Kestrel IIIA engine, which was itself the result of seeing what American engines were achieving when fitted to the rival Fairey Aviation's Fox day bomber – the type could show a clean pair of heels to the front-line fighters of the Royal Air Force. Everyone took note, not least Mitchell.

The Scapa not only proved the new design philosophies Mitchell wanted to impose but also introduced a new element into the Mitchell story and, by extension, that of Supermarine. On 29 October 1932, three months after the first flight of the Scapa, a young Royal Air Force flying-boat test pilot took the train to Southampton and boarded the ferry across the Itchen to collect the prototype, still called the Southampton Mk IV. Flight Lieutenant George Pickering, who had been awarded the Air Force Cross for his exploits with flying boats in Malta, was welcomed at Woolston by Biard and Mitchell. He was briefed and, with little fuss and his customary professionalism, took the machine from Southampton Water to Felixstowe to begin Marine Aircraft Experimental Establishment proving trials. These included a ten-hour endurance cruise around the North Sea and, in May 1933, a cruise to Malta for operational trials with the Royal Navy. Pickering, as the project pilot, was in command for these trials, as well as a subsequent cruise from Malta to Port Sudan. His reports cemented the plan to order the Scapa, as it would be called, into production. He later flew the Scapa to the Hendon Air Pageant on 6 July 1934, completing his last service flight to Woolston later that day. Pickering would go on to join Supermarine and was chosen by Mitchell to be the first Supermarine test pilot, after Mutt Summers, to fly the Type 300 in 1936.

The chief designer was now focused on winning the Scapa follow-on contract. This needed a new approach under specification R24/31, which was very advanced for its time – 160 mph, a low stalling speed for water operations and the ability to operate up to 20,000 feet. Perhaps the most exacting requirement was the need to operate using only one engine, while maintaining height and directional control. This would mean paying attention to the rudder and vertical stabiliser as well as the trim tabs, which could be used to compensate for the loss of thrust on one side.

Mitchell's approach was typical of his philosophy. The team worked on three different solutions: enlarging the existing Scapa design (which had worked with the Southampton); creating a Southampton X lookalike sesquiplane (a biplane with one wing significantly shorter than the other); and a thin-wing flying-boat design. The last of these prevailed, showing the influence of Shenstone's presence on the team with his Junkers experience. The competition for the Scapa replacement came down to Saunders-Roe and Supermarine – interestingly, the initial winner was the former, but Mitchell convinced the Air Ministry to put his design, to be called the Stranraer (maintaining the Scottish theme), into production. Its decision was likely based on the reduced risk of Supermarine with its track record and the financial power of Vickers behind the company.

One has to admire Mitchell's tenacity and his confidence in his personal experience and engineering knowledge. His credit was very good with the Air Ministry, which appreciated that his flying-boat design concept for the Stranraer seemed to tick all the requirement boxes. In fact, the Stranraer design outperformed all comers with its redesigned hull, which although wider and deeper, did not produce any more drag than the smaller, lighter Scapa. Mitchell, with a small team, had produced a world beater that even had a new innovation: a tail gunner. The Stranraer was the first British flying boat so equipped. Even though it was only armed with a rifle-calibre Lewis machine gun of First World War vintage, it would be enough, the experts thought, to frighten away another flying boat. The Germans were designing floatplane fighters, and Britain needed something to counter them.

The Stranraer seems to have taken a while to reach proto-type stage, but that's because the Air Ministry was late with the specification, understanding that Mitchell was busy with racing seaplanes. Mutt Summers was again the maiden flight test pilot, on 27 July 1934, and tests were flown by George Pickering that same afternoon on the Solent and Southampton Water. Pickering took her to Felixstowe on 24 October. He reported that the Bristol Pegasus engine was reliable.

The Stranraer was also the first project on which Mitchell felt he could bring in his new team of engineers and designers. He could develop the talents of those who had joined with the Schneider successes ringing in their ears. This is the first flying boat on which there is evidence that Alan Clifton and Trevor Westbrook worked; both important names in the post-Mitchell era of Supermarine. As a result of Shenstone's wing and Shirvall's radical hull influence on Mitchell, the Scapa and then the Stranraer were faster and more economic flying-boat designs.

The Stranraer started a series trend on offensive armaments: bombs and anti-ship torpedoes, soon to be joined by depth charges. The fact that the flying boat flew on active service into the Second World War and is featured in Air Ministry propaganda books published in 1942 indicates its utility to the Royal Air Force. It was only succeeded on front-line squadrons by the American Catalina in March 1941. Mitchell would have been proud when Vickers received an order from the Royal Canadian Air Force for the Stranraer to be built in Montreal, where it was nicknamed the Whistling Bird Cage because of the noise of the wind through the rigging wires and sheer complexity of the biplane wing structures. Civilian-owned surplus Stranraer flying boats transported passengers and 'mercy missions' on the west coast of Canada with Queen Charlotte Airline until 1958. Their exploits* in harsh conditions without rebuilds shows the wisdom of the Mitchell design and the Supermarine craftsmanship. One is exhibited in the RAF Museum in Hendon, needing only small rectification work on the fuselage and wings.

In 1931, Faddy was joined in the drawing office by Bill Fear, who had also worked at Parnall, so knew about innovation and good design. That flexibility and inherent freedom to innovate would result in the strangest, most adored and fantastical amphibian of all time: the Walrus.

This amazing biplane had started life as a Royal Australian Air Force specification, issued by the Air Ministry as 6/34, and this machine became the Seagull V. The attention that the Seagull II and III had received from officialdom in London was transferred to the colonies and resulted in an order for six Mk III variants for the Royal Australian Air Force in 1925. Mitchell's design proved reliable and functional, allowing the RAAF to carry out a survey of Papua and the associated Mandate Territories as well as the Great Barrier Reef – at least 2,000 nautical miles flown – despite the fact that the Seagull's original specification did not call for long-range aviation. Versatility was the main feature of the design, allowing flat-deck operations, catapult launches and amphibious operations from shore stations. Mitchell had developed his skill at creating a

---

* These are covered in *The Accidental Airline* by Howard White and Jim Spilsbury (Harbour Publishing, 1988).

keel for the Seagull III that could withstand rough water as well as the high forces of a catapult launch from a cruiser.

Despite Australian support, the Royal Air Force's view was lukewarm, and Mitchell was faced with a design that was not his usual perfection as it did not meet the full Air Ministry specification. The Seagull family did, however, morph into the Seagull V with a powerful Bristol Pegasus II engine as a pusher rather than a tractor mounting. Design evaluation of the single-engine amphibian needed to develop further, and often the step forward on the linear progression to the Walrus was taking an existing design and re-engineering the airframe with appropriate modifications to the tail surface to give lateral control with a more powerful engine, for example. The torque generated by the newer engines from Rolls-Royce and Napier meant that stability on the water and the air required a way of channelling the airflow. As military aviation designs continued to grow in size and power, in order to carry bombs or depth charges, aerial ordnance needed special provisions that Mitchell and his team soon learned how to develop. These modifications included the development of water rudders to allow for tight turns on the surface in close proximity to warships, or ramps to transfer from the sea to the land.

The Seagull V design shows some of the latest thinking of the time, including a pusher engine mount to reduce exposure to the sea; enclosed cockpit, which came from the Southampton flying-boat cruise and conditions in the Arabian Gulf; and a spacious cabin for navigation and the rest of the crew. It was robust as it needed to be catapult-launched, land in rough seas and be craned aboard the parent warship. Mitchell designed the Seagull V around the RAAF requirement, but the Royal Navy needed something with more power. The Royal Air Force also asked for a naval catapult-launched observation and gunnery-spotting flying boat for the Royal Navy's cruisers. This was issued as specification 2/35 – the Walrus.

Superficially, the Walrus looks like a Seagull V, but with lessons learned, including a more powerful engine for a lesser increase in speed and service ceiling. Yet it was originally rejected by the Air Ministry. Denis Le Penn Webb states that the ministry was less than keen originally, although asked to be kept informed but that 'we do not envisage any role for an aircraft of this type with HM Forces'.[8] Strange. Left hand and right hand in the ministry. The view of the 'experts' at Calshot was summed up by Squadron Leader Dickie Brice, a flying-boat captain, who asked why Supermarine bothered with a design that would be shot out of the sky, as he put it. Luckily the Fleet Air Arm had other ideas. Lieutenant Caspar John, later an admiral, borrowed a Seagull V for the Mediterranean Fleet exercises in 1934 and the Royal Navy loved its versatility and ruggedness for naval-gunfire spotting duties. The design showed that ugly-looking didn't matter with a flying boat; it was so successful that the last Walrus was not delivered until the first quarter of 1944.

George Pickering was actively involved in the production test flying of the Walrus amphibian; the model was so rugged he rolled one on its acceptance flight and the men in the delivery shed came out to watch and cheer. This would become a norm for every Walrus delivered. Pickering would take each aeroplane off the line at Woolston, and, usually with a works passenger, take off from

Southampton Water and head out over the Solent. He would climb to a safe altitude and then loop – yes, take an amphibian biplane upside down – to confirm its structural integrity. According to Joe Smith's biographer, Mike Roussel, Pickering would return to Woolston and carry out a loop at 300 feet to show the production staff that the Walrus was fully airworthy.[9]

One bridge Pickering used to fly over – presumably with Mitchell's knowledge, as it was right outside his office window – was the Itchen Floating Bridge. Now replaced by a toll bridge, the ferry was an important part of the Supermarine story as it connected the city with Woolston on the other side of the Itchen. Pickering would purposely fly low over the floating bridge, which was actually a ferry, to watch the reaction of the occupants. He was not beyond landing a Walrus in the Solent to drift and fish on a quiet day. He was Mitchell's type of test pilot.*

Mitchell had joined Pickering in the production testing of the Seagull for the Royal Australian Air Force in August 1935 and, six months later, he couldn't wait to join his test pilot in a Walrus development prototype for a flight over Southampton Water. Joe Smith was on board too.

---

* Jennie Pickering Sherborne remembers that low flying was in her father's blood and he is credited with being the first of several daredevil pilots to fly under the Winchester Bypass Bridge, situated in a cutting to the east of the city. The bridge was always known as Spitfire Bridge until it was demolished to make way for the M3 motorway. There is no true evidence, but the story fits the coincidentals. She recalled, 'My father would fly over our thatched cottage near Fordingbridge, and you could hear him coming, especially in a Spitfire. He would be very low, and we would rush outside to watch. He could come back over and drop a small silk parachute carrying a note inside.' Jennie still lives in the cottage.

Mitchell was undoubtedly the doyen of the flying boat. But war clouds over Europe would soon test his engineering skills to the limit.

Mitchell's first fighter, the Type 224, nearly damaged Supermarine's reputation beyond repair, but Mitchell and his assistant Faddy worked to learn the lessons and refine their designs.

12

Towards a Fighter

The banner could not have been more explicit in calling the prime minister and leader of the National Government, Ramsay MacDonald, a traitor. Lucy Houston was never a lady to mince her words: 'DOWN WITH MACDONALD THE TRAITOR' it read, strung between the masts of her steam yacht moored in the Thames opposite the Palace of Westminster.

Mitchell had watched with interest when, in 1932, Lucy Houston took a further step in her crusade for British air defences by offering £200,000 (or around £12 million today) to strengthen the armed forces, especially the air defence of the metropolitan area, saying that she alone had 'dared to point out the dire need for air defence of London', which, she said, the government had shamefully neglected. The same year, on 10 November, the former prime minister, Stanley Baldwin, made his infamous 'bomber will always get through' speech. Bombers were considered fast and rugged – and sufficient in number to always ensure that some would reach the target with devastating effect. Mitchell simply didn't believe him.

That obvious neglect of the air defences is what had led the Air Ministry the previous year to issue a specification for a new fighter to protect the metropolitan area.

At the beginning of the decade that saw the world speed record break the 400-mph barrier, the current fighter aircraft available for the Fighting Area of the Air Defence of Great Britain – the countryside around Greater London – were aeroplanes that had changed little since the end of the First World War. They were faster, certainly, but the firepower and manoeuvrability were about the same; they were biplanes that even kept open cockpits and fixed undercarriages. For all intents and purposes they looked little different from the fighters that Biggles flew in the boys' adventure books.

Even before the outcome of the final Schneider Trophy race at Calshot had been decided, the Air Ministry in London had begun to consider what a new fighter might require. There was considerable evidence from trials at the Aeroplane and Armament Experimental Establishment (A&AEE) at Martlesham Heath that four rifle-calibre machines would not be adequate for a new type of all-metal bomber that France, Germany, Italy and even the British aircraft industries were developing.

The election of Adolf Hitler as chancellor of Germany is often taken as a massive change of policy in Berlin but, in reality, Germany, even under the left-of-centre Weimar Republic, had been secretly rearming for several years. A key prelude to Hitler's rise to power was the change of status of the Rhineland, which had been occupied by France from 1 December 1918. This included the complete demilitarisation of the territory on the west bank of the Rhine to the French border. It was enforced by the Inter-Allied Rhineland High Commission, which was nominally Belgium, France and the UK, with the USA as observer; but, in effect, it was France who ran the Rhineland.

The occupation was designed under the Treaty of Versailles to give France and Belgium a buffer zone against future German attack; it was also a guarantee for Germany's reparations obligations. When Germany fell behind on its payments in 1922, the industrial Ruhr valley was occupied by French troops from 1923 to 1925. Everyone in positions of power in Europe thought that the French withdrawal from the southern zone in 1925 demonstrated that Berlin understood the rules on demilitarisation, and everyone sat back and rejoiced. It was not to last.

The Versailles Treaty, flawed and rarely enforced except by France, had prohibited German rearmament and even the development of aeroplanes. Germany's response was to concentrate on gliders, which were not covered by the treaty (but which gave the aircraft industry the benefit of new research on wing design and shedding drag for its wartime military aircraft) and to team with the Soviet Union. In Russia, engine development and pilot training became mutually beneficial; ironic, really. Heinkel, Junkers and Messerschmitt all benefitted from German policy, together with Daimler-Benz, the aero-engine manufacturer.

In London, the air branch of the Secret Intelligence Service (SIS) had been collecting information about German and Italian aeronautical developments since the Schneider Trophy races in

1929 had shown the European interest in new technologies. British secret intelligence had been running agents in Nazi Germany but gained more from the technical expertise of young officers who went on holiday to Germany. Although Mitchell was not briefed directly by SIS, he was in receipt of industry private briefings from the Air Ministry, which made use of detailed work by the SIS.

In fact, intelligence from inside the Dornier *Flugzeugwerke* (aircraft factory) at Friedrichshafen on Lake Constance had indicated as early as 1930 that Germany thought it could design, develop and build a 'bomber type' faster than current British or French fighters – this might be why the *bomber will always get through* mindset of the senior politicians prevailed. The SIS knew that Germany was developing a shoulder-wing, twin-tail bomber-type aeroplane under the cover of government mail aircraft with a planned speed of 250 mph at altitude. In 1932, the *Heereswaffenamt* (army weapons office) became more open and issued public tenders for a freight aeroplane for the *Deutsche Reichsbahn-Gesellschaft* (German railway company) which could also be a high-speed mail for Lufthansa.

The Air Ministry was deeply concerned that the current fighters in service would not catch a new generation of monoplane bombers. They were right. The new Dornier Do 17 'Flying Pencil', the Heinkel He 111 or the Junkers Ju 88, all allegedly designed as mailplanes, were in fact high-speed bombers. The Ju 88 was so fast, it was later used in the Bay of Biscay and the Mediterranean theatre of operations as long-range fighter aircraft by the Luftwaffe.

In the Royal Air Force, the Bristol Bulldog was the dominant fighter and, although only introduced in 1929, its conventional

RIGHT: With obvious roots in Admiralty Air Department boats of the First World War, the Channel was created with commercial crossings of the English Channel in mind.

ABOVE: Mitchell (right) aboard a Swan II proving flight, in the wicker basket seat, for the Southampton–Channel Islands service, likely flown by Henri Biard in June 1926.

LEFT: Henri Biard, the intrepid company test pilot, with Mitchell outside the finishing shop at Woolston with the S4. The picture was probably taken in June 1925.

ABOVE: Mitchell (centre) had high hopes of the S4 for the Schneider contest at Baltimore in October 1925. It was certainly ahead of its time.

ABOVE: Ready for the 1927 season, Mitchell (centre) and the Supermarine racing team gather before the S5. Flt Lt Webster, the winning pilot, stands behind on a float.

LEFT: Supermarine S5 at RAF Calshot during an engine test of the Napier Lion prior to departure to Venice in 1927.

RIGHT: From the Mitchell family album, another fine view of the S5 showing the beaching and travelling gear required for a racing seaplane.

THE S.5. AT CALSHOT.

BELOW: Half a million Italians and their guests lined the Lido in the Venice lagoon with Flt Lt Worsley powering the S5 to second place.

LEFT: Two great aeronautical engineers of the twentieth century, R. J. Mitchell and Sir Henry Royce, came together in the quest for speed and the Schneider Trophy.

RIGHT: Mitchell (second left) at the installation of the Rolls-Royce R-type engine into the S6 at Woolston in 1929. This is always a tricky moment for any designer or engineer.

LEFT: The sleek design of the S6 is clear from this view, including the floats, which needed different shapes to allow for the immense torque developed by the Rolls-Royce R-type engine.

RIGHT: A rear picture of Flt Lt Waghorn boarding the S6 at Cowes. He went on to win the 1929 Schneider contest with a record 328.63 mph. The Rolls-Royce engine appears to be running.

LEFT: Despite two straight wins, the British government pulled support for the third and final race in 1931, but the RAF High Speed Flight was reformed just in time. OC High Speed Flight, Sqn Ldr Orlebar, is centre.

RIGHT: Ready for the race. The S6b embodies everything that Mitchell and his team had learned from the Schneider contests; this went on to help the development of the Spitfire.

TOP: The Royal Aero club published souvenir brochures for the 1929 Schneider contest at Calshot.

MIDDLE: In 1930, the aviation event of the year was the Hendon Air Pageant; a formation of Southampton Mk II flying boats would have thrilled the crowd of 180,000.

BOTTOM: A famous picture taken on 5 March 1936 at Eastleigh for the first flight of the K5054. L–R: Mutt Summers; Harold 'Agony' Payn; Mitchell; Stuart Scott-Hall; and Jeffrey Quill.

ABOVE LEFT: Mitchell was honoured by King George V with the award of the CBE in 1932. He is pictured here in court dress for the investiture, including sword.

ABOVE RIGHT: Not everything Mitchell designed was a success. The Southampton X departed from his normal twin-engined philosophy and did not enter production.

ABOVE: The very air-minded King Edward VIII visited Martlesham Heath in Suffolk in 1936 to see the Type 300. Mitchell, pictured in front of the wing and nearest the propeller, had flown up with George Pickering in the company Miles Falcon.

LEFT: Canadian Beverley Shenstone's experience with wing design and aerodynamics was vital to the Spitfire design. CENTRE: Joe Smith was chief draughtsman for the Schneider racers, the Walrus and the Spitfire. RIGHT: Alan Clifton ran Supermarine's Technical Office during the transition from seaplanes to high-performance fighters.

ABOVE: By 1939, the Supermarine Works at Woolston was a thriving aeronautical powerhouse, producing the Walrus and the Spitfire for British and allied governments. In twenty years, a muddy tidal site had become vital to Britain's defence.

radial engine meant its combat speed was limited to a maximum of 178 mph, so the fighter was likely to be outrun by a modern bomber.

Secret technical briefings from the SIS were very persuasive. In October 1931, the Air Ministry issued a detailed specification F7/30 for a Single Seater Day and Night Fighter for a competitive tender to British aircraft manufacturers, although the initial planning had been carried out in 1930 when word of German developments had reached Whitehall.

It specified a new high-speed fighter (at least 250 mph) which had all the hallmarks of a 'bomber destroyer' rather than a pure fighter (one designed to engage other fighters). The winning design would need to climb to 15,000 feet at the highest possible rate of climb – about 1,000 feet a minute – have good manoeuvrability, be of all-metal construction, have a pilot field-of-view all around and carry four 0.303-inch machine guns. Interestingly, the air chiefs wanted this machine, which could be a biplane or a monoplane, to have a landing speed not exceeding 60 mph (to make it easier for young pilots to master), which meant that engine and wing design would be very important given the speed range from about 250 down to 60 mph.

The document contains fourteen highly detailed sections with very specific requirements, many of which strike the reader as coming straight out of the First World War, including the provision of armaments that might include the Lewis gun with 400 rounds of ammunition for each weapon. This was clearly inadequate, and Mitchell was not the only one to think so; his rivals at Hawker and Gloster also preferred the Vickers machine gun and, later, the Browning. The endurance was given by the requirement that the new fighter should fly at full throttle for thirty minutes at ground level, plus for two hours at full throttle at 15,000 feet. There was an option to configure the new fighter as a 'pusher' to give the pilot a clear field-of-view forward. Many of the provisions were deliberately loose to engender a feeling that close cooperation and collaboration between the design team, the Royal Aircraft Establishment and Air Ministry would be needed. Mitchell was concerned that this would lead to interference and stifle individual innovation by the designers.

As a result of the competition being announced there was intense industry speculation about the bold move by the Air Ministry to create a revolutionary fighter/bomber destroyer. The British public were also aware that *The Times* had reported in an editorial that the French *L'Armée de l'Air* had overtaken the Royal Air Force in terms of numbers of combat aircraft.

Jeffrey Quill later recalled, 'In 1931, industry in Britain was still suffering from the effects of world recession, and the issue of the F7/30 specification sparked off intense competition among aircraft companies.'[1] The Supermarine team were soon hard at work.

Mitchell had started to develop his own supply chain of sub-component manufacturers and assemblers for the S6b, and now widened the scope with the help of Westbrook and his new team of engineers including his design chief leader, Alf Faddy, and the aerodynamics expert, Beverley Shenstone.

The stumbling block was power. It was imperative to find the right engine, of British design, with a secure supply train that could be relied upon in times of conflict. Mitchell took the unusual step of asking Sir Henry Royce if the engine and airframe design team could collaborate as closely as possible. The Schneider Trophy successes had demonstrated that the Rolls-Royce R-type was a constant high performer that had showed its merit when tested to its limit. Now there was the Goshawk engine in development with an unconventional evaporative cooling system, which removed the heat as steam and returned it as water to cool the engine.

As Jeffrey Quill explained, 'we had in Britain an aircraft design team at Supermarine who were world leaders in the technology of high-speed aircraft, and an engine design team at Rolls-Royce who had brought the 60 deg V-Twelve supercharged engine of high specific power, low specific weight and low frontal area to a new pitch of efficiency and performance'.[2] However, Mitchell was not over-confident. According to Alan Clifton, Mitchell recognised that he was not a specialist in fighter aeroplane design and engineering. It is reported that he sought the views of Royal Air Force pilots at Martlesham to understand what their priorities for such an aeroplane would be.

Type 224 general characteristics[3]
- Crew: 1
- Length: 29 ft 5¼ in
- Wingspan: 45 ft 10 in
- Height: 11 ft 11 in
- Wing area: 295 sq ft
- Airfoil: root: NACA 0018; tip: RAF 34

- Empty weight: 3,422 lb
- Gross weight: 4,743 lb
- Powerplant: 1 × Rolls-Royce Goshawk II V-12 evaporative/ steam-cooled piston engine, 600 hp
- Airscrew: two-bladed fixed-pitch propeller

Performance
- Maximum speed: 228 mph at 15,000 ft
- Service ceiling: 38,800 ft absolute ceiling
- Time to altitude: 15,000 ft in nine minutes thirty seconds

Armament
- Guns: 4 × 0.303 in Vickers Mk IV machine guns

Mitchell was aware how much was depending on the work for the future of Supermarine, even with the support of Vickers' chairman, Sir Robert McLean. McLean was an entrepreneur and corporate mogul, usually dressed in a rather baggy double-breasted suit, who thought the Air Ministry had failed industry with its restrictive specifications and dictatorial attitude. Mitchell was happy for McLean to deal with the high-level politics of procurement, while his private thoughts were supportive of his chairman: to his mind a specification should be clear and broad, allowing designers and engineers to work a few miracles to meet it.

Mitchell led the day-to-day design and development effort at Supermarine, conscious that he needed technology to counter the high temperatures, which even at 660 hp the Rolls-Royce Goshawk was showing in tests. He decided that he would innovate again. He designed a cranked wing with a fixed undercarriage, both of which could act as surface condensers, allowing the steam to return to water, be collected and returned to the engine in a closed circuit.

Ernie Mansbridge, who worked on aerostructures, told the author Alfred Price that 'we were a bit over-cautious with the wing and made it thicker than it needed to have been'.[4] That also added to the drag, and it was obvious that a true aerodynamics approach was required: the over-dependence of the cooling system on the wing structure needed to change, as the engine still frequently overheated during test flights. Mitchell in fact became 'rather sensitive about the aeroplane', according to Jeffrey Quill.[5]

It has to be said that as the brainchild of Mitchell, the man who led the design of some of the world's most beautiful flying boats and racing seaplanes, the Supermarine Type 224 was just plain ugly. There is an old adage that 'if it looks right, it flies right'. The Type 224 fell short of expectations, and this was apparent from the first flight at Eastleigh on 19 February 1934 in the hands of Vickers' chief test pilot, Mutt Summers. Quill later recalled, 'The aeroplane was not a success; the top speed was disappointing, the rate of climb was below specification requirement, the steam cooling system was far from being satisfactorily developed, the aircraft was overweight and the drag patently too high.'[6]

Mitchell saw immediately that the Type 224 would not do. After the first flight, he re-grouped the design team and recruited more young men into engineering and young women into the draughting office, placing advertisements in local newspapers and 'poaching' a new generation from other engineering businesses.

It was at this time, in 1934, that the name 'Spitfire' seems to have been applied to the Type 224, according to another Supermarine test pilot, George Pickering, whose logbook refers to it as such a year before the Type 300, which officially became the Spitfire, had been flown. Many at Supermarine would probably have preferred to leave the project unnamed because names tend to cause controversy; better to build a winner and name it afterwards.

The British companies that entered the competition for F7/30, besides Vickers Supermarine, were Blackburn, Bristol, Westland, Gloster and Hawker. All famous names. All with competent design and engineering support, and most eyeing the Rolls-Royce Goshawk engine as likely to be the winning powerplant, as it was so favoured by the Air Ministry, without the air chiefs actually saying anything. The specification was tough, though, and Blackburn soon pulled out when it was clear that its F3 would not fly safely. The two Bristol entries were still-born, being able to match few of the specification's key user requirements, and it saw the end of the company's brief foray into single-engine fighters. Hawker had put its eggs in the biplane basket, but with an eye to developing a single-engined high-performance fighter next – and that became the Hurricane. Gloster stuck to what it knew best and offered a biplane fighter but with an enclosed cockpit. Amazingly, the Gloster competitor was faster than the Type 224, showing a greater rate of climb in comparative trials at A&AEE, and then at RAE Farnborough, and won the competition. The Gloster Gladiator – the first fighter with an enclosed cockpit in the Royal Air Force – entered service in 1937 and stoutly defended Malta in 1940–41.

Perhaps sadly, the Type 224 prototype was later reduced to

wreckage at the Orford Ness firing range in 1937. However, by that time there was a new Spitfire flying.

But if Europe was facing a crisis, so was Mitchell. In May 1933, he was diagnosed with rectal cancer. At that time the only treatment was surgery under less than promising conditions. Cancer surgery was risky in the 1930s, with little or no antibiotics, and little understanding of the causes or treatment of cancers, except using the surgeon's knife. Even then, there were considerable risks. So much so that Mitchell nearly died when he was operated upon in London that August, and even then not everything malignant could be removed.

If part of the rectum or colon had been removed during surgery, which was often the case, a colostomy was required, fitting a bag or pouch to collect the faeces. This was the result of Mitchell's surgery, along with almost constant pain, and the prognosis was not good; perhaps four or five years if he rested.

Mitchell had the latest model of colostomy fitted but was not impressed. It was yet another challenge for him and it is said that he organised for the pattern shop at Woolston to make some replacement parts he had designed to make the bag and apparatus more comfortable – and to make it more efficient so that he could return to productive work. The principle is still in use today. It was just another application for his brilliant brain. Flight Lieutenant John Boothman later commented that Mitchell had once told him:

if he had his life again he would not have been an aeroplane designer but a surgeon – this was a long time before

169

he was sick – and I remember about 1932 or 1933 an occasion when, having been out shooting with him early in the morning, there was a most gory procedure going on in the kitchen when he was explaining the inside of a rabbit to his son.[7]

The best kept secret at Supermarine from 1933 onwards was the diagnosis of Mitchell's cancer – or, rather, the fact that it was life-threatening. Pre-war reticence about discussing cancer is evident from published accounts of the Spitfire or about Mitchell the man. The fact that he was stoic in his suffering will be inspiring for many contemporary readers. According to his obituary in *Flight*, 'Mr Mitchell had been seriously ill for many months and had in fact not been really well for several years, although his manner and habit of never complaining disguised the fact even to those who knew him really well.'[8]

Most of Mitchell's colleagues were unaware of any illness, even when their pragmatic leader started developing a reputation for ill-humour and sudden outbursts in meetings. Mitchell was well liked; apprentices almost worshipped him for his kindness, which included picking up people in his Rolls-Royce when travelling in Southampton, and asking how their work was going. One Supermariner recalled, 'He never seemed to forget that he had once been an apprentice.'[9] But, as Joe Smith remembered, he would also occasionally 'let rip with us'[10] when work was not up to scratch. As far back as 1930, Le Penn Webb thinks that Mitchell suffered from bouts of anger. 'None of us knew at the time,' he wrote, 'about the trouble' that would cause his death.[11]

With retrospect, it was clear that he had developed a real urgency about the projects underway and he knew the situation for him was terminal; he, of course, faced up to it.

Mitchell did not like noise when he was working, so he would take himself off home to think, sketch and calculate. This was especially true as the Vickers investment in Supermarine was going through major construction to make the premises at Woolston more fit for purpose. Mitchell's office overlooked the water and the slipways; the latter had to be broken up by drilling before being replaced with reinforced concrete to take the weight of the heavier machines now coming out of the production shed adjacent. After his first series of operations for cancer, Mitchell was obviously weakened. The company decided to create a personal lift, just big enough for one, to take Mitchell from his car parking space to his office above the factory floor.* Mitchell's work rate didn't let up through all of this; it may well have been a means of escape from the pain of cancer.

He did have time, however, for buying and selling shares on the Stock Exchange, which he began around this time. His son Gordon reports that, with his salary of £2,500 in 1934 (worth around £152,000 in current value), he felt able to take a certain amount of risk in an activity in which he was reasonably successful.

Mitchell liked to clear his mind while tackling a tricky engineering or design issue, or after working late in his office. He liked sport, particularly sailing a small dinghy, often single-handed on

---

* After his death and after the bombing in 1940, the salvage team found the lift intact and were more than a little surprised to find that it was mahogany lined with stainless-steel fittings. It was salvaged and, of course, re-used in Southampton.

the Itchen. Just upstream from the Supermarine works, there was also the Ridgeway Golf Course situated to the east of the railway line, where he would play the nine holes after work. For Mitchell the skill and concentration required for golf made it a favourite pastime. Despite his grave illness, Mitchell continued to play sport, drive and sail.

Flying would prove to be another source of comfort. Mitchell was almost unique among engineers and designers in taking flying lessons in 1933. He wanted to understand flight from a pilot's perspective. In 1934, Mitchell joined the Hampshire Aeroplane Club, which had recently moved to the airfield at Eastleigh. Founded in 1926, it was one of the first to offer flying lessons in Hampshire, using the de Havilland Gipsy Moth.*

He honed his flying skills with George Pickering in a Miles Falcon 6 after his initial exercises – take-off, climb, turns, approach and landing. Pressure of work meant that it took him six months to go solo – not surprising, as he seems to have been galvanised by the cancer diagnosis and thrown himself into work. This is perhaps the only element of the Mitchell story as fictionalised in *The First of the Few* that is true. In his remission phase of cancer, post yet another operation, Mitchell used flying as an escape – the

---

* It moved to Eastleigh just after Southampton Corporation bought the fields which had been used for flying since 1912. Although in the Borough of Eastleigh, the Corporation named it Southampton Airport – one of the four largest in the country because of the cross-Channel operations to Jersey and other business destinations. The Royal Air Force moved in in 1935 and knew it as Eastleigh, until the Corporation persuaded them to name it RAF Southampton. Eastleigh was also where Supermarine had its final assembly and finishing shops for initially the Type 300 and then for production Spitfires.

concentration needed to fly, especially as a student or low-hours private pilot with the Royal Aero Club certificate cleared the mind. He even took part in Hampshire Aeroplane Club flying competitions, and had a forced landing in a field near what would four years later become RAF Middle Wallop. It was also useful for business, as he could fly to Derby to meet with Rolls-Royce at critical moments. Pickering used to fly Mitchell to Derby Hucknall in open-air biplane DH Moths, which usually meant an overnight stay, or to the Royal Aircraft Establishment at Farnborough. Pickering and Mitchell were stalwart members of the Hampshire Aero Club and pleased to prop up the bar there after a busy day at the works or on the Eastleigh airfield.

Only in Germany was there a similar chief designer with the same feeling for flight. At Focke-Wulf, Kurt Tank also undertook test flying of his work in what legendary British test pilot Captain Eric (Winkle) Brown later described as 'understanding the design from the sharp end'.[12] Mitchell didn't go that far, but Quill and Pickering certainly appreciated being able to talk to the boss about flight regimes and performance in a more constructive way than if he had not been a pilot. It is not a fantasy to conclude that Mitchell's airmindedness allowed him to be unconstrained in design and engineering. In this way he allowed himself to 'father' the improved version of the Type 224, the sleek Type 300 – which would become known as the Spitfire.

The Type 300 was the result of lessons learned in failure.
It would become the Spitfire, but only after considerable work
on marrying the machine guns with the Shenstone wing.

13

Towards the Icon

Reginald Mitchell worked even during his protracted surgery and convalescent periods from 1933, but he was frequently absent for long periods, according to his staff. The family house Hazeldene was turned into a meeting place and design study – drawing board, pencils, rubber erasers, draughting paper – so that he could work while recovering from surgery and the constant tiredness that cancer often causes. Even the garden became a venue for his trusted team to meet, led by Faddy, with Clifton and Shenstone never far away. Having the tools of his trade nearby was the only way Flo could keep her husband from driving to work at Supermarine. She must have often wondered about the unruly but talented group of engineers who crowded around the kitchen table, and as a former school teacher would bring all her management skills to bear so that Mitchell was not too exhausted.

It is clear that the failure of the Type 224 haunted him. He had discussed the general arrangement of the new Fighter* (as the project was habitually called at Supermarine) with Faddy and chief draughtsman Joe Smith but, although he had some ideas for taking the design of the Fighter forward, he realised from the outset that he could not give it his full attention. Earlier in his career, during the development of the Schneider Trophy-winning S6 series of high-speed racing monoplanes, he had learned to delegate. Without a team around him, Mitchell could not have issued the right instructions for the work to be carried out and completed in record time.

And there was good reason to work quickly. War clouds had clearly gathered over Europe as early as 1933 if anyone had cared to look up and see them. Hitler withdrew from the European Disarmament Conference in Geneva in October 1933 and later left the League of Nations. War seemed inevitable when all talks about limited arms and the armed forces collapsed. The public announcement on the creation of the German Luftwaffe in 1935 was preceded in Whitehall by secret intelligence which confirmed that the training programmes in the USSR and the design facilities in Germany were creating a new large and modern air force.

The Air Ministry was keen to modernise and issued Scheme A on 19 July 1934 after Parliamentary approval was granted. This first of a dozen expansion schemes called for forty-one additional fighter squadrons in service by 31 March 1939. The government was now well aware that air defence was the priority.

---

* Later, George Pickering's logbook shows it as the SS – Supermarine Spitfire.

Mitchell, feeling increasingly unwell, yet not immune to the tensions in Europe, urged his team on to drive forward the new Fighter and expunge the shadow of the failure of Type 224. They were ready. Faddy, Clifton, Smith and Shenstone all worked on a new design, which was submitted to the Air Ministry on 19 July 1934. It refined the Type 224, keeping the Goshawk engine, but took advantage of the new technologies about which Mitchell cared so passionately – retractable undercarriage and faired radiator to reduce drag and allow for greater speed. The famed elliptical wing was yet to make an appearance: the team had gone for a straight tapered wing to house a machine gun and its ammunition. The key would be keeping the new design under 5,000 lb, and if possible 4,700 lb.

In Derby, the head of the experimental department at Rolls-Royce, Ernest Hives, and his team had been designing, developing and constructing a V-12 piston-engine with higher specific and continuous power than had ever been thought possible before. The PV-12, as it was known internally – soon to be more widely known as the Merlin – had completed an initial 100-hour bench test which showed that 1,000 hp might be possible, even if the maximum continuous power achieved had only been 790 hp. It was a big engine with a 27-litre capacity and that meant adequate oil, cooling and fuel would be needed even for a point-defence fighter.

Hives needs to take his place in the Spitfire story. The contribution that he made to the development of successful powerplants for the fighting aeroplanes of the Royal Air Force is difficult to over-state. After the passing of Sir Henry Royce in April 1933, Mitchell turned to Hives, who had been at Rolls-Royce since before the First World War and had been involved in some of the experimentation for the Schneider racers, as well as developing flying-boat engines. Of such importance to the war-aircraft industry – Avro (Lancaster), de Havilland (Mosquito), Fairey (Fulmar) and Hawker (Hurricane), which all used Rolls-Royce engines – he was created a peer in 1950. His perseverance and continual endeavour to get the best out of materials and men included never minding about mistakes – just putting them right quickly, as he told an American guest after the Second World War.

Like Mitchell, Hives was a team player and a hard worker. As one senior officer later commented, 'That man Hives is the best man I have ever come across for many a year. God knows where the Royal Air Force would have been without him. He cares for nothing except the defeat of Germany and he does all his work to that end, living a life of unending labour.'[1] He was without doubt a workaholic and therefore got on famously with Mitchell.

Mitchell was a great organiser and understood the characteristics of his staff, which allowed him to get the best from them. As Jeffrey Quill later commented:

At the time the Spitfire was designed, Mitchell's design team . . . had more practical knowledge of high-speed aeronautics than any other design team in the world. They were mentally adjusted to, and dedicated to, the search for the ultimate in aerodynamic efficiency and the achievement of the highest possible speeds. They were not going to allow themselves to be constrained by convention or other extraneous considerations from achieving these aims. They were young and, I believe, very single-minded.[2]

With Shenstone, for example, Mitchell realised that he had the benefit of German post-Masters education and work experience with the growing, technically advanced German aircraft industry. If Mitchell was going to create a world-class fighter monoplane, he needed to absorb – or at least have his team absorb – the very latest that Germany and the USA could offer in terms of experience and research. So Shenstone organised a trip to America. The Americans were already spending twice what the British aircraft industry was able to afford. This was concentrated in the National Advisory Committee for Aeronautics (NACA), which among other things was working on laminar flow wing profiles and other innovative ways of giving aeroplanes lift and reducing drag. Shenstone had experience from Junkers and the German academic scene to offer America, and had worked with designers from Heinkel.

Before travelling to America to visit the major manufacturers in 1934 – by steamship, of course – Shenstone had been in Germany with Hives. The close working relationship with the Derby-based engineers was born out of the Schneider races, and from the lessons learned from the Type 224, which was rejected by the Air Ministry around this time.

For Shenstone in 1934, the visit to America was eye-opening. He was able to bring back thoughts and experience of US wing profiles and the way in which the science of aerodynamics was mixed with the art of finishing and flush riveting. Mitchell gladly accepted Shenstone's written report* and applied the thinking to his and Faddy's ideas for a better, faster monoplane fighter that Vickers would financially support. It was more than a re-worked Type 244: the Type 300, as the first documents call it, would be better powered and have a radical new wing design.

There is a delightful story[3] in the Faddy family about one of the frequent Sunday lunches they hosted, when Mitchell and Faddy would get together and talk designs. In 1934 (the exact date is lost), after a fine roast beef lunch prepared by Mrs Faddy, and while the ladies were clearing away, the men started discussing the new fighter. Faddy took a pencil and started to sketch on the tablecloth but, realising that such actions might be seen as vandalism by Mrs Faddy, he started on the wallpaper behind his chair. After about thirty minutes, he and Mitchell were satisfied with the arrangement and sat back to admire, just as Mrs Faddy came in with a wet cloth and wiped it away. Mrs Faddy was delightful, if a little daunting, remembers her son David.† Some sources say it was the kitchen in the family home in Bitterne, but David's remembrance was the dining room.

Luckily, Faddy remembered the sweeping lines, the stream-lined fuselage, and the beginnings of the elliptical wing. Vickers-Armstrong later recorded in the company magazine that Faddy was:

---

* Sadly, extensive searches have failed to locate it.

† A graduate of the Royal Aircraft Establishment (RAE) apprenticeship scheme and a designer/engineer of detail on such aeroplanes as the ill-fated TSR 2 strike bomber.

a product of the time when aircraft engineering was largely a matter of experience and flair, he exerted considerable influence on many Supermarine designs, but it is certain that his own choice for memorial would be the Spitfire, for the detail design of that famous aeroplane was very largely the work of his hand.[4]

Back at Woolston, on the Monday morning Faddy quickly transferred the dinnertime ideas to paper, and Mitchell used his traditional rubber eraser to correct some of the lines. Mitchell was a true engineer when it came to drawings that would need to be traced for printing and distribution: he used the minimum of soft pencil and only then for the clearest of lines. As Joe Smith later recalled,

> He was an inveterate drawer on drawings, particularly general arrangements. He would modify the lines of an aircraft with the softest pencil he could find, and then remodify over the top with progressively thicker lines, until one would be faced with a new outline of lines about three sixteenths of an inch thick. But the results were always worthwhile, and the centre of the line was usually accepted when the thing was redrawn.[5]

The first rendering of the new fighter went straight to the drawing office for tracing, printing and distribution.

The elliptical wing was nothing new at Supermarine. Faddy, Mansbridge and Smith were aware that the initial thoughts for the

Type 179 flying boat had featured an elliptical wing; and they had seen the Short Crusader racing seaplane for the 1927 Schneider heat (most people referred to the Short's wing as a lobe-form). In Britain before the First World War, researchers had begun to understand that the vortex flow generated by the wing passing through the air needed to be spread across the whole wing, rather than just at the tip, to reduce drag. Shenstone had used this work on elliptical wings by the pioneering engineers Frederick Lanchester* and Max Munk† in his postgraduate work.

Both Shenstone and Mitchell had seen the clean lines of the Heinkel He 70 fast mail aeroplane, which first flew in 1932. Mitchell had apparently already discussed the use of glycol coolant instead of water in the BMW engine of the German machine with his friends at Rolls-Royce, as he was keen to reduce the size of the radiators needed, which in turn would reduce weight and drag. Rolls-Royce was aware of the He 70 and liked the engineering so much that in 1935 the company acquired one for engine trials and it remained in use until 1944. It has been suggested that the Heinkel's elliptical wing was a direct influence on the Type 300. However, Shenstone later explained:

> The Heinkel 70 did have an influence on the Spitfire, but in a rather different way. I had seen the German aircraft at the Paris Aero Show and had been greatly impressed by

---

* A British polymath engineer with a deep interest in railway locomotives and aeroplanes in the early twentieth century.

† A German-born émigré to the US who was a wing specialist at NACA. He died in 1986.

the smoothness of its skin. There was not a rivet head to be seen . . . When we got down to the detailed design of the F37/34 (which was to become the Spitfire) I referred to the Heinkel 70 quite a lot during our discussions. I used it as a criterion for aerodynamic smoothness and said that if the Germans could do it so, with a little effort, could we.[6]

Mitchell was always influenced by the latest technological developments. So much was he impressed with the He 70 that he wrote to Ernst Heinkel at Rostock, expressing his astonishment that it was faster than the contemporary fighters in Royal Air Force service. What particularly impressed him was the fact that 'we have been unable to achieve such smooth lines in the aircraft that we entered for the Schneider Trophy Races',[7] meaning the S6b. Part of Heinkel's success – which Mitchell could not yet achieve – was the use of wind tunnels to prove, for example, half-size designs before they were built as real aeroplanes. But all of this exchange of letters, and even plans at various international conferences, doesn't mean that the Spitfire was directly influenced by German designs; rather, that Mitchell took advantage of modern technology. He was not hemmed in by a need to use only his own ideas, or even those of his team; he was open to innovation.

Shenstone commented later when president of the Royal Aeronautical Society 1962–63:

The elliptical wing was decided upon quite early on. Aerodynamically it was the best for our purpose because the induced drag caused in producing lift, was lowest when this shape was used: the ellipse was . . . theoretically a perfection . . . To reduce drag we wanted the lowest possible thickness-to-chord, consistent with the necessary strength. But near the root the wing had to be thick enough to accommodate the retracted undercarriages and the guns . . . Mitchell was an intensely practical man . . . The ellipse was simply the shape that allowed us the thinnest possible wing with room inside to carry the necessary structure and the things we wanted to cram in. And it looked nice.[8]

Faddy, with his colleagues R. J. Fenner and Bill Fear – known as the Three Fs – had been working together on monoplane fighters since the Type 224 and produced the general arrangement diagrams. Faddy is credited, too, with persuading Mitchell to adopt Shenstone's elliptical wing, to give room for the ammunition for the eight machine guns, and for the undercarriage to retract sufficiently flush to reduce drag. Mitchell was skilled at bringing together the viewpoints of his team and working to find the best solution to any problem. Harry Griffiths, assistant to metallurgist Arthur Black, recalled that:

When a problem was being discussed in the drawing office he would stand by the drawing-board listening to all the arguments as to what should be done – on these occasions he had the habit of rolling a pencil back and forth on his hand (it was always a very black pencil!) – and when he had heard enough he would push everyone aside, draw a few lines on top of the existing drawing saying, 'This is what you will do,' throw the pencil down and march back to his office.[9]

On 5 December 1934, Mitchell took the team's wing design to the Air Ministry, where it was described as 'a distorted elliptical wing with the main spar at right angles to the fuselage'. This was all groundbreaking stuff, and radical for the senior officers in Whitehall.

It is at this point that Henry Cave-Browne-Cave re-enters the story. Cave-Browne-Cave had first come into contact with Supermarine as the company prepared the Southampton flying boats for the Far East Cruise. By 1934, he was director of technical development at the Air Ministry before taking command of the Royal Air Force Academy at Cranwell. His admiration for Supermarine's design, technology and build skills is underlined by his authorisation of the first payment of £10,000 to prime the pump of the Type 300 development programme, which he described as a 'most interesting development'. This farsighted move was supported later by the Chancellor of the Exchequer, Neville Chamberlain, who authorised funding for the production of the first batch of 310 fighters.

On 3 January 1935, the Air Ministry caught up with the Type 300 development and issued specification F37/34 based on a rapidly created Operational Requirement (OR17) for a high-speed monoplane single-seater fighter based on the Supermarine submission. To add to the bureaucracy, but to cross the Ts and dot the Is, the Type 300 was given its own funding stream in the procurement plan. The world has Neville Chamberlain and the various senior civil servants to thank for allowing the first payment to be made to Supermarine without the usual formality but with a great deal of lobbying from McLean and the Vickers Board. McLean at Vickers and Arthur Sidgreaves, managing director at Rolls-Royce, had won approval for an initial private venture concept which could not be tinkered with by the Air Ministry, which is why the Type 300 had the specification written around it, and not vice versa.

Specification F37/34, received by Supermarine on 5 January 1935, was based on a rapidly created Operational Requirement (OR17) for a high-speed monoplane single-seater fighter. The key performance requirements, later specified in the first Vickers Supermarine contract, were:

- a horizontal speed of not less than 195 mph at 15,000 ft
- landing speed not to exceed 60 mph
- service ceiling not less than 28,000 ft
- provision for four machine guns

The specification was for a four-gun fighter; but it was immediately clear that four rifle-calibre machine guns would not be capable of substantially damaging or destroying the new German bomber designs with their all-metal construction. The head of the Operational Requirements Section in the Air Ministry, Squadron Leader Ralph Sorley, initially pressed the Air Staff for the Vickers or Lewis gun weapons from the First World War to be changed for American Browning, a Belgian design for which the British had now bought a licence. The Browning was a generation better mechanically, fired more rounds per minute and needed less maintenance, but still lacked the hitting power of a heavier calibre. Even so, the Browning stood a better chance of hitting and severely damaging a bomber in a two-second burst – the only opportunity the fighter pilot might have in a single pass.

One of the fascinating 'rabbit holes of history' occurred at this time when a thirteen-year-old girl confirmed the lethality requirements of the future British fighter aeroplane. She was the daughter of Captain F. W. Hill, whose successes in designing armament systems to counter Zeppelins in the First World War meant that everyone in Whitehall knew him simply as 'Gunner'. Hill played an important part in the Spitfire story with the armament fit and with the development of gunsights as well. In July 1934, before the specification F37/34 had been issued, a meeting chaired by Air Commodore Arthur Tedder,* then director of training in the Air Ministry, confirmed the need for eight guns. Hill's initial work, checked by his daughter, Hazel, showed that a modern fighter would need eight rifle-calibre machine guns firing 1,000 rounds per minute to have any chance of damaging the new German bombers from Dornier, Heinkel or Junkers. Air Intelligence had established that the Luftwaffe had 'armoured' the crew compartment around the pilot and the engine cowlings.

---

* Tedder was one of the great characters of the Royal Air Force in its first fifty years. He became Eisenhower's deputy for the Liberation of Europe in 1943.

In his memoirs, Claude Hilton Keith, the assistant director of Armament Research & Development at the Air Ministry, wrote: 'The battle was brisk and was carried into very high quarters before the implementing authority was given. My Branch had made out a sound case for 8-gun fighters and if this recommendation had not been accepted and we had been content with half-measures, it might indeed have gone ill for us during the late summer of 1940'.[10]

Ralph Sorley is, to many, an unsung hero of the development of the leading fighter designs which would emanate from Hawker and Supermarine. He helped draft a specification, F5/34, which called for an eight-gun fighter in November 1934. Sorley had been a fighter pilot with the Royal Naval Air Service, winning a gallantry medal for day and night bombing operations, so he spoke from a position of knowledge. Sorley served in the Mediterranean aboard the seaplane carrier *Ark Royal*. He showed himself to have a courageous spirit on 20 January 1918 when he took part in the successful attack by Short seaplanes of No. 2 Wing on the imperial German warships *Breslau* and *Göben*, winning both the Distinguished Service Cross and a share of the prize money for the destruction of the former warship. With the formation of the Royal Air Force, Sorley undertook staff duties in Palestine and Iraq, returning to flying with the MAEE at Felixstowe in 1924; he later commanded the establishment in 1940 after a tour of duty in the Air Ministry from 1933. His relatively low rank in 1934 belied his influence in the corridors of power, and he never formed an opinion without having the facts at his fingertips. This 'speaking from a position of knowledge' impressed Mitchell, who recognised a like-minded thinker. Sorley already had a good understanding of seaplanes and flying boats, and would have been an entertaining guest at the Mitchells' table, even though there are no formal records that he dined at the Chandler's Ford house. Contemporaries called him thoughtful and innovative, which might account for his excellent relationship with Mitchell. Sadly, no copies of their correspondence seem to exist.

Sorley had absorbed the technical expertise of the knowledgeable Captain F. W. Hill, and, armed with data from Orford Ness firing trials, he visited Mitchell and the team at Woolston on 26 April 1935 to assess progress on the new Supermarine fighter. Sorley wanted to know if Mitchell could up-gun his new design to eight wing-mounted guns. He was keen that Spitfire (and Hawker Hurricane) production was entered into immediately, even if that meant the Gladiator production run would be cut. Sorley also wanted a provision for eight 20 lb bombs to be removed from the specification, as there would be very little use of such a small bomb and that was not the purpose of the new monoplane bomber-destroyer.

Again, Shenstone and Faddy came to the fore with expertise in creating the wing shape. But Mitchell's team were struggling with provision of wing-mounted weapons, and he gave the task of finding space for weapons and 300 rounds of ammunition – that two-second burst – to Jack Davis, a technical draughtsman at Woolston. It was not only space but weight that had to be considered, as well as how to stop the guns from freezing. It was Faddy who came up with the simple solution of ducting hot air from the Merlin powerplant along the inside of the wings to raise the temperature in the gun compartments. At least the provision of bombs could now be jettisoned, saving weight and space.

As Alfred Faddy's son David told the Royal Aeronautical Society in a speech in the 1990s, 'Aircraft of the Spitfire generation could not be designed by a single individual; many different skills were required. I certainly believe that the design of the Spitfire was the work of a team,' adding that 'aircraft engineering was largely a matter of experience and flair' in the early days. When it later entered service, the Spitfire 'provided full-scale practical evidence of flexible airframes and transient aerodynamics in combat manoeuvres,' said David Faddy in the lecture. He might have added that Mitchell allowed the team to progress these structural ideas independent of the theoretical work at RAE.

Back in Whitehall, things were moving unusually fast. Air Marshal Hugh Dowding, then in charge of research and development, had read Sorley's report and the recommendations passed by his boss, Air Commodore R. H. Verney, director of technical development, for a policy decision on production. Dowding thought it needed the Chief of the Air Staff's approval and consequently Air Chief Marshal Sir Edward Ellington was asked to rule, which he did, confirming the changes and the need to progress to test flights as soon as possible.

Mitchell immediately set to work on modifying the Supermarine Fighter to take eight guns rather than his planned four, but it took time. By 1935, there were about 150 key people working on the revisions. The immediate modification was not possible and a re-issued specification F10/35 was issued around a new design. By July 1935, the specification had been finalised for an eight-gun fighter. It was going to be a cracker.

High above the Hampshire countryside on 11 May 1936, the Type 300 on a test flight, flown by Mutt Summers. The picture was taken from the company's Miles 'chase plane', flown by Jeffrey Quill with Mitchell aboard.

14

A Legend Is Born

The first flight was a special occasion. Mitchell drove to Eastleigh and parked on the edge of a grass airfield to watch the new fighter take to the air. A photograph taken after the flight shows Mitchell surrounded by his colleagues: Mutt Summers, works manager Harold 'Agony' Payn, Stuart Scott-Hall, the Air Ministry resident technical officer, Jeffrey Quill, who had just joined Vickers, and, in the centre, Mitchell himself.

London's Royal Air Force Club has one of the best aviation art collections in the world, including almost every type of aircraft flown by the service and nearly every great leader. It also recognises the engineering genius of the great figures of the early days of fixed-wing designs from the great houses of Avro, Hawker and, of course, Supermarine.

Among the displays is one paying due homage to Mitchell, including facsimile copies of the report of the Type 300's first test flight on 5 March 1936. The document is marked for 'Messrs Mitchell, Smith, Pickering', and handwritten is the notation

'Mr Faddy's copy'. It is headed Flight Record No. R/300/1, indicating that it is the first report for the Type 300, which is also identified by its then nomenclature: F37/34 (the Air Ministry specification), Fighter and its serial K5054. Nothing about being the Spitfire!

It records the first four flights by Mutt Summers with an indication of the test regime, by date, the flight times and duration. The data shows how the flight-test programme was progressed as Summers developed his understanding of the Type 300's performance.*

First Flight	Second Flight	Third Flight	Fourth Flight
5.3.36	6.3.36	10.3.36	14.3.36
1635	1525	1725	1700
8 min	23 min	31 min	50 min

After the first flight, on landing Summers said, 'Don't touch anything' – this reflected the need for some engineering discussions prior to the next day's flight, rather than in some way indicating that the design was perfect.

Having said that, it is clear from the first report, written on 13 or 14 March, that there were some immediate conclusions that this was a winner, including Summers' note that 'the handling qualities of this machine are remarkably good', but also noting something that would catch many a novice pilot out: 'there is a

---

* As typed on the data sheet.

slight tendency when across the wind for the machine to roll'. Other interesting titbits are that the air reservoir was insufficient for undercarriage and flap operations, and that the cockpit canopy was difficult to open or 'nigh impossible' at speed.

Summers records that the Type 300 achieved 270 mph at 3,000 feet, with the Merlin producing 2,700 rpm at 6 lb of boost. However, the report also says that there were technical issues with the speed recording, and a subsequent flight showed that at 17,000 feet, the Type 300 achieved 255 mph indicated in air that was −15°C with the engine producing 2,100 rpm with 6.5 lb boost set.

There is also a rather alarming but heartening note at the end of this report: 'As part of the engine cowling had torn away and turned backwards, most likely the indicated speed given here is low owing to the extra drag of the cowling.' The cowling had started to show signs of cracking in the early flights, possibly due to the complex curve of its metalworking, which required the use of the English Wheel method of bending the sheet metal. This was a skill that wooden flying boats and even racing seaplanes did not require.

The great results of the first few flying tests before George Pickering and Jeffrey Quill took over vindicated the role that Mutt Summers played in the early development (even though many wondered why the chief test pilot of Vickers, Supermarine's parent company, had been given the job). It was all to do with experience.

There were, however, initial concerns about its speed, which fell short of Mitchell's expectations. Quill reports that 'it was something of a crisis and R. J. was a very worried man',[1] fearing that the Hawker Hurricane would be the ministry's preferred model. But the aeroplane was modified with a new propellor and in May achieved a speed of 349 mph – a far better outcome.

Incidentally, Mitchell wanted to call it the Shrew, the Air Ministry wanted to call it the Scarab or Shrike, and Vickers' chairman, Sir Robert McLean, said he held the casting vote and it would be the Spitfire.

Ernest Mansbridge was Mitchell's trusted representative at the A&AEE at RAF Martlesham Heath in 1936 when the Type 300 was ready for service trials. It was delivered on 26 May and was tested the same day. Flight Lieutenant Humphrey Edwardes-Jones, the first Royal Air Force pilot to fly the Type 300, recalled: 'Usually the first flight of a new aircraft did not mean a thing at Martlesham, they were happening all the time. But on this occasion the buzz got around that the Spitfire was something special and everybody turned out to watch – I can remember seeing the cooks in their white hats lining the road.'[2] Edwardes-Jones' report on the aeroplane was enough to start the Whitehall cogs moving. The young test pilot relayed on the telephone, in guarded tones, that young pilots could fly this revolutionary machine. It was a gamble by the Air Ministry to ask for the funding to order the first batch of fighters but approval by the Chancellor of the Exchequer, Neville Chamberlain, clinched it. On 3 June 1936, the first 310 Spitfires were ordered, even before the A&AEE had reported to Parliament in September.

Shortly before the Type 300 took to the air, the Secretary of State for Air, Viscount Swinton, told Parliament that the government was adding to the Royal Air Force Expansion Scheme with the aim of 123 squadrons of 1,500 front-line aeroplanes in place within five years.[3] The two single-engined fighter types – the Hurricane from Hawker and the new Supermarine fighter – would be a huge part of that expansion because the emphasis would be on air defence of the homeland, especially the metropolitan area – in other words, London.

Part of the expansion was a series of new monoplanes. The Fairey Battle and Bristol Blenheim bombers were given wide publicity, with *Flight* magazine, the aviation bible of its day, devoting whole sections to how wonderful were these new machines. It kept quiet about the fighters being developed.

In fact, details of the new fighter would be kept very secure even from *Flight*, with its reputation for promoting British aviation companies, products and government policy. It wouldn't be until 25 June 1936 that Mitchell would see the first public mention of the Spitfire in *Flight*. Even then there would only be a photo and caption of the aeroplane – the detail that it was on its fifth test flight and being flown by George Pickering would be omitted. *Flight*'s caption writer oozed praise on 'what is described as the world's fastest fighter' and he describes it as a 'very small size and with retractable undercarriage'. On 8 July, King Edward VIII met Mitchell again and inspected the Spitfire on a visit to Martlesham, climbing up to the cockpit. The Spitfire's first public appearance was on 27 June at the Hendon Air Display, where it went so fast that the audience could hardly grasp the uniqueness of this new fighter.

Later in the year, *Jane's All the World's Aircraft*, the handbook of every aeroplane in production in every country of the world, would first mention the Spitfire in its 1936 edition. Its matter-of-fact details include the manufacturer's name as Supermarine Aviation Works (Vickers) Ltd and lists three directors: Sir Robert McLean (chairman), Squadron-Commander J. Bird (the previous owner) and R. J. Mitchell (chief designer). The entry describes the Spitfire – for which it gives no technical information, unlike most other entries – as: 'flush-rivetted, stressed skin construction with exceptional cleanliness and stiffness to the wings and fuselage for a structure weight never before attained in this class of aircraft'.

Supermarine had never put an aeroplane into mass production, but Mitchell believed they were up to the task. In the event, there were many teething problems (including the pitch of the propeller, oil leaks and cockpit ergonomics) before the first deliveries in August 1938. For Supermarine, used to hand-crafting flying boats, this was a difficult job. Alf Faddy was the aeronautical engineer who really made the Spitfire what it was to become. As the Section Leader in charge of the detailed design, he would work nonstop after the first flight in March 1936 until full production in 1938 to bring the Spitfire into production.

By September 1936, shortly after the third anniversary of the surgery, Mitchell's pain returned. He learned to rely more and more on Faddy, Smith, Clifton and Westbrook – these were the doers in his organisation, and he trusted them completely. He called them his 'senior team'. But he still went to the airfield every time the Type 300 took to the air and would brook no argument. The overall performance of the Spitfire would have given Mitchell a real boost in his last months. He was gravely ill, knew there was no cure, and he must have been in considerable discomfort. Its success vindicated the creation of the fighter design team under Alf Faddy, using the expertise of Shenstone and others in a combined effort that Mitchell watched over like the conductor in an orchestra.

However, Mitchell was not yet finished.

In 1936, Mitchell was gravely ill. He persevered but the effects of his cancer can be seen in his face. He spent much of his time on new designs, including a bomber and a twin-engined Spitfire replacement.

15

Future Imperfect

Once Mitchell was satisfied that Faddy and his team were on the right track with the Spitfire, he turned his amazing brain to three other issues: a new long-range fighter, a high-speed amphibian and a bomber.

It is a sad fact that war often propels the development of high technology. For the Germans, the outbreak of the Spanish Civil War in July 1936 was a godsend for the testing and evaluation of new aircraft types and tactics; supporting the right-wing forces led by General Francisco Franco against the Republicans seemed appropriate in every way for the Third Reich. The Luftwaffe, born the year before, was founded as 'flying artillery' for ground forces. Consequently, the newly developed Messerschmitt Bf 109, the Dornier Do 17 'Flying Pencil' bomber and the Heinkel He 111 medium bomber were deployed to Spain as the Condor Legion. The Legion was tactically commanded by a succession of airmen who would become household names a few years later: Adolf Galland and Werner Mölders, for example. The destruction of undefended civilian 'targets' such as the Basque market town of Guernica, a road junction that Franco needed to capture the port of Bilbao just a few miles to the west, on 26 April 1937 has become symbolic of the Civil War and indiscriminate use of air power. It wasn't the only civilian target, but Pablo Picasso's painting has made it internationally infamous. The bombing by the Condor Legion was judged a great success in Berlin and led to the so-called terror campaigns against Warsaw, Rotterdam and London in the Second World War. German fighter aircraft had proved themselves against the Soviet-supplied Spanish Republican Air Force, which was badly led and under provisioned. Most importantly, the 'finger four' tactical fighter formation developed in Spain led to significant advantage to the Luftwaffe in air battles over France and England in 1940.

In Whitehall, the chief of the Secret Intelligence Service, Sir Hugh Sinclair, had created an air department within his service based in Broadway House; the Air Ministry had been seconded to work in collecting technical intelligence from Germany and Spain, and the so-called Passport Control officers at embassies in Berlin and Madrid, and consulates in Germany, were using their networks. At least one pair of enterprising Royal Air Force officers cycled around Germany and mapped aircraft factories. This later led to the commissioning of the photographer and aviator Sidney Cotton to outfit a Lockheed 12A with the latest cameras and set up a charter business where his aeroplanes 'accidentally' flew over the Reich's factories.

All this was, of course, secret, but the Air Ministry would verbally brief people who needed to know, like Mitchell at

Supermarine and his colleagues at Vickers. The information was also leaked to Winston Churchill, then a back-bench Member of Parliament, who used the information on the growth in numbers and capability of the Luftwaffe to embarrass the government of the day into increasing defence spending. Reports about the inefficiencies of the Italian and Soviet machines were often ignored because it did not strengthen the case for an uplift in money, especially for the building of new airfields and the formation of new squadrons, which in turn meant more training aeroplanes.

In 1937, as the Spitfire was being developed at Eastleigh and each modification flight tested at the Royal Air Force's Martlesham Heath establishment, Mitchell found solace in thinking about the fighter's successor. Mitchell knew that the Air Ministry would be looking for a longer-range fighter to escort bombers to Germany and which could pack a bigger punch than the eight machine guns of the Spitfire or Hurricane.

Initially, Supermarine allocated the designation Type 324 to the project for a conventional tractor-engine layout and Type 325 for a pusher version. Both would have tricycle undercarriage, which was very much a new development in the late 1930s, demonstrating yet again that Mitchell was not afraid of new aeronautical engineering developments.

From his bed in Hazeldene, Mitchell examined the engineering behind a twin-engined fighter with a central-fuselage-mounted gun pack of up to twelve machine guns. Later – perhaps because he was given access to the intelligence reports from the Spanish Civil War, which indicated that the German bombers supporting Franco were better armoured than had been first thought – Mitchell then considered a gun pack of six 20 mm Hispano-Suiza cannon,* and the Air Ministry agreed, as the Westland Whirlwind twin-engined fighter was fraught with delays. Supermarine designated it the Type 327.

Supermarine wasn't alone in its quest to fulfil the Operational Requirement and specification F18/37, which called for a 400-mph long-range fighter. The divergence of design opinion among Britain's aircraft manufacturers immediately showed: Hawker favoured a single-seat conventional fighter; Gloster looked at a twin-boom fighter with a pusher propeller; Bristol's design team offered three engine options and a conventional layout.

Right up until his death, Mitchell persevered with the Type 327, considering an Alclad aluminium alloy structure, new innovated Fowler landing flaps and two Merlin engines that would be geared to cancel out torque by having propellers that rotated in opposite directions, thus cancelling the swing of the aeroplane on take-off; this would bedevil the later de Havilland Mosquito. However, illness prevented any real progress and the Supermarine team, now under Mitchell's technical assistant Payn, Smith and Faddy, was too busy getting the first Spitfires off the production line and to RAF Fighter Command to spend time on the twin-engined design. Eventually, Mitchell's great rival at Hawker, Sydney Camm, received a development contract for the airframe which would become the Typhoon in the next decade with sterling

---

* The Air Ministry had bought a licence for this weapon system before the Second World War and production had been assigned to the British Machine and Research Company (BMARC).

service at D-Day in 1944. Did the world miss an opportunity for a really innovative machine? Possibly.

During this time, Mitchell also developed a potential replacement for the Walrus, the single-engine amphibian biplane first flown in 1933, for which Supermarine was authorised to start detail design on 17 April 1936, just over a month after the Type 300's first flight. The Walrus had been a significant design for Supermarine. In fact, it would be the company's bread and butter until the Spitfire entered production and Air Ministry payments started to arrive in 1938.

Its successor was no less robust, demonstrating that Mitchell's engineering skills far outweighed any design input he may have had. The Air Ministry would name this new version the Sea Otter. It was a logical development from the Walrus, in a very similar mould. In Mitchell's mind, this upgraded biplane would have a new hull form and a redesigned top wing, but the engine would be conventionally fitted as a puller (against the Walrus' pusher configuration). It was heavier, bigger and altogether more powerful than the Walrus. In the event, there was no space in the Woolston or Itchen works for the new amphibian to be built and it was sub-contracted to Saunders-Roe on the Isle of Wight. Production continued until 1944, so successful was the design. It was robust enough to be looped on its very first flight and was vital for the Royal Navy until radar was fitted to major warships – and many Allied aircrew owed their lives to the robust amphibian landing on the sea to rescue them.

Mitchell's pencil was still not satisfied. In the last few months of his life, he gave birth to a radical new design of high-speed amphibian. This machine would replace the Walrus and Sea Otter for the Royal Navy and the Royal Air Force, which had begun to consider (but were yet to implement) the use of amphibians for search and rescue. It wasn't until 1940 that the Air Ministry would issue its specification S12/40 for a new observation flying boat; yet Mitchell had been considering a Sea Otter replacement long before.

The groundwork for the hull shape, the use of materials and the engineering concepts were put in place by him in the mid-1930s. Mitchell wanted to move on from biplane amphibians by using the Supermarine variable-incident, cantilever wing, and utilise new powerplants that were planned but yet to be built. This developmental thinking would result in the Seagull ASR 1 Amphibian, but not for another decade after Mitchell's death. Initially, Mitchell's successors were not able to spend much time on his original concepts due to the difficulties with launching the Spitfire. But he would have been proud of the creation by Joe Smith's team when they responded to the Air Ministry engineering conference in April 1941, which took his thoughts and created the winner.

One final production consumed Mitchell's thoughts in his last year. He might have been suffering pain from terminal cancer but his mind, it appears, was clear as a bell. It seems extraordinary now, but there could have been a Supermarine bomber leading the offensive against Germany at the same time as the Spitfire was defending Britain's skies. Had Mitchell lived, and had the proto-type bomber's fuselages and ancillaries survived the disastrous German raids that destroyed much of the Supermarine factory in September 1940, that might have happened.

The B12/36 design – it was never given an official name and was just known as the Bomber in the same way that, in its early days, the Spitfire was simply termed the Fighter – was Mitchell's very special project into which he poured his engineering genius. He envisaged a four-engined, high-flying, high-speed machine with that great innovation, a pressurised cabin for the crew. No longer would aircrew have to breathe oxygen through face masks above 10,000 feet – and they would be able to move about and fly the bomber almost in short sleeves. The notion of a pressurised cockpit was being developed by Junkers in Germany but it was not adopted for Allied bombers until the Boeing B-29 Superfortress came into service in the US Army Air Force in the Pacific in 1944. The Mitchell B12/36 could have been operating over Germany and the occupied nations four years earlier.

The Bomber very much encapsulates Mitchell's philosophy: creating the best possible design by pushing the boundaries of technology and engineering. It was also something into which Mitchell could pour his heart and soul, as he knew he was dying, yet still wanted to do his utmost to prepare the Royal Air Force for the forthcoming war. He believed that a superior bomber would give Britain the strategic edge in a future conflict.

The Air Ministry specification stemmed from Air Staff Operational Requirement 40, which called for a bomber of sufficient reach and endurance to attack the German industrial Ruhr and even the major cities of Augsburg and Nuremberg. Berlin too would have been in range. That meant a range of 1,500 nautical miles carrying a 4,000 lb bombload. To put that into perspective, the American B-17G Flying Fortress, which carried out daylight raids over two years, habitually flew to Berlin with just 2,000 lb of ordnance.

Other key user requirements included limiting the main wingspan to 100 feet, and design for production so that the main components were not only road transportable, but could also be carried in the British rolling stock of the time and fit under bridges and in tunnels.

Four top aviation companies were sent the secret document in 1936. The Air Ministry initially thought that Vickers, Boulton Paul and Armstrong Whitworth would come up with winning designs, and had relegated Supermarine to fourth place. The officials had not reckoned with the tenacity of Mitchell, who needed something to get his teeth into – he didn't solely want to work on the Spitfire after the debacle of the Type 224 (which perhaps explains a private utterance Mitchell made to Alf Faddy, saying he did not want to get so deeply involved in a fighter again).[1] A four-engined bomber intrigued Mitchell and he thought his design, designated Type 316, would beat the competition.

He responded to the Air Ministry within weeks. Mitchell's outline was radical: a swept-wing mainplane with a straight trailing edge and bombs carried in the massive wing that would generate lift, as well as in the lower fuselage. The wing would use the single-spar technique of the Spitfire design and allow for fuel to be carried in the leading edge of the wing. Perhaps there would be room for 2,500 gallons of fuel. Mitchell called in the expertise of his aerodynamicist and wing expert Beverley Shenstone to finesse the design and capacity. Although Shenstone was now working on refining the Spitfire wing, this was his other project of priority.

Mitchell also startled the boffins in Whitehall with the asser-
tion that the upper fuselage, cockpit and defending gun turrets
could be within a pressurised hull. Because the Type 316 would
fly higher than the operational norm, Mitchell drew a ventral gun
turret in a dustbin into the design and this, he argued, would
be lowered below the fuselage to provide defence against enemy
fighters attacking from below. There would be a nose and a tail
gun turret with Browning 0.303-inch rifle-calibre machines guns
set below the gunner's direct eye line, with shielding to allow for
a clear view of potential fighters. The aeroplane would be stabil-
ised with a very large single fin and rudder. The whole machine
would have four 1,000-hp Rolls-Royce Merlin engines when available but could have the Bristol Hercules or the Napier Dagger
powerplants as an interim. Using his close personal relationship
with Rolls-Royce at Derby, Mitchell calculated that the Merlin
would deliver a maximum combat speed of 360 mph (rather than
the 250 mph specified) and that the wing, with Shenstone's help,
would be so efficient as to double the range to 3,000 nautical
miles. A large wing and pressurised (sealed) fuselage would also
allow for several hours of flotation if the bomber was forced down
into the sea. Mitchell embraced the challenges with relish. It was
exactly what his mind liked – the attention to detail and yet the
scope of vision that allowed new developments.

Mitchell believed that the Type 316 needed to go into production as soon as possible – both as a deterrent to Hitler's ambitions,
and because he knew that he himself was dying. Whitehall turned
around the Type 316 submission very quickly and by Christmas
1936 Mitchell was back with a revised approach, the Type 317,

with a twin tail for better handling in the air and access to hangars on the ground, and he had managed to increase the wing* area and therefore the bomb load. The twin tail would also allow the bomber to fit the railway criteria in the specification.

Operating from short fields was also a consideration. Despite its size and weight, the Air Ministry expected the new bomber to have a maximum take-off distance of just 500 feet, clearing trees of 50 feet at the end of the runway. Although all air stations were grass in 1936, there were plans to build concrete runways on bomber bases to allow a greater payload to be carried. There was even a discussion about whether to have catapult fixings on the bomber's fuselage to allow for some form of assisted launch, rather like aboard an aircraft carrier. The Royal Aircraft Establishment at Farnborough was already working on such systems in 1936.

Always ones to double their chances, the Air Ministry also wanted the B12/36 design to be built as a troop carrier as well as a bomber as specified in the design, which said that the winning contender should be configured to carry twenty-four fully armed fighting men with their basic equipment, food and water. In the 1930s, many of the so-called bombers, such as the Bristol Bombay or the Handley Page Harrow, were better suited to support roles than actually taking bombs to the enemy. Ironically, at the end of the Second World War, bombers such as the Lancaster and its smaller brother-in-arms the Halifax were employed as troop transports, bringing home prisoners of war.

---

* Through Shenstone's expertise, the world's first delta-winged bomber.

The Air Ministry liked what it saw. Supermarine was given a development contract to build two Type 317 prototypes, powered by Hercules engines (the Merlin was not available as it was reserved for fighters). The actual order document came to Southampton on 22 March 1937 and a similar document went to Short Brothers at Rochester and resulted in the Stirling heavy bomber. Boulton Paul decided to focus on the Defiant turret fighter and Armstrong Whitworth abandoned the AW 42 design to work on transport aircraft. Vickers, still manufacturing the Wellington bomber from the team that included Mitchell's nemesis Barnes Wallis, also pulled out directly and added its weight to Supermarine's design. It was clear that Mitchell's vision had won over the Air Staff and the ministry officials. The Type 317 was the preferred design and it had a Shenstone-influenced wing just like the Spitfire. It was quite an achievement to come from fourth place to first.

With the support of Vickers, the now seriously ill Mitchell went ahead with the detailed design for the Type 317 (its now twin-tail design would also be used for the Handley Page Halifax and the Avro Lancaster). His drawings showed a bomber with a 93-foot wingspan, an overall length of 71 feet 6 inches and accommodation for six crew members – two pilots, navigator, radio operator, bomb aimer/front gunner and tail gunner. It was presumed that the radio operator would man the ventral gun as required – which was likely to be constant when over enemy territory.

The main bomb carriage was in the wings: Mitchell's calculations showed that the Type 317 would eventually be able to carry individual bombs of 2,000 lb and a full load of as much as 20,000 lb,* using a technique developed by Poland's PZL company, then one of Britain's closest allies. This again shows Mitchell's openness to work with other design teams and use modern techniques, especially from Europe. Mitchell had allowed an elliptical wing with German origins on the Type 300 and had examined the Italian winning seaplanes at Schneider events, noting down the best design features for future exploitation. Aeronautics in the 1920s and 1930s had been a fruitful arena of cooperation between design teams in France, Italy, Poland and Great Britain.

On 26 February 1937, Mitchell knew that the Air Ministry had down-selected the Type 317, but he also knew that unless he had urgent treatment for his cancer, he had only a few months to live.

---

* Although they were yet to become available as the Royal Air Force inventory consisted of 250 lb and 500 lb high-explosive bombs.

Mitchell at home in Hazeldene, the house he designed in Portswood. Always a dog lover, he is seen here with Bondy in the garden.

16

Last Days

Every 15 August from 1933 until 1936, Mitchell made a note in his diary to remind himself of the anniversary of his first cancer operation. The surgeon, Mr Gabriel, had said that if the cancer had not returned within four or five years, Mitchell would be in the clear.

Mitchell must have known that the cancer had not been eradicated or had returned even as he sat watching the Type 300 take to the air for the first time on 5 March 1936. But he wanted to build the very best fighter that he could. He had a great team of engineers and designers around him and he was not going to be stopped by mere cancer. It appears that he even cut short his convalescence because he wanted his ideas – and, importantly, those of Faddy, Shenstone and the team – to take to the air before he succumbed to the disease that was eating away at him. He recorded in his diary:

Now I think I have a winner. I have laboured over her for months, probably years, and all the stages of her life have been put into you, my diary. My death is drawing nearer and my cancer is spreading but the doctors say there is nothing they can do. Every day until the end I will stand over my drawings and diagrams making them better.[1]

In a newspaper interview, Mitchell's son Gordon said he knew his father's prognosis was bleak, though he remained positive. Gordon, then at school in Bristol, remembered his father's letters were still upbeat – Mitchell was constantly offering Gordon advice.

He continued flying until just six months before he passed; his logbook records 28 November 1936 as his last flight. As Mitchell grew weaker, the cold and blustery Moth was too much for him. Supermarine acquired a Miles Falcon 6, one of the finest private cabin monoplanes available. In fact, the Falcon 6 had flown for the first time as recently as 12 October 1934, so the four-seater was new and exciting. Pickering took Mitchell flying in the company aeroplane on 10 March 1936, just after the first flight of the Type 300. As late as September that year, Pickering and his boss were flying to Vickers at Brooklands, probably the last time that Mitchell went to head office. They chose the Moth again because the weather was so good. 'There is no doubt,' says Jennie Pickering Sherborne, 'that my father and R. J. discussed the Type 300 which was being thoroughly tested.'[2] One of Mitchell's last flights was on 2 November 1936 when he accompanied Pickering on a production test flight of a Walrus and they went over the Solent for handling, which Mitchell is most likely to have taken control of for part of the time. It would have ended, Jennie thinks, with her father's party piece, a loop over the Itchen before the amphibian touched down on the water near the floating bridge.

By February 1937, doctors had determined that, at best, Mitchell had four or five months to live. On 15 March Flo wrote in a letter to R. J.'s brothers Eric and Billy, 'Sometimes I feel that I shall be unable to carry on – you can imagine how distressing it all is – then I have a great urge to know all that he would like, for I have never known anyone with such wonderful judgement and clear sightedness. I keep a little book when I am in the bedroom & I write down all his ideas which will to me be a sacred guidance.'[3]

The burden of pain was very great and yet everyone who met with him remarked on his stoic attitude and good humour. Visitors included the local parson and, of course, Faddy and his team to discuss points of production design. Among the frequent visitors were George and Gladys Pickering. George was one of the two test pilots – the other was, of course, Jeffrey Quill – who would fly every mark of Spitfire and its naval variant, the Seafire. Mitchell had no shortage of friends despite his work ethic, and those he treasured, including the Pickering family, remember him as warm and caring.

Jennie Pickering Sherborne treasures and keeps safe her father's deep affection for Mitchell. She recalls, 'R. J. certainly played a large part in both my parents' lives at that time and I know shared the same doctor – Dr Picken. He actually brought me into the world in August 1936.' Dr Christopher Picken was a general practitioner in Southampton and in his twenties when he joined a general practice in 1930. He later joined the Royal Army Medical

Corps and served with distinction in North Africa, Italy, Belgium and Germany.* Mitchell was in good hands.

When he could, perhaps after test flying, Pickering would join his wife, Gladys, at Hazeldene to talk to Mitchell, who was always keen to know about the works, output and progress with fulfilling the Walrus order. According to the recollections of his private secretary Vera Cross, Pickering and Mitchell would chat for hours and often be joined by Faddy and Smith so Mitchell could be briefed on the Type 300's progress.

Gladys would wheel Jennie to Hazeldene in a perambulator along with her older sister Ann. Jennie remembers her mother talking about Mitchell's love of the garden and the flowers, bees, butterflies and birds. It seems strange but there are very few photographs of Mitchell, his family and the home at Hazeldene. 'I have always found it interesting that R. J., a national hero in the mid-1930s, was not photographed more. I know from my mother that his wife Flo was timid and disliked pictures, but R. J. never struck her as shy,' remembers Jennie. Mitchell had a soft spot for the Pickering girls. When Ann wanted to paddle in the garden pond, he would boil water to warm it up. Gordon records that Mitchell offered his sun lamp, designed to give heat when he was in pain, to Ann Pickering when she had whooping cough. When Gladys protested that Mitchell might need it, he apparently answered that what he had, no sun lamp could cure. Mitchell also found solace in

---

* *British Medical Journal* obituary 1973: 'He was a man of great integrity, professional excellence and quiet modesty who rarely had a bad word to say about anyone and his friendship was valued highly by his colleagues. His sense of humour and unfailing courtesy were a constant delight.'

his three black Labrador puppies which all helped to deaden the blow of not getting his beloved Bomber into the air.

Mitchell was leaving behind a world approaching chaos. In Europe, Germany was eyeing the occupation of the Sudetenland in Czechoslovakia (it happened in 1938) and talking about expanding its living space or *Lebensraum*. There was the threat of conflict spreading from Asia, where Japan had invaded the Korean peninsula and China. In Britain, Edward VIII, a great supporter of Supermarine flying boats, had abdicated, and Neville Chamberlain succeeded Stanley Baldwin as prime minister in May 1937. Against this backdrop, Mitchell did not think that he had done enough to provide Britain with the means to defend itself, but there was universal support for him, channelled through the stalwart Miss Cross in his final days.

On 16 March, Air Chief Marshal Sir Edward Ellington wrote to Mitchell from his headquarters in Adastral House on London's Kingsway to express his sympathy and admiration:

This is to say how extremely sorry I am to hear of your serious illness. I think I have never told you before how much your great service to the Royal Air Force and aviation as a whole are valued. I am fully aware, as are all the other members of the Air Council, of the unsparing manner in which you have devoted your great abilities to the task of design, and I wish you to realise that however incomplete you may feel your work to be at the present time we know that you have always given us of your best. More especially I should like to recall how your success with the

Schneider machines placed British aeroplane design at the top of the world.[4]

Mitchell replied four days later saying that the chief's letter had made him feel very happy. Among Mitchell's other correspondents was the highly influential Air Marshal Sir Wilfrid Freeman, the Air Member for Research & Development, who praised the B12/36 bomber in particular, hoping it would be 'a great success'. In Mitchell's reply on 20 March, he confessed to Freeman that he might well not be able to finish the design work but reckoned that his staff were up to the job should the Air Ministry place an order.

The Mitchell family decided on, and Vickers-Armstrong's chairman Sir Charles Craven decided to fund, the hiring of a private aeroplane to take Reg, Flo and a nurse, just identified as Miss Jones, from Southampton via Paris to Vienna. The destination was the American Clinic, a pioneering cancer hospital run by a Frederic Pearson and where a certain Professor Freund was viewed as Europe's most capable cancer specialist. In all, the Mitchells spent five weeks in Vienna where R. J. was subjected to tests but sadly to no avail. Mitchell returned to Southampton on 25 May 1937 and knew it was just a matter of time. All that the medical profession could do now was prescribe pain killers and hope that they would be sufficient without dulling the great man's brain.

In the last months, Gladys Pickering was a frequent visitor, as Jennie explains: 'I know that when his health was failing fast my mother visited and sat with him regularly to support and help his wife. I have absolutely no idea whether she was the last person to be with him before he died, but certainly one of the last.'

Reginald Mitchell died at home at noon on 11 June 1937. He was just forty-two years old. The world had lost one of its greatest engineers and Gordon had lost a devoted father. He had been able to rest in the early summer sun during June, being too weak to work even in his study at home. In the garden, which he had crafted with Flo and Gordon over the last five or six years, he loved the roses and the blue tits, his favourite garden bird according to correspondence with Gordon. It was so like the man to have been impressed by the skill of this very small bird to build a nest and raise over half a dozen chicks. He did not live to see the chicks fledge, just as he did not live to see his greatest legacy, the Spitfire, enter service with the Royal Air Force.

The Spitfire will always be remembered as the legacy of Mitchell. This superb single-seat air defence fighter is probably the best-known aeroplane in the world. This is the Type 300 prototype camouflaged for war after the Munich Crisis in 1938, by which time Mitchell was dead.

17

Legacy

In a speech at the annual reception of the National Spitfire
Project, held in 2024 in the Henry VIII wine cellars at the UK
Ministry of Defence, Sir Rich Knighton, the then Chief of the Air
Staff, spoke of his enduring admiration for Supermarine's 'Team
Spitfire' and the wonderful technology it embraced. He is an aero-
nautical engineer who grew up in Derby so understands the engine
development as well as the airframe. He said:

> In the late 1930s, the Spitfire Mark I was a huge leap
> forward in Royal Air Force fighter capability. British engin-
> eering excellence delivered just in time as war beckoned
> once again in Europe. The Spitfire was the right capability
> at the right time, but those early Spitfires were not with-
> out their challenges. The Spitfire needed to be constantly
> adapted and modified throughout the war as its roles,
> operating locations, and threats changed – from the early

introduction of Miss Shilling's orifice* to enhance engine performance, to the added firepower of Hispano cannons, and the sheer brute force of the later Griffon-engined Spitfires. The Spitfire was always there – a loyal servant to Britain and twenty-nine others.

Bringing the Spitfire into production was fraught with difficulties. It even triggered a ministerial inquiry into its lateness. In late 1940, the enemy made its presence felt, causing further delays in Spitfire production, when the Supermarine factory was bombed. The *Luftwaffe* was well aware of the location of Woolston Works and the additional Itchen Works which opened in 1938, as one of the bomber aircrew admitted after he was shot down that he had flown Dornier flying boats to Southampton before the war. The raid destroyed the fabric of the factories but not the jigs and precision equipment, which was moved in short order to sites around Southampton, including a steam laundry and a motor garage. The opening of a 'shadow factory' for a second production line out of range of most German bombers at Castle Bromwich got the first Spitfires to RAF Fighter Command in time for the Battle of Britain. The intervention of Lord Beaverbrook, the minister for aircraft production, pushed production on; Beaverbrook had a knack for cutting through red tape and ignoring middle-ranking bureaucrats with their devotion to process. Plans and contingencies had been in place since the late 1930s, so Supermarine's war

---

* A small washer to regulate the fuel flow in the carburettors of the Merlin engine which was leaking in the original design.

effort continued at pace. Mitchell was always remembered, but he had trained a team to take the fighter through more than seventy variations before production stopped in 1948. This was part of his legacy.

With the death of Mitchell, Vickers took the opportunity to restructure Supermarine in 1938 and absorb it and Vickers (Aviation) Ltd into Vickers-Armstrong Limited and so register the company with the Society of British Aeroplane Constructors (SBAC). McLean resigned from the SBAC but ensured there would be Vickers and Supermarine representation to protect the reputation of the company and the legacy of Mitchell. Even today, that reputation is still guarded, not just in Britain but in thirty nations which flew the iconic machine and a few more besides.

Our understanding of Mitchell's role from 1933 onwards is clouded with myth, conjecture and a certain amount of innuendo, caused mainly by the appallingly inaccurate Hollywood propaganda film *The First of the Few*. Authors and film makers continue to insinuate that Mitchell designed the Spitfire all by himself and have concocted stories that belie the skills of his team at Supermarine. When, in 1955, Alfred Faddy died of the same cancer as Mitchell, *The Aeroplane* magazine wrote 'some of the [Supermarine Spitfire] documents are marked "Mr Faddy's copy" and yet, sadly, no-one has been able to trace who he was.' This is remarkable and sad. Faddy's son, David, said in a speech in the 1990s that '[Mitchell's] achievements were undoubtedly remarkable but it is also true that the emphasis on him has been rather at the expense of other people in the design team'.[1] As Jeff Quill wrote in his autobiography, 'the amount of adulation and notoriety which has very properly been accorded to Mitchell has to a large extent swamped the notice and credit which is due to so many of his design staff'.[2] David adds Joe Smith, Beverley Shenstone, Eric Lovell-Cooper, Ernie Mansbridge, Alan Clifton and Arthur Black to the list of the design team. These were the boys who toiled night and day for the Father of the Spitfire.

One can't help but think that Mitchell would not have been pleased to receive all the credit.

But these are not the only myths that abound. Even documentary makers have, in recent years, included the erroneous myth that Mitchell met with German *Luftwaffe* pilots and immediately saw the evil in them, wanting to build a fighter to combat the menace. The real story is that Mitchell was dissatisfied with the Type 224 design and knew he could do better. Faddy deserves to be recognised for his constant support and innovative thinking, which led Vickers, the parent company, to fund development of a new design. Through its connections with Whitehall, the senior Royal Air Force officers took note. The Air Ministry issued the specification for which the Type 300 was designed at least a year before the Luftwaffe became public knowledge. In fact, there is no evidence that Mitchell travelled to Germany – although he did go to Austria for medical treatment where, again, he met no Luftwaffe pilots.

The German connections to the Supermarine Type 300 and hence the Spitfire have often perplexed historians and enthusiasts. Speak in public to a certain demographic about the German influence on the Shenstone elliptical wing – often called 'Mitchell's Wing' in error – and the audience starts to bristle. Too many have seen *The First of the Few* and believe it to be a documentary. Just imagine, if Germany had been allowed to develop racing seaplanes in the 1920s, where the Schneider Trophy might reside today. Not the Science Museum in London, but Berlin?

However, Mitchell's legacy is more than just the greatest fighter aeroplane flown by thirty nations; it is his ability to develop and galvanise a whole generation of engineers to create one of the most innovative aviation companies in the world.

He was not so much a designer, more a gifted engineer who brought together a team that not only designed some of the greatest flying boats during the golden age of such machines, but also developed world-beating racing seaplanes. Mitchell's medical condition was one of the great tragedies of British aeronautical engineering history. It is impossible to know where Mitchell's brain would have taken Supermarine in the war years: had he lived, the greatest British bomber might have been designed at Southampton – although it would have been built at Castle Bromwich because there simply wasn't the space – or there might have been a twin-engined, long-range fighter to replace the Spitfire, which would have taken the air war to the enemy. Mitchell, the great engineer, was also an innovator of structures and ergonomics: for example, the hull form of the Southampton and its development into the Scapa, or the S5/S6 racers which proved ideas for the Type 300.

Mitchell trained his people well. He and Smith were described in the Putnam book *Supermarine Aircraft since 1914* as 'design engineers of distinction' and that is right – engineers first, innovators second, and as a result they produced amazing designs. There is no doubt that Mitchell was visionary right down to allowing his team to take the lead in various aspects of the major designs, from the Southampton flying boat to the Spitfire. John Shelton, a Staffordshire historian and prolific Mitchell author, talks of him as a head trainer at a thoroughbred stable yard, an analogy that works well. I think of him as a conductor of a vast orchestra of skilled performers where the leader of the orchestra was Faddy, and the virtuoso violinist was Smith. The metaphors abound. They are all correct about the Father of the Spitfire.

Like many other aeronautical engineers, Mitchell was modest and highly self-critical – the last words on his legacy are left to Denis Le Penn Webb in his autobiographical notes:

Unlike some men who achieve considerable success when young, it was quite obvious that [Mitchell's] success had not gone to his head and it never did. A man in a million.[3]

Epilogue

In 1996, Jeffrey Quill, the chief test pilot of Supermarine for twenty years, worked with Gerald Gingell, head of technical publications at Supermarine in the 1930s, to ensure that the many people involved in the Spitfire were recognised and received due credit. Quill wrote that, besides the Spitfire, the other great Mitchell legacy was the design team he had assembled at Supermarine – a team that was able to carry on after the Father of the Spitfire had passed.

Through Quill's leadership, a group of veteran Supermariners were brought together – most in their eighties – to create a book covering the period from 1932, when design work on the Type 300 started, until the end of the Second World War in Europe in 1945. It is very much part of the legacy of Mitchell as, sadly, most of the records of Supermarine were destroyed when the US computer firm IBM took over the Supermarine design and administrative centre at Hursley Park near Winchester. Quill and the Supermariners used every contact they could to compile *The Spitfire Book* and lodge copies in various learned establishments to ensure its safe keeping.

The key to Supermarine's success seems to have been a tight ship. Between 1932 and 1937, the book records that Mitchell had just five others in the chief designer's office: Frank Holroyd (assistant chief designer);* Harold 'Agony' Payn (technical assistant); G. Spencer (office administration); his secretary, Vera Cross; and Miss Wood, the typist. Miss Cross was the stalwart supporter of Mitchell in his last years, often answering correspondence on his behalf without reference to him; alas these letters and telegrams have not survived the break-up of Supermarine.

The book continues to list the various other teams including the drawing office, led by Joe Smith until 1937 and then by Eric Lovell-Cooper, and the senior designers, including Alf Faddy, in charge of the Spitfire Design Team. The draughtsmen and drawing-office staff total 151 in the period and it is a clear endorsement of Mitchell's leadership and the good terms and conditions at Supermarine that there was very little if any staff movement in the crucial period. One section, the tracing office, was totally female with twenty-nine 'ladies with pens'. There were also jig and tool design staff who made the equipment to make the Spitfire, and laboratory staff for everything from metallurgical research to photography.

In another office was Alan Clifton, the chief technician, with a dedicated team of experts. The terms and job titles seem so

---

* There is a discrepancy in the historical record here. Denis Le Penn Webb recorded that Holroyd was dismissed by Vickers in 1932 following the cancellation of the Type 179. However, *The Spitfire Book* notes that he was assistant chief designer 1932–37. See supermariners.wordpress.com, which notes that Holroyd does not appear to have been involved in the design of the Spitfire.

mundane in the modern world where everyone has to be a manager or director, but in the 1930s, in engineering, the chief technician, for example, was a key player in the design of any product. The titles in those days did not have to be glamorous; even chief designer did not mean that Mitchell was solely responsible for any design, just that he carried the weight of the decision-making, and reaped the glory, including being Father of the Spitfire.

Appendix 1

Timeline to the Spitfire

YEAR	MITCHELL'S LIFE	SIGNIFICANT EVENTS
1895	Born 20 May near Stoke-on-Trent	
1901	·	Royal Aero Club formed
1903	Starts school	December, first powered flight
1908		First British aeroplane flies
1910	Watches local flying display	First seaplane flew
1911	Begins apprenticeship	November, first British seaplane
1912		Schneider competition announced
1914		Schneider race at Monaco First World War begins
1916	Designated reserved occupation Joins Supermarine	Hubert Scott-Paine buys Supermarine
1918	Appointed assistant works manager Building Shorts under licence Marries Florence	First World War ends Royal Air Force formed Arthur Shirvall joins Supermarine

YEAR	MITCHELL'S LIFE	SIGNIFICANT EVENTS
1919	Appointed chief designer	Schneider race at Bournemouth James Bird joins the company Versailles Peace Conference Paris Air Show Regular flying-boat service
1920	Appointed chief engineer First design at Supermarine Gordon Mitchell born	
1921		Seal/Seagull first flight Joe Smith joins Supermarine
1922		Sea Lion II wins Schneider Trophy
1923	Joins Woolston Tennis Club	Supermarine acquired by James Bird Sea Eagle first flight Sea Eagle in King's Cup Air Race Alan Clifton joins Supermarine
1924	Meets HRH the Prince of Wales Receives specification for the Southampton	Spanish navy orders Scarab Swan first flight Seagull II in King's Cup Air Race Eric Lovell-Cooper and Ernest Mansbridge join Supermarine
1925		S4 sets British air-speed record Schneider race at Baltimore Southampton first flight Seagull catapult trials Jack Davis joins Supermarine
1926	Designs a light aeroplane	RAF High Speed Flight formed Southampton Mediterranean cruise Commercial flights by Swan
1927	Appointed technical director	S5 wins Schneider Trophy Nanok first flight Hythe Works acquired
1928		Vickers buys Supermarine Seamew first flight Jacques Schneider dies
1929		S6 wins Schneider Trophy

YEAR	MITCHELL'S LIFE	SIGNIFICANT EVENTS
1930		Alfred Faddy joins Supermarine Argentine Southampton delivered Air Yacht first flies Trenchard retires as CAS
1931	Future flying boats to be twin-engined	S6b wins Schneider Trophy
1932	Awarded CBE	Scapa first flies Beverley Shenstone joins Supermarine
1933	Cancer diagnosis; colostomy December, flying lessons	
1934	July, first solo flight	Type 224 flies & is rejected Type 300 begins to take shape
1936	Cancer returns November, last solo flight	5 March, Type 300 flies
1937	April, Vienna treatment 11 June, dies Southampton	

Appendix 2

Air Ministry Specifications of the 1930s

During his time as chief designer, chief engineer and technical director of Supermarine (Aviation) Works Limited, Mitchell and his team of engineers like Harold Payn, Alan Clifton and the section leader of a design team, Jack Rasmussen, who led Air Ministry liaison, were always busy – never more so, perhaps, than following the Air Ministry's stream of rearmament specifications for aeroplanes. There were 159 between 1930 and Mitchell's death in 1937. There is a visible increase from 1935 when the Luftwaffe was formally announced.

Mitchell would not have asked for them all as the company was not interested in basic training aeroplanes (e.g. 3/30, the third specification issued in 1930) and several were issued and then cancelled, including ones for very specific types for the Royal Navy. But there were ten specifications which were directly against a Supermarine design or product, so they are worth examining to show the depth and breadth of the team's work.

The first up was the Air Ministry's interest in a monoplane four-gun fighter F7/30 to which Mitchell bid in the Type 224, and it was followed the next year by the specifications for the Scapa and Stranraer and the rarely discussed Type 231 (a design that does not feature in any of the standard references and is presumed to have been a twin-engine biplane), which had been proposed for C26/31 to replace the Valentia with a light bomber/transport. Then there was a gap until 1934 for the Seagull V for the Royal Australian Air Force, rapidly followed by F37/34 which was written around and specified the Type 300 which had been submitted privately by Vickers on behalf of Supermarine. Two specifications were issued for the Walrus biplane amphibian to which only Supermarine was invited.

Two specifications that did really excite Mitchell were F37/35 for the twin-engined fighter, for which Mitchell had already allocated the Supermarine Type 313. This was later supplemented by F18/37 about the time of Mitchell's death, to which Joe Smith allocated Types 324 and 325. Two bomber specifications came out in 1936; Mitchell bid for B12/36, while P13/36 resulted in the Avro Manchester, Handley Page Halifax and Vickers Warwick. Mitchell's team always claimed that if he had not died, his bomber would have been better and may have saved lives because of its performance.

Mitchell believed that his design was superior because of reduced drag and the unique feature of a pressurised crew area. Certainly the schematics that survive show a streamlined, modern-looking bomber. Its construction was planned to be far more advanced than the older Vickers Wellington – the standard

Bomber Command medium bomber – and a decade ahead of the Boeing Superfortress, which didn't enter service in Europe. Just who influenced Mitchell in his thinking on the B12/36 is unclear; again, the relevant papers were destroyed in September 1940 by enemy action.

Another debate among historians is whether a twin-engined Spitfire, the Type 313, with its Merlin engines, would have been better than the Westland Whirlwind which was already planned and flew in 1938 armed with the same armament that Mitchell had proposed, the Hispano-Suiza 404 cannon grouped in the nose, but powered by the lacklustre Rolls-Royce Peregrine engine. Only 114 were built and it was taken out of service in 1943.

Appendix 3

The Mitchell Designs

Supermarine Channel (1919)

Mitchell was designated chief designer of Supermarine in 1919 at the age of twenty-four at a time when surplus wartime designs were being converted to civilian use. The Channels, a series of passenger-carrying flying boats converted from the AD Boats, were probably where Mitchell first gained his insights into spiral development because even five years after the end of the war, techniques had developed. An extra cockpit was inserted into the hull and a more powerful Hispano-Suiza engine fitted with a small water rudder to control the flying boat when taxiing on the water. The Channels were regular sights between Southampton and Bournemouth, over the Cowes Regatta and even cross-Channel to St Malo and Le Havre. Export orders followed from Japan and Venezuela; Chile bought the last Channel Mk II for naval service.

Channel Mk I

Power: a single Beardmore 160-hp engine
Crew: five (pilot and four passengers)
Span: 50 ft 5 in (upper wing), 39 ft 7 in (lower wing)
Length: 30 ft
Empty weight: 2,356 lb
All-up Weight: 3,400 lb
Range: 300 miles

Supermarine Commercial Amphibian (1920)

In its search for a safe and comfortable commercial amphibian seaplane, the Air Ministry commissioned a competition to take place at Felixstowe from 1 September 1920. Among the target specifications were a speed of not less than 70 knots and a range of 350 nautical miles, as well as the need to be able to fly for three minutes 'hands off' in level flight at 3,500 feet. These were quite ambitious for the time because they also included water-taxi capabilities which were almost never included in specifications. Supermarine entered with the Commercial Amphibian which would be pitted against the Fairey III and the Vickers Viking. Supermarine's team, including the young Mitchell, used the AD Boat form which had been so successful in the Channel; the Linton Hope hull form had special attention. It was flown to Suffolk by Captain J. E. A. Hoare on 17 September. Supermarine came second and received a £8,000 prize with the rider that the Commercial would have performed better with a more powerful engine. Alas, the Commercial crashed in October 1920 and was not rebuilt – but Mitchell and Supermarine had learned the power lesson. Never again would Mitchell be involved with a project that did not have sufficient engine thrust.

Commercial Amphibian

Power: a single Rolls-Royce Eagle 350-hp engine

Crew: three (pilot and two passengers)

Span: 50 ft (upper wing), 47 ft (lower wing)

Length: 32 ft 6 in

Empty weight: 3,996 lb

All-up Weight: 5,700 lb

Range: 312 miles

Supermarine Sea King I and II (1920)

The Sea Lion, which had been entered in the 1919 Schneider contest, led to the Sea King I, which appeared at the 1920 Olympia Aero Show. Mitchell made a number of important changes to the Sea King I, including increasing the height of the vertical tail empennage and giving the rudder more chord to allow for better handling on the water. When these modifications were complete, Supermarine referred to the design as the Sea King II. Mitchell's small team managed to create the Mk II in a record six months and there was even talk of a two-seat version with an observer handling a Lewis gun. The Mk II was Mitchell's first design from scratch and over which he had design authority, and it shows that his knowledge of basic seaplane aerodynamics was taking shape.

Sea King II

Power: a single Hispano-Suiza 300-hp engine
Span: 32 ft
Length: 26 ft 9 in
Height: 11 ft 7 in
Empty weight: 2,115 lb
All-up weight: 2,850 lb
Maximum speed: 125 mph
Range: 250 miles

Supermarine Seal II (later named Seagull) (1921)

A maritime flying-boat design at the outset, this was based on the 1920 design of the Supermarine Commercial Amphibian, probably known at Woolston as the Seal I. The Seagull II became the core business of Mitchell's team and the Woolston works between 1922 and 1924. As the government trials progressed, the design was amended – something that was so simple in the days of woodwork and canvas. It was a remarkably reliable flying machine throughout the 1920s, especially with the Royal Australian Air Force. There is a good case to be made for the Seagull development being vital to one of Mitchell's greatest designs, the Walrus, when the Seagull II was fitted with a pusher Bristol Jupiter engine. The Seagull V led directly to the Walrus.

Seagull II

Power: a single Napier Lion IV 492-hp engine
Crew: three
Span: 46 ft
Length: 37 ft 9 in
Empty weight: 3,820 lb
All-up weight: 5,691 lb
Maximum speed: 85 mph

Supermarine Sea Lion II (1922)

The Sea Lion II was modified for the 1922 Schneider Trophy race at Naples and won at around 145 mph, despite being a private venture against state-sponsored French and Italian competitors. The Sea Lion II was a publicity stunt by Hubert Scott-Paine, who wanted the publicity for Supermarine, which was suffering from a lack of business. It was a derived variant of the 1919 winner with a new engine and better fuels from Shell Mex. Mitchell was at the forefront of the modifications, giving Henri Biard, the pilot, a flying boat which can be rolled and looped as well as flying at 160 mph.

Sea Lion II

Power: a single Napier Lion II 450-hp engine
Crew: one
Span: 32 ft
Length: 24 ft 9 in
Empty weight: 2,115 lb
All-up Weight: 3,275 lb
Range: 360 miles

Supermarine Sea Eagle (1923)

Hargreaves made the initial design, but it was Mitchell who did the donkey work on a folding-wing amphibian powered by a Rolls-Royce Eagle engine mounted between the biplane wings over the enclosed cabin. This design could carry six passengers and a crew of two – the pilot and the mechanic, the latter being a necessary feature given the unpredictable nature of the power plant – yet operate on a single engine. It was clear that fee-paying passengers wanted to be protected from the elements especially on take-off and landing in a swell or moderate sea. The first registered commercial flying-boat service was flown by the British Marine Air Navigation Company, with an Air Ministry subsidy, on or about 25 September 1923, linking the Channel Islands with the English mainland. The Sea Eagle was fast for its day, coming third in the King's Cup Air Race, beaten by a Siddeley Siskin fighter. Hargreaves, Mitchell and his bosses, Hubert Scott-Paine and James Bird, were delighted. The Sea Eagle was inspected by Edward, Prince of Wales, on 27 June 1924; a contemporary picture is a definite period piece as the prince is wearing the uniform of a Captain Royal Navy with ceremonial sword at his side. One Sea Eagle may well have been the first airliner ever christened on 13 October 1923 – the name chosen showed no real imagination – *Sea Eagle*.

Supermarine Sea Eagle

Power: a single Rolls-Royce Eagle IX 360-hp engine
Span: 46 ft (21 ft 1 in when folded)
Length: 37 ft 4 in
Height: 15 ft 11 in
Empty weight: 3,950 lb
All-up weight: 6,500 lb
Maximum speed: 93 mph
Range: 230 miles at 84 mph

Supermarine Sea Lion III (1923)

According to one reference work,* creating a Schneider Trophy competitor from an existing design, which had already been modified, was the worst job of Mitchell's career. The background is that Hawker and Blackburn, commercial rivals of Supermarine, were going to enter the Cowes heat of the races in 1923 but not Supermarine, until Scott-Paine realised that both machines would be beaten by the US-government-sponsored entry – $2 million. Mitchell set to work almost alone to redesign the hull of a Sea Lion II and create the heavier but more streamlined Sea Lion III. The extra weight and resultant large wing area was due to the adoption of an encased Napier Lion III engine, again to reduce drag and to give an altogether cleaner, more modern look to the biplane racer. Test pilot Henri Biard was initially concerned that the Sea Lion III would be hard to unstick from the water because a rapid take-off was a key element to putting in a good time for a race. The Americans naturally won that year's race but Mitchell later had the satisfaction of seeing the aeroplane delivered to the

---

* C. F. Andrews and E. B. Morgan, *Supermarine Aircraft since 1914* (Putnam, 1981).

MAEE at Grain. However, it sadly crashed on 5 July 1924, killing the test pilot, Flying Officer E. E. Paull-Smith. Another important development was the decision by all participating countries that the Schneider Trophy races would be better conducted by racing seaplanes on floats or pontoons in future.

Supermarine Sea Lion III

Power: a single Napier Lion III 525-hp engine
Span: 28 ft
Length: 28 ft
Empty weight: 2,400 lb
All-up weight: 3,275 lb
Maximum speed: 175 mph
Range: 350 miles

Supermarine Scylla and Swan (1924)

In the confusing linear progress of Mitchell flying boats, it doesn't come more confusing than Scylla and Swan. Design work for a twin-engined replacement for the First World War design known as the Felixstowe F5 for coastal reconnaissance and anti-submarine warfare began in 1919. The Air Ministry issued a specification, 21/22, which meant funding for the project. Mitchell, only just in post as chief designer, opted for the simplicity of the two-bay wings of equal span which folded forwards to save storage space. There was seating for a dozen passengers in the hull below the cockpit, which was fitted with side windscreens for the crew of two, who were otherwise unprotected from the elements. The Rolls-Royce engines were positioned leading over the front edge of the wing, which had a span designed to be large enough for the engine mounts. Mitchell, by 1921, had designed a military variant, the Scylla, along with the commercial offering, the Swan, in which Instone Air Lines showed interest for a service from Southampton to the Channel Islands. The Air Ministry in London ordered both designs from Supermarine – the Scylla in 1921 and the Swan a year later. The Scylla was a five-seat twin-engined maritime flying boat which is believed to be the first twin-engined amphibian ever ordered, but it was not ordered into production as Mitchell came up with a modification to the Swan, which the Air Ministry appears to have preferred to the Scylla, and which led directly to the Southampton. The first flight of the Swan was on 25 March 1924, while the Scylla had been used from December the previous year as a taxi trials aircraft at Felixstowe. Considerable confusion reigns with the Scylla, as it appears the drawings and supporting paperwork disappeared, possibly when the Supermarine works was bombed in September 1940. The Swan performed well in trials and was modified to Mk II standard as a result. The first flight of the uprated Swan – with Henri Biard at the controls – was 9 June 1926. The Swan remained experimental and was believed to have been scrapped in 1928 but not before it had been the technology demonstrator for the forthcoming Southampton, which was already entering service.

Swan Mk I

Power: twin Rolls-Royce Eagle IX 360-hp (replaced with two Napier Lion IIB 490-hp) engines
Crew: two with ten passengers
Span: 68 ft 8 in
Length: 48 ft 6 in
Empty weight: 7,800 lb (Eagle); 9,170 (Lion)
All-up weight: 11,900 lb (Eagle); 13,710 lb (Lion)
Maximum speed: 92 mph (Eagle); 108 mph (Lion)
Range: 300 miles

Supermarine Scarab and Sheldrake (1924)

Mitchell's designs were becoming more sophisticated with each iteration of the biplane, single-engined flying boat, yet they all paid due respect to the lineage of the Channel designs which themselves went back to First World War designs from the Admiralty. The Scarab was a Sea Eagle design with a Rolls-Royce Eagle IX engine modified to carry up to 1,000 lb of bombs and other ordnance which attracted the interest of the Spanish *Armada* and its newly formed *Aeronáutica Naval.* Coming at the same time that James Bird took over Supermarine, the order for a dozen Scarab amphibians boosted the company's morale in February 1924 – it also gave Mitchell the opportunity to refine the Sea Eagle with a water rudder for manoeuvring on the sea and yet keep the key quality of comfort for the crew, who could stay dry in all conditions because of the hull shape. For Spain, fighting the Rif War* in

---

*   The Rif War (Spanish: *Guerra del Rif*) was an armed conflict fought from 1921 to 1926 between Spain (joined by France in 1924) and the Berber tribes of the mountainous Rif region of northern Morocco. This conflict allowed Spain to keep its enclaves of Ceuta and Melilla in Morocco – with slightly less of a legal case than Britain's retention of Gibraltar. This war saw the first combined landing operation involving warships and aircraft.

North Africa, the Scarab would be a reconnaissance asset as well as being able to deliver 100 lb bombs, albeit without a bomb sight. The Spanish aeroplane was delivered by seaplane carrier, but as deck cargo, as the hangar lift was found to be 4 in too narrow! The Sheldrake, a frequently seen duck which frequented Southampton Water and the Solent, was a hybrid of the Scarab with increased weight and boosted by a more powerful Napier Lion V engine. It was also armed with a forward-firing Vickers machine gun and a rear-cockpit-mounted Lewis gun, both of rifle calibre. The Sheldrake took part in the Hamble Air Pageant on 12 May 1927, appearing as a Scarab with a gunner's cockpit aft of the mainplane and a tractor propeller. The Sheldrake was faster than the Scarab, breaking through the 100-mph barrier for the first time.

Scarab and Sheldrake compared

Scarab power: a single Rolls-Royce Eagle IX 360-hp engine
Sheldrake power: a single Napier Lion V 450-hp engine
Scarab and Sheldrake crew: three
Scarab and Sheldrake span: 46 ft
Scarab length: 37 ft
Sheldrake length: 37 ft 4½ in
Scarab empty weight: 3,975 lb
Sheldrake empty weight: 4,125 lb
Scarab all-up weight: 5,750 lb
Sheldrake all-up weight: 6,100 lb
Scarab maximum speed: 93 mph
Sheldrake maximum speed: 103 mph
Estimated range of both: 250 nautical miles

Supermarine Sparrow I and II (1924)

This landplane is rather an anomaly in the Supermarine stable and can only partly be attributed to Mitchell. The Sparrow I was designed to contest the Air Ministry prize for a new light aeroplane for the private flyer, including flying schools as a two-seat trainer. Mitchell had the design responsibility, but features appear to have been taken from the early AD Boats, especially the lower mainplane. It was first flown by Henri Biard on 11 September 1924 but suffered from a very temperamental Blackburne Thrush engine. Not ideal in a training aeroplane. It failed to complete the test and even when the high-wing monoplane Sparrow II appeared in 1927 it was of little commercial use, instead being used for testing aerofoil sections. It was passed to Halton Aero Club and probably disposed of in 1933.

Sparrow I

Power: Blackburne Thrush 35-hp engine
Crew: two
Span: 33 ft 4 in (upper wing)
Length: 23 ft 6 in
Empty weight: 475 lb
All-up weight: 860 lb
Maximum speed: 72 mph

Sparrow II

Power: Bristol Cherub III 32-hp engine
Crew: two
Span: 34 ft
Length: 23 ft
Empty weight: 605 lb
All-up weight: 1,000 lb
Maximum speed: 65 mph (depending on wing type)

Supermarine S4 (1925)

Iconic in its own right, this Mitchell design was ahead of its time in construction, technology and innovation. The construction was entirely from wood which allowed a streamlined body strengthened by two steel frames and a monocoque after end. Napier worked with Supermarine's team to create a 700-hp Lion engine and Fairey-Reed created the all-metal propeller. Mitchell knew that the racers would find rough water during the take-off and landing phases of the Schneider events, so the floats were given the same attention as a flying-boat hull, having watertight compartments. Henri Biard took the S4 into the skies after a very long take-off run on 25 August 1925. It flew very little before being shipped to Baltimore for the 1925 heat of the trophy – other than breaking the British air speed record at 226.75 mph. It was written off in curious circumstances on 23 October, again with Biard at the controls. It showed Mitchell that he needed to rein in his ambitions for super-streamlined designs and return to more traditional branching with struts and wires in his next seaplane racer.

S4

Power: Napier Lion VII 680-hp engine
Crew: one
Span: 30 ft 7½ in
Length: 26 ft 7¾ in
Empty weight: 2,600 lb
All-up weight: 3,191 lb
Maximum speed: 226.75mph

Supermarine Southampton (1925)

One of the most successful Supermarine designs of the 1920s. It was possible to mount the Napier Lion engines in the centre section of the biplane wing design because Mitchell had selected a centre section design for the wing bracing, which required no cross-wires in the centre – this is known after its designer as the Warren type. It also allowed a gravity fuel feed from the upper wing tanks, rather than the previous hull tank, giving more space in the hull compartments. There was a sump fuel compartment for long patrols and eventually a powered pump was installed. The propellers were two-bladed and fixed.

The first eighteen Southampton flying boats delivered were wooden-hulled Mk I airframes. After research and consultation, metal was specified for the final forty-eight Mk II aircraft. In a programme begun in 1929, all surviving wooden-hulled Southampton Mk Is were rebuilt with metal hulls. The days of teak and mahogany were over. The Southampton Mk I first entered service in August 1925 and quickly gained notoriety for long-distance formation flights, 'showing the flag' to the empire and others in Africa and Asia. The most notable endurance flight was a cruise of four flying boats to Singapore via Malta, Alexandria and Bombay (now

Mumbai), covering 27,000 nautical miles as the Far East Flight in 1927 and 1928.

Southampton Mk II

Power: twin Napier Lion 500-hp engines
Crew: five
Span: 75 ft
Length: 49 ft 8½ in
Empty weight: 9,696.5 lb
All-up weight: 15,200 lb
Maximum speed: 95 mph
Range: 545 miles
Endurance: over six hours

Supermarine Nanok (1927)

This three-engined flying boat was a modified version of the Southampton design, upgraded to provide greater range and weight-carrying capabilities. The plan was for the Royal Danish Navy to use the Nanok on long patrols and if necessary for it to be fitted with a torpedo under each mainplane. The design was tested by the Air Ministry at Felixstowe but did not achieve the contracted performance, so despite flying on 21 June 1927, it was shelved. Denmark bought a Southampton instead.

The unwanted airframe was converted into the first Air Yacht design for the Guinness family, with accommodation for twelve passengers and range of more than 200 nautical miles. The aeroplane would often transit the Irish Sea to Dublin and on to County Galway. It was named the *Supermarine Solent*.

Nanok

Power: three Armstrong Siddeley Jaguar IV 430-hp engines
Crew: five
Span: 75 ft
Length: 50 ft 6 in
Empty weight: 10,619 lb
All-up weight: 16,311 lb
Maximum speed: 113.5 mph

Supermarine S5 (1927)

Mitchell was never one to be despondent. The S4 disaster in America just spurred him on to greater things. He re-examined his design philosophy and, of course, realised that the S5 would have a shorter span of wooden wings, and the monocoque Duralumin fuselage's overall length was shortened compared to the S4. The struts and braces of the new design, and a different construction technique, would make it heavier, but the powerful Napier engine drove it through the air quicker. If in doubt, more power! The S5 also benefitted from wind-tunnel testing on models and the support of the Air Ministry through an official specification, 2/26, for a 265 mph racing seaplane. The S5 was entered in the 1927 contest after Mitchell worked hard to improve the water taxiing (even using a speedboat to tow the S5 to check its buoyancy) and the general handling by 'tweaking' the design. To fly, race and win, the Air Ministry created the High Speed Flight, and Flight Lieutenant Oswald Worsley first flew the S5 on 7 June 1927. Two were built and, after trials at Felixstowe, they were disassembled and taken to Italy to the race where one of them, with a direct-drive Lion engine, flown by Flight Lieutenant Sidney Webster, won that heat with a new world-record speed of 281.66 mph.

A third S5 was built but sadly written off in the Solent on 12 March 1928 when Flight Lieutenant Sam Kinkead flew into the water in hazy conditions.

S5

Power: Napier Lion VIIA 900-hp engine
Crew: one
Span: 26 ft 9 in
Length: 24 ft 3½ in
Empty weight: 2,680 lb
All-up weight: 3,242 lb
Maximum speed: 319.57 mph

Supermarine Seamew (1928)

The Seamew was looked upon by many as a smaller version of the Southampton Mk I. Mitchell envisioned a small, shipborne amphibian which would be used from cruisers and battleships to scout ahead of a naval formation. The crew was a pilot and two gunners, probably one of whom would double as navigator and/ or radio operator. The first drawings appeared in October 1924 and show a biplane with twin tails, canted up to protect them from the wash when the aeroplane was in the water. The overall arrangement was improved the following January with a better weight distribution by having the rear gunner closer to the centre of gravity immediately behind the mainplane. Mitchell was too busy to develop the design that year, prioritising the S4 racing seaplane and the Southampton flying boat. In 1926, the design and technical teams could concentrate on the detailed design to accommodate two Armstrong Siddeley Lynx engines with four-bladed propeller and to ensure the hull reflected the need to operate in open water from a warship. A drawing was also created of a four-seat civilian version but it was not shown to the public until the May 1929 issue of *Flight*. The military version was progressed earlier, first being flown on 9 January 1928 with Henri Biard at the controls. The design seems to have been prone to limitations in climb and balance, causing a series of negative reports from the Air Ministry, leading to the cancellation and scrapping of the two prototype airframes.

Seamew

Power: twin Armstrong Siddeley Lynx IV 238-hp engines
Crew: two/three
Span: 45 ft 11½ in
Length: 36 ft 5½ in
Empty weight: 4,675 lb
All-up weight: 5,800 lb
Maximum speed: 95 mph

Supermarine S6/6a (1929)

The penultimate racing seaplane was the S6. This is the beginning of the close collaboration between Rolls-Royce and Supermarine – or, rather, Sir Henry Royce and Mitchell. A powerful engine was needed to drive a larger machine faster. The Napier Lion had been instrumental in many Mitchell designs up to now, but had reached the end of its development potential. Royce was an old man in 1928 and living in retirement in West Wittering on the South Coast. He began work on a superior twelve-cylinder engine there in November and the R-type was born. It would go on to be developed into the Merlin and power most of the early successful Second World War warplanes in Britain and America. Mitchell wanted an engine that could develop 1,500 hp at a time when most piston-engines were giving a quarter of that power. To this engine, he would design the fuselage using the tried and tested basic form of the S5 but with a far greater use of metal, especially light alloys of aluminium and steel. This included the fin and the innovative fuselage skin cooling ducts for the engine. An important footnote is that Rodwell Banks, the pioneer who brought Fighter Command its 100-octane fuel in

1940, also contributed to the 1929 Schneider race with a special fuel mix.

The Air Ministry issued specification 8/28 and work was completed at Woolston in July 1929. The two S6s were flown by Squadron Leader Augustus Orlebar, one of the senior test pilots at the Marine Aircraft Experimental Establishment, on 10 and 25 August respectively. The British team won the 1929 Schneider event on the Solent, and the Ramsay MacDonald government pledged Britain would defend the trophy win and attempt a third consecutive victory in 1931, thus clinching the trophy for all time.

S6

Power: Rolls-Royce R-type 1,900-hp engine
Crew: one
Span: 30 ft
Length: 25 ft 10 in
Empty weight: 4,471 lb
All-up weight: 5,771 lb
Maximum speed: 357.7 mph (world speed record)

Supermarine Southampton X (1930)

The X was specified as a follow-on to the Southampton Mk II. It was a time of expansion for Supermarine and heightened interest in Mitchell, his team and seaplanes, so designs were developed often overlapping each other. In the event, it was clear that the evolution of the design was limited. Mitchell had to rethink his design concepts and that was all to the good.

Southampton X

Power: three Bristol Jupiter IV 570-hp engines
Crew: five
Span: 79 ft
Length: 55 ft 6 in
Empty weight: 13,975 lb
All-up weight: 23,000 lb
Maximum speed: 130 mph

Supermarine Air Yacht (1930)

In an age of luxury sailing and steam yachts anchored off every French, Italian and Spanish resort, a flying yacht attracted the attention of the very rich. In 1930, a most unusual Supermarine design appeared to attract a private customer for luxury travel around the coasts of Europe. The Air Yacht was initially designed by Mitchell as a three-engined reconnaissance flying boat for the Royal Air Force and had been stored at Hythe. At first glance, the design appears to draw on the Dornier Wal, a German project for a twin-engined flying boat for exploration and pioneering flights away from the usual ports. Built in the mid-1920s, it was a minor commercial success in South America and the Far East. The Supermarine Air Yacht took note of the general arrangement with stud lower mainplanes and mainplanes attached to the fuselage with a series of studs and braces. It is not an unpleasing design, with a triple tail and powered by cowled Armstrong Siddeley Panther engines which could lift ten people – six passengers – and give a good deal of comfort in the style of ocean-going steam yachts of the period. It was bought on sight by an American lady and entered private ownership on 11 October 1932 but was paid off a few months later, after a series of mishaps which were weather-related and the result of a too adventurous owner rather than the design.

Air Yacht

Power: three Armstrong-Siddeley Panther IIA 525-hp engines
Crew: four crew, six passengers
Span: 92 ft
Length: 66 ft 6 in
Empty weight: 16,808 lb
All-up weight: 23,348 lb
Maximum speed: 102 mph

Supermarine S6b (1931)

The Air Ministry in London was ordered by the MacDonald socialist government to withdraw support from the British entry to the Schneider 1931 event just two months after the pledge to support what everyone in Britain hoped would be a final victory. The final private support from Lady Houston was agreed in January 1931 and, even by the standards of the day, that left little time for Mitchell and his team to swing into action. That meant Mitchell was compelled to make as few changes as possible in the S6 for what was to become the S6b. He had not been idle – he was never idle. He was keen that everything should flow from the uprated R-type engine and its dynamic cooling system on the fuselage sides; float design, a new propeller, the wings and tail would all have to change. It seems that the fuselage was the only thing he did not consider needed changing. Aileron flutter seems to have merited considerable attention after both S4 and S5 accidents.* The first of two S6bs was flown for

---

* Lieutenant Brinton RN had died on his first take-off in a S6 (modified so that many call it S6a). Flight Lieutenant Linton Hope had also been injured – so much so with burst eardrums that he could not race again in another S6a, which was wrecked because of boat wash on landing.

the first time by Squadron Leader Augustus Orlebar, and he found the take-off run challenging because of the engine torque and the need for continuous full right rudder to keep straight. The S6b of Flight Lieutenant John Boothman won on 13 September 1931 – Britain permanently kept the trophy and Mitchell was vindicated. So too were the other key supporters – not least Lady Houston, the Royal Aero Club and the Society of British Aeroplane Constructors. The design work and the proof of its veracity showed that Mitchell's 'technology demonstrator' concept for future designs was highly relevant.

S6b

Power: Rolls-Royce R-type 2,350-hp engine
Crew: one
Span: 30 ft
Length: 28 ft 10 in
Empty weight: 4,590 lb
All-up weight: 6,086 lb
Maximum speed: 407.5 mph (world speed record)

Supermarine Scapa (1932)

The Scapa looks modern even if it's a biplane flying boat. The hull design, superstructure, cowled inline engines and, above all, the enclosed cockpit show a clear progression from the older designs from Supermarine. It was significantly faster than its predecessors. The flying boat benefitted from the support of the parent company in that Mutt Summers, the legendary chief test pilot of Vickers, was the first to lift the Scapa into the air on 8 July 1932. Twelve of the type were initially ordered by the Air Ministry to specification R20/31, later modified as R19/33. The first deliveries began in 1935 and with an out-of-service date of 1939, it was not a long service career, but it was an important one. Besides proving the new hull design philosophy and construction methods, the flying-boat cruises to Sudan and Nigeria, as well as the Mediterranean, were important proving grounds which gave the Air Ministry the confidence in flying boats to operate in what Italy thought was its own sea. It also showed the flag, running defence diplomacy and rule-of-law missions to protect neutral shipping in the Spanish Civil War. Immediately prior to the outbreak of the Second World War, the Scapa was training flying-boat aircrew from the Royal Air Force Volunteer Reserve at RAF Calshot on the Solent. A brief but glorious career.

Scapa

Power: two Rolls-Royce Kestrel IIIMS 525-hp engines

Crew: five

Span: 75 ft

Length: 53 ft

Empty weight: 10,030 lb

All-up weight: 16,080 lb

Maximum speed: 142 mph

Supermarine Giant (1932)

There is nothing like a bit of competition to spur on an aeroplane designer. It was Short Brothers who first went to see the Air Ministry about the German developments of giant passenger-carrying flying boats. In 1929, Supermarine was also interested by a specification for a forty-passenger machine with eight (later six) engines in four separate nacelles on a shoulder wing. Mitchell worked on a 65,000 lb machine and it became known in Whitehall as the Mediterranean Flying Boat project. Alas, the main backer, Secretary of State for Air Lord Thomson, died in the R101 airship crash in October 1930 and momentum left the project. The keel had been laid and a registration number allocated but on 19 January 1932, the project was cancelled by a cash-strapped government.

Giant

Power: six Rolls-Royce 900-hp engines
Crew: seven and forty passengers
Span: 185 ft
Length: 104 ft 6 in
Empty weight: 49,390 lb
All-up weight: 75,090 lb
Maximum speed: 145 mph (estimated)
Range: 700 nautical miles (calculated)

Supermarine Seagull V (1933)

Another classic Mitchell! The Seagull V naval spotter require-ment originated from Australia after prompting from Supermarine which was frustrated by the lack of interest from the Admiralty. Thus a simple one-step hull seemed in order for the venture known as Type 223 at Supermarine. It was first flown by Mutt Summers on 21 June 1933, having been redesignated Type 228. The first Royal Australian Air Force production machine was flown on 26 June 1935 by George Pickering and found to be capable of being looped. Trials at Felixstowe and RAE Farnborough followed to test the landing gear and ability to be catapult-launched.

Seagull V

Power: single Bristol Pegasus IIM2 625-hp pusher engine
Crew: three (two gun positions)
Span: 46 ft
Length: 38 ft
Empty weight: 4,640 lb
All-up weight: 6,847 lb
Maximum speed: 125 mph
Range: 630 nautical miles
Endurance: over three hours

Supermarine Stranraer (1934)

Coming hot on the heels of the success of the Southampton and the Scapa, the Stranraer shows a design that amassed the best technology of the day. Few suffered any kind of corrosion. It was a clean-looking machine with two powerful Pegasus engines and general arrangement which was slightly more than 10 per cent larger than the Scapa; some lessons had been learned about ergonomics for the crew on long flights. It was designed to last and represented new thinking in the Air Ministry, including the provision of bombs to engage enemy shipping. Proof of the flying longevity of the Stranraer is found in two places. First, in the propaganda book published for morale purposes in 1942, *Britain's Wonderful Air Force*, which shows that the flying boat was still operational, if not front line. It is rated with the Short Singapore Mk III, Saunders-Roe Lerwick and London as well as the Short Sunderland. By 1940, Short Brothers and Saunders-Roe (Saro) had taken over the flying-boat mantle from Supermarine, now devoid of its biggest asset: Mitchell. Second, Canada also showed the merits of Mitchell's work, with Alclad alloy plating and the skill with which Canadian builders put licence-built Stranraer boats together. The aircraft flew on into the post-war period after rugged service on both Canadian seaboards. Many a coastal community in British Columbia owes its creation and prosperity to the flying boat in winter or summer, providing links with larger towns and cities such as Campbell River, Victoria and Vancouver.

Stranraer

Power: two Bristol Pegasus X 920-hp engines
Crew: five
Span: 85 ft
Length: 54 ft 10 in
Empty weight: 11,250 lb
All-up weight: 19,000 lb
Maximum speed: 165 mph
Range: 1,000 nautical miles

Supermarine Type 224 (1934)

Often described as the first Spitfire, this was Mitchell's attempt at creating a monoplane fighter for the Royal Air Force. The Air Ministry wanted to move smartly from the biplane era into the new world of streamlined fighters, with good performance even at night and carrying sufficient guns to engage the new bombers coming from French and German factories. Mitchell could confidently use the experience of the racing seaplanes to answer specification F7/30. The Type 224 was all-metal with the thick gull-wing and specially designed radiators for the Goshawk engine, which was suggested by the Air Ministry as the best powerplant available in Britain. In the event, the Type 224 flew with the Goshawk II on 19 February 1934 and was shown off at RAF Hendon that June. There is ample evidence to deduce that Mitchell was not pleased with his first efforts on the Type 224 and the test-pilot reports were disappointing. Many at Supermarine thought the long screw-driver of the Air Ministry was responsible for a bad specification. The Goshawk steam-cooled engine was not a success either. The machine went to Farnborough to be used as a 'hack' aeroplane, then Martlesham Heath, finally ending its days on the Orford Ness gunnery range in 1937. Mitchell was disappointed and, by now, had a good inclination that he was still suffering from cancer. The Type 224 only just outlasted him.

Type 224 Spitfire

Power: Rolls-Royce Goshawk 600-hp engine
Crew: one
Span: 45 ft 10 in
Length: 29 ft 5¼ in
Empty weight: 3,422 lb
All-up weight: 4,743 lb
Maximum speed: 228 mph

Supermarine Type 300 (1936)

The design and development of the Type 300, which became the most iconic aeroplane of the twentieth century, was somewhat tortuous. Mitchell knew that the first 'Spitfire', the Type 224, was not his best effort so he gathered a team around him that could come up with the best possible solution to a modern fighter requirement. With Alf Faddy, Mitchell worked up the general arrangement and Beverley Shenstone perfected his elliptical wing ideas, while Rolls-Royce offered the private-venture Merlin engine. In November 1934, the first sketches were shown to the Supermarine Board in time for F37/34 to be issued on 1 December. The new Air Ministry requirement followed the Supermarine design and was shown to the Air Ministry in May 1935. By the time of the first flight, Mitchell was very sick and no longer working at Woolston. He did summon the strength to witness Mutt Summers take K5054 into the air on 5 March 1936, and later to have Jeffrey Quill fly him in the Miles Falcon 6 to see the fighter in the air, flown by George Pickering. The first batch of 310 Spitfires was ordered on 3 June 1936 which must have delighted the ailing Mitchell. Sadly, the Type 300, delivered to Farnborough and camouflaged for wartime flying, crashed on 4 September 1939, and was consigned to the fire dump. It had disappeared from view by 1944, when the legendary 'Winkle' Brown arrived at the Royal Aircraft Establishment – he said, 'We went to look for the carcass, but it had been broken up and scrapped.'[1]

Type 300

Power: Rolls-Royce Merlin 990-hp engine
Crew: one
Span: 36 ft 10 in
Length: 29 ft 11 in
Empty weight: 4,082 lb
All-up weight: 5,359 lb
Maximum speed: 349 mph at altitude; 430 mph (in a dive during trials)

Supermarine Walrus (1936)

The first production Walrus flew on 18 March 1936 – just days after the Type 300 took to the air. The Walrus I was heavier and had a smaller wingspan than the Seagull V, yet was faster and generally improved. The Walrus was built at the Itchen factory and finished across the water in Hythe. There was a Mk II variant with a wooden hull that was used for training, but it did not fly until 1940. The first order was for 168 MK I amphibians, coming close on the heels of the first Spitfire order in 1936. The two designs were chalk and cheese, and a challenge for Supermarine with its 'cottage industry' style of production. The Walrus was still in production in 1942 and is another of those designs operational throughout the Second World War.

Walrus I

Power: single Bristol Pegasus VI 750-hp pusher engine
Crew: four (two gun positions)
Span: 45 ft 10 in
Length: 37 ft 7 in
Empty weight: 4,900 lb
All-up weight: 7,200 lb
Maximum speed: 135 mph
Range: 600 nautical miles
Endurance: over three hours

Supermarine Sea Otter (1938)

Mitchell had died when George Pickering took the prototype Sea Otter into the air on 23 September 1938. Mitchell had been working on the improved Walrus – originally called the Stingray – from his sickbed since February 1936 at one of his last meetings with Air Ministry officials. As a result, on 17 April, Supermarine received an Air Ministry requirement for an amphibian for use embarked on aircraft carriers. It was, in effect, a cleaned-up Walrus but with a tractor propeller. The production version was heavier, yet faster thanks to the Mercury engine.

Sea Otter

Power: single Bristol Mercury XXX 965-hp pusher engine
Crew: four
Span: 46 ft
Length: 39 ft 10¾ in
Empty weight: 6,805 lb
All-up weight: 10,000 lb
Maximum speed: 163 mph
Range: 920 nautical miles

Supermarine ASR Mk I

Mitchell's last amphibian concept was started in 1936 and res-
urrected in 1940 to meet Air Ministry specification 12/40. It is
recorded here for completeness, although it was completed by Faddy
and Smith in design terms. It is possible to see the design lineage.

Supermarine Bomber Type 316, 317 and 318

Mitchell was a pioneer of new technology and forward thinking. The B12/36 bomber would have been a half generation ahead of its rivals even in 1936. The project had been driven by the politics of rising tensions between Germany and the UK with Mitchell taking up the challenge for better, faster, higher and carrying more payload. Mitchell created five alternatives for the Air Ministry by September 1936. After his death, the project was dropped as there was much to do with the Spitfire's productionisation and the wooden mock-up was destroyed in the September 1940 onslaught against Supermarine's factory. It would have been a fantastic contribution to the bomber offensive.

Supermarine Type 327 Twin-Engined Fighter

The final Mitchell design was for a twin-engined tricycle-undercarriage six-cannon-armed fighter, powered by the Merlin, which he thought should replace the Spitfire in 1942/43. Little is known about it other than the wooden mock-up which is again ahead of its time. Mitchell estimated the performance would be superior to existing fighters with a calculated 465 mph at 22,000 feet. Previously, the Air Ministry even considered replacing the single-engined Spitfire production line with the Bristol Beaufighter which resulted from Air Ministry specification F18/37, for which Mitchell had approved the initial Type 324 and 325 twin-engined fighter configuration. The mock-up and paperwork were destroyed in September 1940 by enemy action.

Acknowledgements

Every author needs a publisher who will take a punt on an idea. A book might take months to research and write, an investment in the author's time, but it is the publisher, with the advice of a good editor, who takes the risk – reputational as well as financial. I have been extremely fortunate that Lorne Forsyth has been prepared to back me in the creation of this book in a crowded market with many pre-conceived ideas. I am sure that without my editor Jennie Condell's support and her post-contractual guidance, I would not have signed a contract with Elliott & Thompson in 2024. Huge thanks must also go to Amy Greaves, Alex Hippisley-Cox, Pippa Crane, Marianne Thorndahl, Eluned Gulbekian and all of the brilliant team at E&T.

Lorne allowed me to develop the theme of the person not the aeroplanes, although with Mitchell the two were interlinked to such a degree that it is often difficult to work down to the personality at key times. I hope I have managed to highlight the great man who was without doubt the 'Father of the Spitfire' but I have also been at pains to point out the other people – members of the Supermarine orchestra – whose own contributions were key to the eventual success of the various designs, culminating in the Spitfire.

To get to the point where I could start to write I spoke with dozens of people, and the most supportive and informative are listed here because of the debt which they are owed: James Holland for the opportunities to talk about Spitfires at the Chalke History Festival over the last decade and where I met many of the descendants of those mentioned in this book from Pemberton-Billing to Faddy. They each offered a little something which has helped with the narrative. Thank you to them. Speaking at Chalke always means talking to other historians and seeking their views: Peter Caddick-Adams, Guy Walters, Saul David stand out. Other historians with great knowledge which they have been prepared to share include Victoria Taylor, Phoebe Style and Howard Mason, and the Aeronautical Heritage Committee of the Royal Aeronautical Society, including Andy Rankine and Peter Elliott. Judy Monger, Joy Lofthouse and the Spitfire Society 'roundel' in Gloucestershire were formative in my early research too.

When researching Mitchell's relationship with the top brass of the Royal Air Force, I asked Group Captain David Baker for assistance. He was an engineering officer in the Royal Air Force and is a former director of flying at Boscombe Down when it was a service flying station. His grandfather and great uncle were the Salmond brothers, Geoff and John, who both commanded the Royal Air Force in the inter-war years. True to his word, he spent several days examining the family papers which are still kept by his mother, Annie Baker MBE, who is 110 years old: the last person alive to have met Lawrence of Arabia, no less. She helped me understand the complexity of the service in the Mitchell era. They pointed me in the direction of Ralph Barker's book *The Schneider Trophy Races*

(Chatto & Windus, 1971), so I ordered a copy from the second-hand booksellers Claremont Books in Market Harborough; inside the flap was a letter from John Waghorn, son of the Schneider High Speed Flight pilot, apparently sent in 1992; and a note saying that the original owner of the book was Peter Woodley. He wrote inside that he had sat in the S6 at Vickers House in 1956. The book is a time capsule, wonderfully written for its time and full of detail.

Among the more pleasurable meetings, lunches, coffees and general chit-chat I have been privileged to enjoy have been with the daughters of the two great Supermarine test pilots – Kate Quill and especially Sarah Quill who shared her father's logbook with me. George Pickering is a character too often forgotten but his daughter Jennie Sherborne keeps his memory alive. Biographers are often blessed with the memories and knowledge carried by the descendants of famous or influential people. Interestingly, daughters often care more about their father's lives than do the sons. Jennie Sherborne is one such example. To these ladies, I am most grateful.

Elsewhere, I have tapped into the memories of aeronautical industry experts Peter Cook, David Kirkpatrick and David Daniel. Hugh Trenchard regaled me with family stories of his grandfather T. E. Lawrence and the politics of the time.

At the Royal Aeronautical Society's National Aerospace Library, Tony Pilmer, Anne Hayward and Georgina Townsend have been generous with their time and expertise.

I am grateful to Air Chief Marshal Sir Rich Knighton, Chief of the Defence Staff, for his foreword, and to Group Captain John Shields for facilitating the approval. Rich is just the right person to write the foreword, as not only does he lead the Royal Air Force, but he is a distinguished aerospace engineer in his own right – Mitchell would have approved of his appointment!

Sadly, there are few Mitchell designs left but those that are preserved static or in flying condition deserve a mention of acknowledgement: Maggie Appleton and her team at the RAF Museum, the Solent Sky Museum volunteers, the Bishop's Waltham Aviation Group (of which I am honoured to be Patron), the opportunities offered to me over the years at the Aircraft Restoration Company, the Biggin Hill Heritage Hangar, Kennet Aviation and Spitfires. com (Goodwood) – Matt Jones, Phill O'Dell and Eskil Amdal in particular. The National Spitfire Project with its ambitious plan for the tallest stainless-steel structure in the world at Southampton will inspire others to remember but also to forge a career in aeronautics just as Mitchell would have wanted.

Through the NSP, I met Julian Mitchell, the doyen of the family, at No. 10 Downing Street in 2023, and he has been kind with his support for my project. Visiting Stoke-on-Trent, it became clear just how much the city loves Mitchell when I spoke with Julian at The Potteries Museum & Art Gallery, complete with Spitfire. I was well received and lavishly hosted by Julian and Julia, then celebrated Oscar's birthday with the family including Annabel, Julian's sister. Thank you so much, Mitchells and Staffordshire.

Paul Beaver
Goodworth Clatford
July 2025

Endnotes

Chapter 1: In the Beginning

1. Gordon Mitchell, *R. J. Mitchell: Schooldays to Spitfire* (IWM/ Tempus Books, 2006).

Chapter 2: Super Marine

1. Solent Sky Museum Newsletter, issue 2.

Chapter 3: Gateway to the Empire

1. C. E. Andrews and E. B. Morgan, *Supermarine Aircraft since 1914* (Putnam, 1981).
2. A facsimile of the full letter is reproduced in John Shelton, *R. J. Mitchell: To the Spitfire* (Fonthill, 2022).
3. Letter to Eric Mitchell dated 9 September 1917. Reproduced in Shelton, *R. J. Mitchell: To the Spitfire.*
4. Dinger's Aviation Pages' biography of R. J. Mitchell: https://dingeraviation.net/
5. Quoted in Mitchell, *R. J. Mitchell: Schooldays to Spitfire.*

Chapter 4: First Designs

1. As discussed in Paul Beaver, *Spitfire People* (Evro, 2015).

Chapter 5: Schneider 1922 and 1923

1. The Supermariners website: https://supermariners.wordpress.com/

Chapter 6: Southampton: the Game Changer

1. Andrews and Morgan, *Supermarine Aircraft since 1914.*
2. Papers held in the Solent Sky Museum.

Chapter 7: Need for Speed

1. Quoted in Shelton, *R. J. Mitchell: To the Spitfire.*
2. Quoted in Mitchell, *R. J. Mitchell: Schooldays to Spitfire.*
3. The Supermariners website: https://supermariners.wordpress.com/
4. Letter held in the Royal Air Force Museum.
5. Letter held in the Royal Air Force Museum.
6. Report from special correspondent Major Oliver Stewart, a Royal Flying Corps ace, as quoted in Dr Julian Lewis, *Racing Ace: The Fights and Flights of Samuel 'Kink' Kinkead DSO, DSC*, DFC** (Pen & Sword, 2011).
7. Quoted in Shelton, *R. J. Mitchell: To the Spitfire.*
8. As reported in the *Sentinel*; quoted in Shelton, *R. J. Mitchell: To the Spitfire.*

Chapter 8: Vickers Takeover

1. Quoted in Paul Beaver, *Winkle* (Michael Joseph, 2023).
2. The Supermariners website: https://supermariners.wordpress.com/
3. Richard Morris, *Dam Buster – Barnes Wallis: An Engineer's Life* (Weidenfeld and Nicolson, 2023).
4. Morris, *Dam Buster.*
5. Morris, *Dam Buster.*
6. Morris, *Dam Buster.*
7. Quoted in Mitchell, *R. J. Mitchell: Schooldays to Spitfire.*
8. Joe Smith, First Mitchell Memorial Lecture, 1954. Quoted in Mitchell, *R. J. Mitchell: Schooldays to Spitfire.*
9. Karenza Morton, *Daily Echo*, 23 April 2005.
10. Quoted in Mitchell, *R. J. Mitchell: Schooldays to Spitfire.*
11. Quoted in Mitchell, *R. J. Mitchell: Schooldays to Spitfire.*

Chapter 9: Schneider 1929

1. Quoted in Peter Reese, *Sir Henry Royce: Establishing Rolls-Royce, from Motor Cars to Aero Engines* (History Press, 2022).

2. Jeffrey Quill, *Birth of a Legend: The Spitfire* (Quiller Press, 1986).

3. Quoted in Pieter Shipster, 'From Ink to Oil: T. E. Lawrence and the Schneider Trophy', *Journal of the T.E. Lawrence Society*, vol. XVI, no.2. (2007).

4. Quoted in Shelton, *R. J. Mitchell: To the Spitfire.*

5. Quoted in Shelton, *R. J. Mitchell: To the Spitfire.*

6. Quoted in Shelton, *R. J. Mitchell: To the Spitfire.*

7. Quoted in Shipster, 'From Ink to Oil'.

8. Quoted in Shipster, 'From Ink to Oil'.

Chapter 10: Leave It to Lucy

1. According to the *Oxford Dictionary of National Biography* (2004).

2. Quoted in Jonathan Glancey, *Wings over Water: The Story of the World's Greatest Air Race and the Birth of the Spitfire* (Atlantic Books, 2020).

3. Quoted in Glancey, *Wings over Water.*

4. Quill, *Birth of a Legend.*

5. Denis Le Penn Webb, *Never a Dull Moment* (Solent Sky Library, 2001).

Chapter 11: Back to Business

1. Quoted in Shelton, *R. J. Mitchell: To the Spitfire.*

2. The Vickers-Armstrong company magazine, quoted on the Supermariners website: https://supermariners.wordpress.com/

3. The Supermariners website: https://supermariners.wordpress.com/

4. The Supermariners website: https://supermariners.wordpress.com/

5. In a commentary for Solent Sky Museum.

6. Papers held at Solent Sky Museum.

7. Unpublished memoir held at Solent Sky Museum.

8. Webb, *Never a Dull Moment.*

9. Mike Roussel, *Spitfire's Forgotten Designer: The Career of Supermarine's Joe Smith* (History Press, 2013).

Chapter 12: Towards a Fighter

1. Quill, *Birth of a Legend*.
2. Quill, *Birth of a Legend*.
3. Andrews and Morgan, *Supermarine Aircraft since 1914*.
4. Alfred Price, *The Spitfire Story* (Arms & Armour Press, 1995).
5. Quill, *Birth of a Legend*.
6. Quill, *Birth of a Legend*.
7. Comment made after the First Mitchell Memorial Lecture, 1954. Quoted in Mitchell, *R. J. Mitchell: Schooldays to Spitfire*.
8. *Flight* magazine, 17 June 1937.
9. The Supermariners website: https://supermariners.wordpress.com/
10. Joe Smith, First Mitchell Memorial Lecture, 1954. Quoted in Mitchell, *R. J. Mitchell: Schooldays to Spitfire*.
11. Webb, *Never a Dull Moment*.
12. Quoted in Beaver, *Winkle*.

Chapter 13: Towards the Icon

1. Air Chief Marshal Sir Wilfrid Freeman in a letter to Lady Hives, quoted in Anthony Furse, *Wilfrid Freeman* (Spellmount, 2000).
2. Quoted in Shelton, *R. J. Mitchell: To the Spitfire*.
3. Recounted to the author by David Faddy, formerly Ministry of Defence Director of Operational Analysis at West Byfleet.
4. Quoted in the Supermariners website: https://supermariners. wordpress.com/
5. Quoted in Mitchell, *R. J. Mitchell: Schooldays to Spitfire*.
6. Quoted in Alfred Price, *Spitfire: A Documentary History* (Macdonald and Jane's, 1977).
7. Quoted in Glancey, *Wings over Water*.
8. Quoted in Price, *Spitfire*.
9. Quoted in Shelton, *R. J. Mitchell: To the Spitfire*.

10. C. H. Keith, *I Hold My Aim* (George Allen and Unwin Ltd, 1946).

Chapter 14: A Legend Is Born

1. Quoted in Shelton, *R. J. Mitchell: To the Spitfire.*
2. Quoted in Shelton, *R. J. Mitchell: To the Spitfire.*
3. Reported in *Flight* magazine, 5 March 1936.

Chapter 15: Future Imperfect

1. Conversation between Mitchell and Alf Faddy, relayed to the author by David Faddy in 2015.

Chapter 16: Last Days

1. Sadly this diary does not appear to have survived but this poignant quote comes from Jennie Pickering Sherborne's article in *The Aeroplane* of September 2011.
2. Interview with the author, 2025.
3. Facsimile of the full letter reproduced in Shelton, *R. J. Mitchell: To the Spitfire.*
4. Quoted in Mitchell, *R. J. Mitchell: Schooldays to Spitfire.*

Chapter 17: Legacy

1. Quoted in Paul Beaver, *Spitfire Evolution* (Beaver Westminster Limited, 2016).
2. Jeffrey Quill, *Spitfire: A Test Pilot's Story* (Arrow Books, 1983).
3. Webb, *Never a Dull Moment.*

Appendix 3

1. Quoted in Beaver, *Winkle.*

Sources and Bibliography

Much has been written about Reginald Joseph Mitchell and his short but amazing career. For over forty years, I have been collecting anecdotes and memories from Supermariners and others. I have a library of texts and books, many of which were consulted for the creation of his biography and the main sources are listed below.

Publications

Andrews, C. E. & Morgan, E. B., *Supermarine Aircraft since 1914* (Putnam, 1981)

Barker, Ralph, *The Schneider Trophy Races* (Chatto & Windus, 1971)

Beaver, Paul, *Spitfire Evolution* (Beaver Westminster, 2016, 2024)

Beaver, Paul, *Spitfire People* (Evro, 2015)

Beaver, Paul, *Winkle* (Michael Joseph, 2023)

Cole, Lance, *Secrets of the Spitfire: The Story of Beverley Shenstone, the Man Who Perfected the Elliptical Wing* (Pen & Sword, 2012)

Fellowes, P. F. M. (ed.), *Britain's Wonderful Air Force* (Odhams Press, 1942)

Glancey, Jonathan, *Spitfire: The Biography* (Atlantic Books, 2006)

Glancey, Jonathan, *Wings over Water: The Story of the World's Greatest Air Race and the Birth of the Spitfire* (Atlantic Books, 2020)

Hillan, Jo & Higgs, Colin, *Supermarine Southampton: The Flying Boat that Made R.J. Mitchell* (Air World, 2020)

Jane's All The World's Aircraft (various)

Lewis, Dr Julian, *Racing Ace: The Fights and Flights of Samuel 'Kink' Kinkead DSO, DSC*, DFC** (Pen & Sword, 2011)

McKinstry, Leo, *Portrait of a Legend* (John Murray, 2008)

Mitchell, Gordon, *R. J. Mitchell: Schooldays to Spitfire* (IWM/Tempus Books, 2006)

Morris, Richard, *Dam Buster – Barnes Wallis: An Engineer's Life* (Weidenfeld and Nicolson, 2023)

Price, Alfred, *The Spitfire Story* (Arms & Armour Press, revised 1995)

Price, Alfred, *Spitfire: A Documentary History* (MacDonald and Jane's, 1977)

Quill, Jeffrey, *Birth of a Legend: The Spitfire* (Quiller Press, 1986)

Quill, Jeffrey, *Spitfire: A Test Pilot's Story* (Arrow Books, 1983)

Rawlings, John D. R., *Coastal Support & Special Squadrons* (Jane's, 1982)

Reese, Peter, *Sir Henry Royce: Establishing Rolls-Royce, from Motor Cars to Aero Engines* (History Press, 2022)

Robertson, Bruce, *British Military Aircraft Serials 1912–1963* (Ian Allan, 1964)

Shelton, John, *R. J. Mitchell: To the Spitfire* (Fonthill, 2022)

Shelton, John, *R. J. Mitchell at Supermarine: From Schneider Trophy to Spitfire* (Standon Books, 2017)

Shipster, Pieter, 'From Ink to Oil: T. E. Lawrence and the Schneider Trophy', *Journal of the T.E. Lawrence Society*, vol. XVI, no.2. (2007)

Webb, Denis Le Penn, *Never a Dull Moment* (Solent Sky Library, 2001)

Archives and Personal Stories

The Aeroplane

The late David Faddy

Flight

Personal archives of the Mitchell family

National Aerospace Library (NAL), Farnborough

Royal Aeronautical Society

RAF Historical Society

RAF Museum Hendon

Personal archives of the late Ian Richardson

Personal archives of the Samson/Baker family

Jennie Pickering Sherborne

Minutes of the Society of British Aeroplane Constructors

Spitfire Society

The Supermariners: https://supermariners.wordpress.com/

Georgina Townsend NAL

Charities

FAST Farnborough

National Spitfire Project

Spitfire Makers Charitable Trust

Spitfire Society

Museums

Army Flying Museum Middle Wallop Hampshire

Solent Sky Museum Southampton

Picture Credits

p. 243   National Aerospace Library, Royal Aeronautical Society

p. 245   National Aerospace Library, Royal Aeronautical Society

p. 246   National Aerospace Library, Royal Aeronautical Society

p. 247   National Aerospace Library, Royal Aeronautical Society

p. 248   National Aerospace Library, Royal Aeronautical Society

p. 250   National Aerospace Library, Royal Aeronautical Society

p. 252   National Aerospace Library, Royal Aeronautical Society

p. 254   National Aerospace Library, Royal Aeronautical Society

p. 256   From *Flight International Magazine*, 25 September 1924, via Wikimedia Commons

p. 258   National Aerospace Library, Royal Aeronautical Society

p. 260   National Aerospace Library, Royal Aeronautical Society

p. 262   National Aerospace Library, Royal Aeronautical Society

p. 263   National Aerospace Library, Royal Aeronautical Society

p. 265   Author's collection

p. 267   National Aerospace Library, Royal Aeronautical Society

p. 269   National Aerospace Library, Royal Aeronautical Society

p. 270   National Aerospace Library, Royal Aeronautical Society

p. 272   National Aerospace Library, Royal Aeronautical Society

p. 274   National Aerospace Library, Royal Aeronautical Society

p. 276   Author's collection

p. 277   National Aerospace Library, Royal Aeronautical Society

p. 278   National Aerospace Library, Royal Aeronautical Society

p. 280   National Aerospace Library, Royal Aeronautical Society

p. 282   National Aerospace Library, Royal Aeronautical Society

p. 284   Author's collection

p. 285   National Aerospace Library, Royal Aeronautical Society

p. 286   Imperial War Museum, via Wikimedia Commons

p. 287   Illustration by James Goulding, from *RAF Bomber Command and its Aircraft 1936–1940* by James Goulding and Philip Moyes (Ian Allan Publishing, 1975)

p. 288   Author's collection

Picture Credits

Plate section:

Page 1: top: National Aerospace Library, Royal Aeronautical Society; middle: Mitchell family archive; bottom: Smith Archive / Alamy Stock Photo

Page 2: top: National Aerospace Library, Royal Aeronautical Society; bottom: Smith Archive / Alamy Stock Photo

Page 3: top: National Aerospace Library, Royal Aeronautical Society; middle: Mitchell family archive; bottom: NAL

Page 4: top: Smith Archive / Alamy Stock Photo; middle: Mitchell family archive; bottom: National Aerospace Library, Royal Aeronautical Society

Page 5: top: National Aerospace Library, Royal Aeronautical Society; middle: National Aerospace Library, Royal Aeronautical Society; bottom: National Aerospace Library, Royal Aeronautical Society

Page 6: top: Chronicle / Alamy Stock Photo; middle: National Aerospace Library, Royal Aeronautical Society; bottom: Author's collection

Page 7: top left: Mitchell family archive; top right; Author's collection; bottom: National Aerospace Library, Royal Aeronautical Society

Page 8: top left: National Aerospace Library, Royal Aeronautical Society; top centre: National Aerospace Library, Royal Aeronautical Society; top right: Author's collection; bottom: Author's collection.

305

Index

*Illustrations and their captions (main text) are
denoted by the use of italic page numbers.*

A

Admiralty, the 13, 16–17, 19–20,
   26–8, 32
Aeroplane and Armament
   Experimental Establishment
   (A&AEE) 46–7, 68, 160,
   168, 196
Aeroplane magazine 225
Agello, Francesco 131
Air Council 59, 117, 118
Air Ministry 31–2, 43,47, 48, 50,
   66, 67, 68, 70, 72, 74–5,
   77–8, 85, 86, 89, 90–1, 117,
   127, 146, 149, 151–4, 155,
   160, 162, 163–4, 166, 168,
   176, 179, 185–8, 194, 196,
   202–8, 210–11, 212, 226,
   237–9, 243, 248, 252–3, 256,
   262, 266, 286, 272, 274, 276,
   278, 280, 282, 285, 286, 287,
   288
   specifications 66, 67, 141, 149,
      150, 153, 163, 185–6, 187,
      188, 191, 194, 204, 206, 207,
      210, 220, 237–9, 252, 274,
      263, 268, 280, 286, 287, 288

Albert, Duke of York (later King
   George VI) 79, 81
America 42, 179–80
   High Speed Records 133
   Schneider Trophy races 55, 57,
      85–6, 133
Apsley, Allen Bathurst, Lord 50,
   60–1, 109, 110
Argentina 75, 80–1, 144
Armstrong Siddeley 115, 141,
   147, 262, 265, 266, 270,
   271
   Jaguar engine 147
   Lynx engine 265, 266
   Panther engine 141, 270,
      271
   Puma engine 37
   Siskin 248
Armstrong Whitworth 101, 208,
   211
Atcherley, Flight Lieutenant
   Richard 120
Australia xvi, 75, 77, 79, 145
Avro 36, 66
   Lancaster xx, 51, 178, 210,
      211

B

Baldwin, Stanley 159, 219

Balloon Factory, HM 11, 13–14

Banks, Rodwell 267–8

Beardmore 160 hp engine 33, 242

Beaverbrook, Max, Lord 224

Bentley 116

Bernard HV220 130

Biard, Henri xxiv, xxvi–xxvii, 34,
54–5, 56, 57, 69, 85, 86, 94,
141, 144–5, 150, 247, 250,
253, 256, 258, 265

Bird, Squadron Commander James
57–8, 70, 102, 198, 248

Black, Arthur 99, 184, 226

Blackburn 55, 168, 250

Blackburne Thrush engine 256

Blériot, Louis 4

Blériot Mammoth 44

Boeing 207–8

Bolas, Harold 27–8

Booth, Harris 27

Boothman, Flight Lieutenant John
132, 169–70, 273

Boulton Paul 62, 208, 211

Brancker, Sir Sefton 50

Brandenberg fighter-seaplanes 29

Brice, Squadron Leader Dickie
155

Brinton, Lieutenant Jerry 131, 272

Bristol Aeroplane Company 13, 87,
115, 146, 168
Beaufighter 288
Blenheim 197
Bombay 210
Bulldog 162–3
Cherub III engine 257
Fighter 42
Hercules 211

Jupiter engine 143, 246, 269

Mercury XXX 285

Pegasus engine 152

Pegasus II engine 154

Pegasus IIM2 engine 277

Pegasus VI 284

Pegasus X engine 279

Britain, Battle of xii, xviii, xxi, 117,
130, 224

British and Colonial Aeroplane
Company 13
see also Bristol Aeroplane
Company

British Empire 23, 43, 65, 88, 144,
146–7, 260,

British Marine Air Navigation
Company 58, 248

Brooklands airfield, Surrey 8, 10

Brown, Captain Eric (Winkle) 98,
173, 283

Browning machine gun xx–xxi,
164, 186–7, 209

Buchanan, Major J. S. 132–3

Bulman, Major George 115

Byron, George, 9th Baron 125, 126

C

Calshot, Southampton 70, 71, 73,
90, 92, 118, 119, 130, 131–2,
155, 160

Camm, Sydney 140, 204–5

Capper, Lieutenant Colonel J. E.
13

Castle Bromwich 224, 227

Catalina amphibious flying boat 81,
152

Cave-Browne-Cave, Grp Captain
Henry 77–8, 148, 185

Chamberlain, Neville 185, 186, 196, 219

Chamier, Air Commodore John 140

Chesapeake Bay xxiii–xxix, 87

Chile 37, 242

Churchill, Winston 16, 19–20, 43, 73, 88–9, 94, 118, 126–7, 147, 203

Clifton, Alan xviii, 99, 152, 165, 175, 177, 198, 226, 230

Cody, Samuel 3, 4, 9, 13

Cowes Regatta 35, 50, 56, 250
  Schneider race at xxvi, 57, 122, *124*, 250

Cross, Vera 106, 218, 219, 230

Curtiss racing seaplanes xxvi, xxvii, 55

Cuxhaven Raid (1914) 20

D

Davis, Eric 'Jack' 138–9, 189

de Broughton, Alfred 12

de Havilland
  Comet 11
  Gipsy Moth 172, 173, 216
  Mosquito 11, 178, 204

de Havilland, Geoffrey 11, 114

Denmark 79, 141, 262

Doolittle, James xxvii

Dornier xvi, 140, 143, 144, 162, 187, 201, 224, 270
  bombers xvi
  Do 17 'Flying Pencil' 162, 201
  Do 24 143
  Do X 143, 144, 145
  flying boats 224
  Wal 270

Dowding, Air Marshal Hugh 190

Duralumin 76, 89, 91, 120, 263

E

Eastleigh airfield 172, 193, 203

Edward, Prince of Wales (later Edward VIII) 60, 81, 120–1, 145, 197, 219, 248

Edwardes-Jones, Flight Lieutenant Humphrey 196

Egypt 74

Ellington, Air Chief Marshal Sir Edward 190, 219–20

Engadine, HMS 20

English Electric 115–16

F

Faddy, Alf xviii, 138–9, 144, 153, 164, 175, 177, 180–2, 189–90, 194, 198–9, 204, 208, 217, 225, 230, 282, 286

Faddy, David 180, 190, 225–6, 228

Fairey Aviation Company 27, 36, 46, 91
  Battle 197
  Fairey III 243
  Fox 149
  Fulmar 178

Fambridge, Essex, 10–11, 16

Fear, Bill 153, 184

Felixstowe F5 flying boats 66, 252

Fenner, R. J. 184

First of the Few, The (1942 film) xvii, 172, 225, 227

First World War 7, 16, 19, 23–4, 26, 28, 31, 42, 44, 68, 113, 187

Flight magazine 84–5, 197, 265
floatplane fighters xix, 28, 151
Fokker, Anton xvii
Fokker Scourge xvii
France 9, 14, 42, 44, 55, 130, 160
Franco, Gen. Francisco 201, 202, 203
Freeman, Air Marshal Sir Wilfred 220

G
García, Adm. Manuel Domecq 80
Germany xvi, 42, 142–3, 160–2, 179, 201–2, 207, 219
Gingell, Gerald 229
Gloster Aircraft Company 87, 88–9, 90, 91, 139, 163
  Gladiator 168
  Gloster III xxvii, xxviii
Gretton, Freddy 125
Griffiths, Harry 184–5
Guinness, Ernest 141, 262

H
Hampshire Aeroplane Club 172, 173
Handley Page 13, 33
  Halifax 210, 211, 238
  Harrow 210
Handley Page, Frederick 10, 11
Hargreaves, F. J. 19, 29, 36, 41, 54, 248
Hawker Aircraft 51, 55, 139, 140, 163
  Hurricane 51, 89, 122, 168, 178, 196, 197
  Typhoon 204

Heinkel xvi, 161, 179
  He 70 182–3
  He 111 162, 201
Heinkel, Ernst 183
Hendon Air Pageant 73, 75, 150, 197
Herkomer, Lorenz Hans 12
Higgins, Air Marshal Jack 86
high-octane aviation fuel 130
High Speed Records 85, 122, 132–4, 263
Hill, Captain F. W. 187, 189
Hispano-Suiza
  cannon 204, 239
  engine 32, 242, 245
Hitler, Adolf 88, 109, 160, 176
Hives, Ernest 177–9
Hoare, Captain J. E. A. 243
Hoare, Sir Samuel 73, 88, 89
Hobbs, Squadron Leader B. D. 36
Holroyd, Frank 99, 105, 145, 230
Hope, Lt Linton 14–15, 27, 45, 46, 51, 131, 272
Hope, Flight Lieutenant Linton Jr 131
Houston, (Fanny) Lucy 123, 125–35, 159, 272, 273
Houston, Sir Robert 126

I
IBM 229
Imperial Airways 48, 58, 59, 71
Italy 42, 53, 55, 74, 83–4, 89, 91, 92, 119, 130, 131, 160, 161, 203, 212
  Schneider Trophy races 53, 55, 83–4, 89, 91, 119, 130, 212

Itchen Floating Bridge 156, 217
Itchen, River 11, 18, 24, 25, 70,
    150, 156, 172, 217

J
Jane's All the World's Aircraft
    197–8
Japan 37, 47, 48, 75, 79, 219, 242
John, Lt Caspar 155
Junkers xvi, 139, 140, 161, 179
    Ju 88 162

K
Keith, Claude Hilton 188
Kerr, Stuart & Company 4–5, 26
King's Cup Air Race 50, 248
Kinkead, Flight Lieutenant Samuel
    90, 93–4, 264
Knighton, Air Chief Marshal
    Sir Rich xi–xii, 223–4

L
L. S. Thompson Speed Trophy
    133
Lawrence, T. E. 59, 117, 118,
    121–2
Lewis machine gun 17, 45, 151,
    163, 245, 255
Livock, Squadron Leader Gerald
    74, 78
Lofthouse, Joy xix
Long, Frank 132
Lovell-Cooper, Eric 45, 62–3, 86,
    115, 226, 230
Luftwaffe xvi, xviii, 16, 162, 176,
    201–3, 206, 224, 226

M
Macchi 54, 131
    M33 xxviii, 54, 84
    M52R 120
    M67 120
    M72 129
    MC72 130, 131
MacDonald, Ramsay 121, 122,
    128, 159, 268, 272
McLean, Sir Robert 101, 102,
    103–5, 137, 166, 186, 198,
    225
Majestic, RMS 85
Malta 74, 150
Mansbridge, Ernest 99, 148, 167,
    181, 196, 226
Marine Aircraft Experimental
    Establishment (MAES)
    67–9, 150, 268
Marine and Armament
    Experimental Establishment
    (MAEE) 68, 69, 188,
    251
Martlesham Heath, Suffolk 46–7,
    160, 196, 197, 203, 280
Messerschmitt xx, 161, 201
    Bf 109 201
Metropolitan-Vickers 101
Miles Falcon 6 172, 216
Mitchell, Billy 3, 217
Mitchell, Eliza Jane (née Brain) 1
Mitchell, Eric 7, 29, 217
Mitchell, Florence 'Flo' (née
    Dayson) 30–1, 60, 108, 134,
    175, 217, 218, 220, 221
Mitchell, Gordon 3, 108, 134, 170,
    171, 216, 218, 221
Mitchell, Herbert 1, 2–3, 7, 97,
    109

Mitchell, Reginald (R. J.)
appointed technical director 58, 97–8
apprenticeship and early career 4–7
awarded CBE 134
battling cancer xviii, 2, 169–70, 172, 175, 177, 198–9, *200*, 204, 211, 285
becomes chief designer/engineer 41
death 221
diary 215–16
family background 1–4
flying lessons 172–3
joins Supermarine 21–6
legacy xiii–xxi, 223–8
marriage 30–1
obituary 170
pictures *xxx, 52, 82, 96, 200, 214*
tennis player 60, 108, 109–10
Morris, Richard 104, 105
Mussolini, Benito 74, 83–4, 89, 92

N

Napier & Son, D. xxvi, 75, 84, 85, 87, 91–2, 114–6, 154, 267
Dagger 209
Lion 55, 260, 261
Lion II engine 247
Lion IIB engine 253
Lion III engine 56, 250, 251
Lion IV engine 246
Lion V engine 114, 255
Lion VII engine 258, 259
Lion VIIA engine 263, 264

National Advisory Committee for Aeronautics (NACA) 179, 182
National Aeronautic Association (NAA) 133
National Physical Laboratory (NPL) 27, 84, 89, 149
National Spitfire Project 223
New Zealand 37
Nieuport Delage 130
Norman Thompson NT2B 20
Northern Ireland 71, 72

O

Oakbank Wharf, Woolston 12, 19
Olympia Aero Show 45, 79, 245
Orford Ness firing range 169, 189, 280
Orlebar, Squadron Leader Augustus 122, 268, 273

P

Paine, Victor 79
Parnall & Sons 27, 138, 153
Paull-Smith, Flying Officer E. E. 251
Payn, Harold 'Agony'/'Ag' 105, 193, 204, 230
Pemberton-Billing Limited 12, 17, 23, 24, 27
PB1 14, 15
PB9 15
PB25 15–16
PB29 16–17
PB31E (Nighthawk) 26
Pemberton-Billing, Noel 8, 9–18, 25, 26, 27, 49, 52, 53
Picken, Dr Christopher 217–18

Pickering, Ann 218
Pickering, Flight Lieutenant George
    150, 152, 155–6, 168, 172,
    173, 176, 197, 216–18, 277,
    282, 285
Pickering, Gladys 217, 218, 220
Pixton, Howard 7
Plymouth Sound 72, 74, 77, 118
Powell, Brian 80
Price, Alfred 167

Q

Quill, Jeffrey 117, 129, 164, 165,
    167, 173, 178–9, *192*, 193,
    195–6, 217, 225–6, 229–30,
    282

R

railway engineering 4–5
Reese, Peter 116
Richardson, Cecil 17, 29
Robinson, Major F. A. de Vere 119
Rolls-Royce xvii, 109, 115–17, 127,
    131, 134, 148, 154, 173, 182,
    276
    Buzzard engine 116, 144
    Eagle engine 244, 248, 252
    Eagle IX engine 49–50, 253, 255
    Goshawk engine 165, 166–7,
        168, 177, 280
    Griffon engine xviii, 117
    Kestrel IIIA engine 149
    Kestrel IIIMS 275
    Merlin engine xviii, 117, 177,
        204, 209, 282, 288
    R-type engine 115, 119, 120,
        129, 165, 268, 272

Rothermere, Lord 128
Roussel, Mike 156
Royal Aero Club xxvii, 11, 36, 87,
    127–8, 133, 273
Royal Aeronautical Society 11, 86,
    132, 133, 138, 183–4, 190
Royal Aircraft Establishment 68,
    98, 134, 164, 168, 173, 180,
    210
    see also Balloon Factory; Royal
        Aircraft Factory
Royal Air Force Academy, Cranwell
    185
Royal Air Force Club 193
Royal Air Force High Speed Flight
    ('The Flight') 87–94, 118,
    122, 129, 132, 134, 263
Royal Air Force (RAF) 31, 42, 43,
    45, 60, 66, 69, 70, 71, 72, 73,
    75, 77, 78–9, 90, 92, 117, 118,
    119, 127, 130, 152, 162–3,
    202, 274
    expansion schemes 176, 196–7
    Far East Flight 77–9
    Felixstowe flying fleet 66, 68,
        69, 72
    Fighter Command 204, 224
    foreign bases 74, 79, 146–7
    Museum 133, 153
Royal Aircraft Factory 13–14, 114
    see also Balloon Factory; Royal
        Aircraft Establishment;
Royal Australian Air Force (RAAF)
    153, 156, 246
Royal Flying Corps 7, 13, 19, 31
Royal Naval Air Service 16, 19–20,
    26–7, 31, 33, 67–8, 188
Royal Navy 20, 24, 43, 46, 65, 71,
    100, 117, 127, 146, 155

Royce, Sir Henry xv, 115, 116–17, 132, 165, 177, 267

S

S. E. Saunders & Company
    see Saunders-Roe (Saro)
Salmond, Air Marshal Sir John 86, 87, 117
Salmond, Air Vice-Marshal
    Sir Geoffrey 50–1, 87, 117
Sassoon, Sir Philip 128, 129
Saunders-Roe (Saro) 56, 76, 100, 151, 205, 278
    Lerwick 278
    London 278
    SRA/1 29
Schneider, Jacques 6, 122
Schneider Trophy races xv, xxiii–xxix, 6–7, 35–6, 83–94, 103, 117–18, 137–8, 183
    1919 45, 53, 245
    1920 53
    1921 53
    1922 51, *52*, 53–55, 247
    1923 55–7, 83
    1925 83, 85–6
    1926 89–93
    1927 *82*, 89, 90, 118, 182, 263
    1929 *112*, 113–23, 268
    1931 122–3, *124*, 127, 128, 130
    victories xiv, 55, 93, *112*, 119–20, 130, 133, 267, 268
Scott-Paine, Hubert 12, 16, 17, 18–19, 21, 25, 29–30, 32, 33, 34, 35, 36, 45, *52*, 53–5, 57–9, 70, 114, 121, 247, 248, 250
Second World War 46, 68, 202, 205, 206–7

Secret Intelligence Service (SIS) 161–2, 163, 187, 202
Seddon, Commander John 28
Shelton, John 228
Shenstone, Beverley 139, 140–1, 151, 152, 164, *174*, 175, 177, 179–80, 182–4, 189, 199, 208, 210, 226, 282
Sherborne, Jennie Pickering 156, 216–17, 218, 220
Shipster, Pieter 121–2
Shirvall, Arthur 99, 107, 148, 152
Short Brothers 13, 66, 84, 87, 88–9, 90, 91, 146, 276
    184 flying boat 20, 28
    Singapore Mk III 278
    Stirling 211
    Sunderland 278
Siddeley *see* Armstrong Siddeley
Siemens 143
Singapore 78–9
Smith, Joe xviii, 98–9, 106–7, 144, 156, 170, 176, 177, 181, 198, 204, 206, 218, 226, 227, 228, 230, 238, 286
Society of British Aeroplane
    Constructors (SBAC) 225, 273
Sopwith 13, 36
    Tabloid 7
Sopwith, Tommy 6–7
Sorley, Squadron Leader Ralph 186, 188–9, 190
Southampton–Isle of Wight service 34
Southwell, Alfred 44
Spain 201–3, 253–4, 274
Spanish Civil War 201–3, 274
Spencer, G. 230

Spitfire xiii–xiv, 176, 189–91,
   193–9, 204, 206, 217, 230,
   223–4
   design 183
   development 203
   K5054 prototype 282
   National Spitfire Project 223
   'Spitfire' name 168, 196
   The Spitfire Book 229–30
Stainforth, Flight Lieutenant
   George 132, 134
Sueter, Commodore Murray 26–7,
   28
Summers, Captain Joseph 'Mutt'
   147, 150, 152, 167, *192*, 193,
   194–5, 274, 282
Supermarine Aviation Works
   Limited xiv–xv, *8*, 11, 13,
   18–20, *22*, 31–2, 34–5, 37–8,
   58, 62–3, 70, 76, 84, 100–10,
   113–23, 127, 145, 155, 171,
   206, 224, 230–1
Supermarine designs
   Air Yacht (*Windward III*)
   141–2, 144, 270–1
   ASR Mk I 286
   Bomber Type 316, 317 and 318:
   287
   Channel 33–5, 37, 242
   Commercial Amphibian (1920)
   46, 48, 243–4
   N1 'Baby' 28–9, 36, 45, 54
   Nanok 79, 141, 262
   S4 *xxii*, xxiii–xxix, 84–6, 89,
   258–9, 263
   S5 *82*, 89–94, *112*, 118,
   263–4
   S6/6a *112*, 114, 119–20, 122,
   131, 267–8, 272

S6b *124*, 129–35, 183, 272–3
Scapa xvi, 148–52, 274–5
Scarab and Sheldrake 254–5
Scylla and Swan 48–9, 66, 69,
   252–3
Sea Eagle *40*, 49–50, 58, 116,
   248–9
Sea King I and II 45, 46, 245
Sea Lion I 36, 45, 54, 84
Sea Lion II *52*, 54–5, 84, 247
Sea Lion III xxvi, 56–7, 84,
   250–1
Sea Otter 205, 285
Seafire 98, 217
Seagull 114
Seagull ASR 1 Amphibian
   206
Seagull II 60, 153, 246
Seagull III 153–4
Seagull V 153, 154–5, 246, 277,
   284
Seal II (later named Seagull)
   47–8, 246
Seamew 265–6
Southampton *64*, 65–81, 146,
   260–1
Southampton Mk I 69–76, 80,
   260
Southampton Mk II 76, 77, 81,
   148, 149, 260
Southampton X 147, 269
Sparrow I and II 256–7
Stranraer 151–3, 278–9
Type 179 Giant 144–5, 182,
   276
Type 223/228 277
Type 224 xvii, *158*, 165–9,
   175–6, 179, 208, 226,
   280–1

Supermarine designs (continued)
  Type 300 xvii, 150, 168, 172–3,
    174, 180–6, *192*, 194, 198,
    212, 215, *222*, 226, 282–3
  Type 316 209, 287
  Type 317 209–10, 211–12,
    287
  Type 324 203, 288
  Type 325 203, 288
  Type 327 Twin-Engined Fighter
    204, 288
  Walrus *136*, 154–6, 205,
    216–17, 218, 246, 284
Swinton, Philip, Viscount 196

T
Tank, Kurt 173
Taylor, Joseph Crabtree 16
Tedder, Air Commodore Arthur
  187
Thomson, Lord Christopher 276
Tinson, Clifford 27
Trenchard, Sir Hugh 87–8, 93,
  117–18, 121, 127, 128
Trippe, Juan 59

U
USSR 42, 142, 161, 176, 203

V
Vasilesco, Carl 12
Venezuela 37, 242
Verney, Air Commodore R. H.
  190
Versailles Treaty (1919) 42, 142–3,
  161

Vickers (later Vickers-Armstrongs)
  xvii, 44, 46, 13, 33, *96*,
  100–10, 113–23, 127, 137,
  140, 143–5, 163, 208, 211,
  243, 255
Viastra 145
Viking 243
Vimy Commercial 44
Wellington 211

W
Waghorn, Flight Lieutenant Dick
  119–20
Waghorn, John 290–1
Wallis, Barnes 103–5, 144, 211
Wallis, Molly 104
Webb, Denis Le Penn 76–7, 102,
  131, 141–2, 145, 147, 155,
  228, 230
Webster, Flight Lieutenant Sidney
  90, 263
Weimar Republic 42, 160
Westbrook, Trevor 102–3, 129,
  144, 152, 164, 198
Westland 168
  Whirlwind 204, 239
Wood, Miss 230
Worsley, Flight Lieutenant Oswald
  90, 263
Wright Brothers 9, 13

Y
Yendall, Harold 27

Z
Zeppelins 20, 26, 29, 187